Praise for *Can We Talk About...*

"If you fall into the camp of the 'curious, confused, and conflicted,' then this book is for you. [Sokatch] promises the reader that 'after you've read it, you'll be able to hold your own in any Israel conversation, at any dinner party.' He delivers on this promise, providing an engaging and evenhanded . . . history of the conflict, from its 19th-century origins to the most recent mini-war between Israel and Hamas in May 2021." —*The New York Times Book Review*

"Earnestly and humanely parses the Palestinian-Israeli conflict . . . An optimistic, evenhanded instruction manual." —*Kirkus Reviews* (starred review)

"Accessible and balanced . . . Flashes of humor, including Noxon's witty black-and-white illustrations, lighten the mood without sacrificing in-depth analysis." —*Publishers Weekly*

"We live in an age diseased with certainty, but Daniel Sokatch has the bravery to come along with an antidote that suggests that there is always so much more than one truth . . . He disrupts and therefore re-nuances the accepted narratives, and he does this with great generosity of style and spirit. This is an important book, exceedingly well written, full of insight and empathy and even humor in the face of all available evidence." —Colum McCann, National Book Award–winning author of *Let the Great World Spin* and *Apeirogon*

"Everything that so often seems lacking in our thoughts, feelings, and arguments about Israel and Palestine—clarity, fair-mindedness, and universal compassion—can be found in this elegantly written and surprisingly entertaining book." —Michael Chabon and Ayelet Waldman

"Daniel Sokatch has done the impossible—he writes a breezy, sometimes even witty book about the always hot-button, depressing, and controversial topic of Israel and Palestine. His is a calm voice of miraculous common sense. He is sardonic but empathetic. He has an eye for irony and hypocrisy. But somehow he weaves a historical commentary that is both authoritative and entertaining." —Kai Bird, Pulitzer Prize–winning author of *Crossing Mandelbaum Gate* and *The Outlier*

"An important overview . . . Balanced, insightful, and highly recommended." —Hussein Ibish, senior resident scholar, Arab Gulf States Institute of Washington

"Essential not just for its frank and accessible narrative, but also for Daniel Sokatch's ability to fill the gulf of knowledge that leaves so many of us outside a vital conversation." —Professor Juliette Kayyem, faculty chair of the Homeland Security Project, Harvard's Kennedy School of Government

"Daniel Sokatch has done a remarkable job telling the story of Israel and the Israeli-Palestinian conflict in clear, understandable terms. No reader will agree with everything he writes. That's good! But every reader should appreciate his honesty, passion, intellect, and humanity." —Daniel Shapiro, U.S. ambassador to Israel, 2011–2017

"Israel, WTF? Like almost everyone, I can hardly think about Israel without feeling furious, saddened, frightened, righteous, and wrong. At last, here is a clearheaded, evenhanded book about a crucial and troubled region that makes all of us bonkers." —Daniel Handler

Can We Talk About ISRAEL?

A Guide for the Curious, Confused, and Conflicted

DANIEL SOKATCH

Illustrated by Christopher Noxon

BLOOMSBURY PUBLISHING

NEW YORK · LONDON · OXFORD · NEW DELHI · SYDNEY

Bloomsbury Publishing Inc.
1385 Broadway, New York, NY 10018, USA

BLOOMSBURY, BLOOMSBURY PUBLISHING, and the Diana logo are
trademarks of Bloomsbury Publishing Plc

First published in the United States 2021
This edition published 2022

ISBN: HB: 978-1-63557-387-9; PB: 978-1-63973-048-3; EBOOK: 978-1-63557-388-6

Library of Congress Cataloging-in-Publication Data is available

6 8 10 9 7 5

Designed and typeset by Elizabeth Van Itallie
Printed and Bound at Sheridan, Chelsea, MI

To find out more about our authors and books visit www.bloomsbury.com
and sign up for our newsletters.

For Bill Goldman (1979–2017), who was my partner in this work, and for Charlie Noxon (1999–2019), who was just beginning to wrestle with it all.

CONTENTS

PART TWO: WHY IS IT SO HARD TO TALK ABOUT ISRAEL?

INTRODUCTION

HAVE YOU EVER found yourself at a dinner party when the topic of Israel came up, and you wanted to flee to another room?

I feel your pain. I'm often asked, "Can't you just explain the Israel situation to me in, like, ten minutes or less?" People want to know, they want to understand, and they want me to wrap it up before their entrées arrive. This book will take more than ten minutes to read, but it won't be a daunting, intimidating undertaking. It will be, I hope, interesting and engaging, and after you've read it, you'll be able to hold your own in any Israel conversation, at any dinner party.

Israel.

I mean, is there any other topic on which so many intelligent, educated, and sophisticated people express such strongly and passionately held convictions, but about which they actually know so little? The problem is compounded because these people on all sides of the issue think they know what they're talking about. They sincerely believe what they think to be true.

It's easy to understand why.

Most of us have heard a lot about Israel: in church or synagogue or at the mosque, from parents and grandparents, on visits and vacations, on college campuses. And, of course, in the news: Israel boasts one of the largest communities of foreign correspondents in the world. We encounter Israel online, in Facebook posts and tweets, on podcasts and in blogs. We grew up reading about it in books like Leon Uris's *Exodus* or James Michener's *The Source*. We've seen *The Ten Commandments* and *The Prince of Egypt*. And we're used to seeing Israel in the headlines, where it takes up space completely disproportionate to its actual physical size, population, and global footprint.

Don't believe me? Try this little exercise: Google "Ukraine conflict." I get about 107 million results. Next, try "North Korea conflict." I get 95 million. Now google "Israel conflict." Hits: 181.8 million. The population of Ukraine is 45.5 million; Ukrainians are in a conflict with Russia, population 143.5 million. North Korea's population is 25 million. They're right across the most militarized border in the world from 50 million South Koreans. And Israel? It's a country of 9.2 million people locked in a conflict with all of 4.75 million Palestinians. See what I mean?

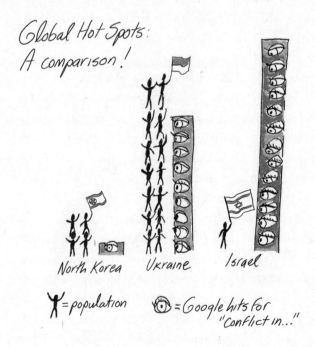

Global Hot Spots: A comparison!

North Korea   Ukraine   Israel

👁 = population   👁 = Google hits for "Conflict in..."

No doubt, as a result of all this information, all these stories, people have very strong feelings about the subject. But that doesn't mean those feelings are actually based on . . . well, facts—on an actual understanding of the situation and of what got us here. Indeed, these powerful loyalties, allegiances, and convictions are often based on something else: on a received, subjective history, a tribal narrative that reinforces whichever side of the conflict a given person identifies with. However, as the saying goes, everyone is entitled to their own opinion, but not to their own facts.

Once these narratives are set in people's minds . . . well, good luck trying to convince them that their understanding of the conflict is wrong. In fact, entire public relations industries are devoted to *reinforcing* highly partisan narratives of the Palestinian-Israeli conflict.

Another Google exercise: Take a look at the plethora of websites, YouTube videos, and other online effluvia claiming to "explain the conflict." As you'll see, most are actually devoted to explaining why one side or the other is right, just, and blameless and the other side perfidy incarnate. This may be satisfying on an emotional level, but it doesn't get anyone closer to understanding what's really going on. It's just another front in a propaganda war.

Many otherwise intelligent people make the case "for Israel" or "for Palestine," but tell only part of the story. They don't acknowledge, or genuinely don't see, that Israelis and Palestinians are both right and both wrong—that they are both victims of forces beyond their control, of each other, and of themselves.

And what about the millions of people who refuse to choose from the various One True Narratives out there? What are *you* supposed to think? And why should you even care? Is there any way to truly understand what often seems to be the world's most complicated, intractable, and ancient conflict?

This book is an attempt to explain why Israel and the

Israeli-Palestinian conflict seem to drive so many otherwise reasonable people completely bonkers. This is the story of why Israel turns some classic Jewish liberals into uber-conservatives on one issue alone. It is the story of why some otherwise compassionate and judicious progressives feel driven to single Israel out for boycotts, sanctions, and a level of condemnation they would never dream of applying to, say, any of the dozens of worse state actors out there. It's the story of why Israel inspires such fierce loyalty and allegiance from certain evangelical Christians who have never met an actual Jew or for whom actual Jews are basically souls to be saved or kindling for the Apocalypse. And it is the story of why it sometimes seems like Israel is the answer to "what's wrong with the world" for half the people in it and "what's right with the world" for the other half. For those people watching from the sidelines, this is the story of why you should care, why Israel matters, and why supporting those Israelis and Palestinians working to resolve their conflict is so important, not only for the Middle East, but also for the world.

In this book I'll try to explain the history and basic contours of one of the most complicated conflicts in the world without propagandizing and without making you yawn. But while I won't engage in propaganda, I *do* have an agenda, and I come from and with a particular perspective. I believe that the Israeli-Palestinian conflict is, essentially, a struggle between what the historian Benny Morris has called "righteous victims": two peoples, both with legitimate connections and claims to the land, who have been victimized by the outside world, each other, and themselves. It is a conflict about land and also about memory and legitimacy; about the right to exist and also about the right to self-determination. It is about survival and about justice. It is about competing narratives understood by their adherents to be singularly "true." These narratives are fueled not only by lived experiences, but also by stories and religious traditions and family and media consumption and political persuasions—and by various degrees of ignorance, willful or otherwise. I believe that the biggest obstacle to resolving the conflict between Israelis and Palestinians is not a lack of political imagination, but a lack of political will.

To put it even more simply: I believe that everyone, Israelis and Palestinians alike, should have their equal rights and security guaranteed. There are partisans of this conflict who think that only some people deserve those things, and I believe they are wrong.

As for my perspective, I am a product of the liberal American Jewish community, and like many Americans, for a long time my main exposure to the debate about the Israeli-Palestinian conflict was to the Israeli side of the story. In fact, the Israeli narrative often takes up more space than the Palestinian one in the American conversation. In a sense, it will do that here, too, but with a difference. Here, I approach the story of Israel, and the story of its conflicts with its neighbors and with the Palestinians, as a person intimately familiar with various aspects of the "pro-Israel" narrative held by most Americans.

And while this is only one narrative of the conflict, it is an influential one, one that I believe is in serious need of review, critique, and most of all, evolution. I can't speak for Palestinians (or, for that matter, for Israelis), but I can try to provide a more balanced and nuanced approach to this often fraught subject than what's out there already.

I care deeply about the place, and that concern has led me to a concern for the conflictual relationships in which Israel is entangled. My brother once said that, when it comes to Israel, I "take the *New York Times* personally." He was right. Israel can inspire and confuse; it can give you hope, and it can give you insomnia. Today, I run the New Israel Fund, the largest nongovernmental organization working for democracy and equality for all Israelis. I get why this story is so difficult. What most people feel about it is true: it *is* complicated. But together, we can begin to make sense of it all.

You are probably not going to agree with, or perhaps even believe, everything you read here. There are few topics more strewn with emotional land mines than this one. You might learn about events that upset you, read about things you've never been told about before, or disagree with my analysis or the conclusions I draw. You might even object to the words I use to describe aspects of the conflict. But that's okay; conversations about Israel are rarely quiet, and they're also rarely boring. I'll tell the story, explain my positions, and you'll draw your own conclusions.

There's a lot of information in the following pages, and some terms and references that might be unfamiliar to you. If you find yourself getting lost or confused, please refer to the "Lexicon of the Conflict" at the end of the book. There, you'll find some of the most important basic terms of the discussion. As you'll see, when it comes to Israel, what you call a place, a political movement, or even a war can be one of those land mines I just referred to. The lexicon will help you keep the story straight and navigate, or at least better understand, the minefields.

ISRAEL, WTF?

I still remember the first time I realized Israel made people a bit un-hinged. It was the mid-1980s, and we were at a second cousin's bar mitzvah in Chicago. I must've been sixteen or seventeen. Earlier that year, my family and I had gone on our first trip to Israel, as part of a "mission" sponsored by the United Jewish Appeal, a Jewish philan-thropic organization. My mom, dad, and younger brother had a good time, found it all interesting, and after ten days or so, happily returned to the routine of their lives. But me? I was hooked.

In that 1980s Lincolnwood, Illinois, town house, drifting past the deli platters and kibitzing relatives, I heard an old great-uncle hold forth on Israel to a group of young cousins. I walked over to listen, my own recent experience in Israel still shimmering in my head. He was fulminating about Israel's enemies, inexplicably angry—nobody was arguing with him—and clearly exercised. If Israel were destroyed in a nuclear attack, he said, he hoped that it would take the rest of the world down with it. Astonished (and vaguely terrified), I spoke up: "You mean, you hope Israel would take all its enemies down with it, right?"

He glared at me with the irritated look old Jewish guys of his generation reserved for idiots: "No. I said, 'I hope the *whole world* will go up in flames if Israel is destroyed.'"

"But what about your grandchildren here in Chicago?" I asked.

He shrugged, and repeated: "The whole world."

From that moment on, Israel became my primary interest—obsession, even—and it's been that way ever since.

I lived in Israel during the golden period of Yitzhak Rabin's prime ministership, in the mid-1990s. This transformational, hopeful, unfinished period had a huge impact on me and on my perspective on Israel. One moment in particular stands out even all these years later. Walking home to my apartment in Jerusalem one day in the summer of 1994, I (and everyone else on the street) looked up to see a massive commercial jetliner fly low from the east, circle the city twice, and then head back the way it had come. All around me, people murmured in astonishment: Who was in that plane? What was it doing here?

What we had just seen was geopolitically impossible. Directly east of Israel and the Israeli-occupied West Bank was Jordan, a state with which Israel had long been formally at war. Airplanes simply didn't fly in from the east, from Jordan to Israel, let alone circle Jerusalem, unless they were planning on bombing it. When I reached the street where I lived, I saw the tough Israeli guy who owned my corner market standing outside, listening to the news on his transistor radio. "Who was on that plane?" I asked him.

He looked at me, eyes full of tears and wonder, and said, "It was the king!"

And that's how those of us living in Jerusalem experienced

the peace accord that had just been announced between Israel and Jordan. To honor it, King Hussein, an old fighter pilot, flew his royal Jordanian jet around Jerusalem in a salute to the city he'd once ruled. At Ben Gurion Airport, near Tel Aviv, Prime Minister Yitzhak Rabin, an old soldier and chief of staff of the Israeli army that conquered East Jerusalem in 1967, spoke with him from the control tower. To me, that image represented hope and the potential for reconciliation and for new beginnings between old foes.

It continues to inspire me today, which is a good thing. Where the Middle East is concerned, we all need some inspiration. Because even if we aren't in the midst of one now, there will be another round of Israeli-Palestinian violence. And this conflict—fueled by deeply held beliefs, sacred texts, and painful histories—will continue to impact all of us throughout the rest of the world. It is in all our interest to understand the problem if we want to help to solve it.

This book is meant to help you understand Israel, the complex and confusing responses the subject inspires in all kinds of people, and the hundred-plus-year-old conflict between Arabs and Jews on the sliver of land between the Jordan River and the Mediterranean Sea. Part 1 tells the story of how we got here, and part 2 takes a look at some of the thorniest issues that define the debate today. This book subscribes to neither of the two camps that tend to define the debate, the "Israel always right" camp and the "Israel always wrong" one. It is my hope that it will help you reject the dominant dichotomy and begin to understand that when it comes to Israel, things are never black and white. Israel is all about the grays.

Part One

WHAT'S GOING ON?

CHAPTER 1

JEWS AND ISRAEL
Where Do We Start?

How far back do we have to go? When does our story begin? In 1967, or 1948, or 1917, or 1882, or 70 C.E., or earlier than that? The answer is: All the above.

THE (BIBLICAL) BEGINNING
(c. Twentieth Century B.C.E.–70 C.E.)

The idea of Israel in the Jewish imagination first appears in the Hebrew Bible, at the very beginning of the Jewish story as we understand it today. In Genesis 12:1, God tells Abraham, "Go from your country and your kindred and your father's house to the land that I will show you." A few verses later, we learn where that land is: Canaan, the Promised Land, the land that will later be known as Israel. And so, Abraham (said to live at the time of this story in what is now Iraq) picks up and leaves, eventually settling near Shechem

("Nablus," in Arabic), in what is now the West Bank, and then near Be'er Sheva, in the Negev Desert, in what is today the South of Israel. Exactly what territory God promises Abraham in the biblical story is unclear—the Book of Exodus tells us God granted the Israelites everything from the Nile River to the Euphrates River, while in the Book of Joshua, the Israelites conquer only Canaan—but it includes modern-day Israel and the Palestinian territories in the West Bank and Gaza. As you can see, from the very beginning of the story, things were complicated.

The Hebrew Bible is, among other things, the origin story of the Jewish people and Judaism. For some people, it is a repository of stories, folklore, and wisdom that may or may not contain a spark of divine inspiration. For others, including tens of millions of fundamentalist Christians, it is the literal word of God. Regardless, the Promised Land story stuck, and the Jewish connection to Israel was forged. Over the centuries, the Jews who lived in the Land of Israel understood their connection to the place in which they lived to be rooted in the promise God makes to Abraham in Genesis 15:18: "To your descendants I give this land."

Thousands of years of war, conquest, expulsion, and exile never uprooted the faith of the Jews (or at least of many of them) in that promise. Indeed, the power of the very idea of Israel as the Jewish homeland—the idea that Jews, no matter where and when they were born, could dream of meeting, as they still say at the conclusion of the Passover seder, "next year in Jerusalem"—served as a unifying principle through millennia of hardship. And for those who take the Bible literally, the establishment of the State of Israel in 1948 represented a partial fulfillment of God's promise to Abraham. The conquest by Israel of the West Bank in 1967, and the subsequent (and ongoing) settlement enterprise aimed at reestablishing a physical Jewish presence in the territories that form the biblical heartland of the Jewish imagination, is for those biblical literalists the necessary next phase of the Jewish story.*

Now, back to Abraham. His grandson Jacob moves the Jewish tribe to Egypt to avoid famine in Canaan and to reunite with his own son Joseph, of *Amazing Technicolor Dreamcoat* fame, who had risen to prominence as the right-hand man of the pharaoh. There, the Israelites live happily enough for a time, until "a new king arose of Egypt, who did not know Joseph. And he said to his people, 'Look, the Israelite people are much too numerous for us'" (Exodus 1:8). To prevent this from becoming a problem, the new pharaoh enslaves them—which sets the stage for yet another musical (and animated film), *The Prince of Egypt*, with the rise of Moses and the Exodus of the Israelites from Egypt. After forty years of wandering in the Sinai Desert (now part of Egypt), the Jews make it back to the Promised Land, probably around the thirteenth century B.C.E.

At around 1000 B.C.E., the biblical figure of David, Goliath slayer, appears. According to the Bible, David founds the Kingdom of Judah and establishes his capital in Jerusalem. His son Solomon builds the first Jewish Temple, at the city's heart. As we will see, David, the city he may have built, and the Jewish Temple figure prominently in the arguments over Jerusalem today. And the disposition, definition, and status of Jerusalem remain perhaps the thorniest, most emotional, and seemingly irresolvable aspects of the conflict.

In the centuries following the time of David, Jewish kingdoms rose and fell in what is now Israel and the West Bank. By

---

* This is the Jewish version of the same kind of faith-based views on land ownership that motivated the Muslim conquests of the Middle East and the Indian subcontinent; the Crusades; the rise of the British Empire; Manifest Destiny and the "white man's burden" in the United States; and Soviet hegemony over Eastern Europe after World War II. In other words, countless countries have engaged in what they understood to be divinely (or at least ideologically) sanctioned land grabs.

587–586 B.C.E., the Babylonians besieged, conquered, and destroyed Jerusalem, exiling much of the population of the city. A few decades later, the Persians conquered Babylon, and seventy years after their exile began, Jews were permitted to return to Jerusalem and rebuild their Holy Temple. Sometime around 200 B.C.E., after centuries of debate about what it should actually contain, the Hebrew Bible was canonized into the book we are familiar with today. Half a century later, a group of Jewish rebels (and, by all accounts, religious fanatics) called the Maccabees revolted against the ruling Seleucid Empire, which was attempting to impose its Greek culture on the people of Judea (as the southern part of what is now Israel and the West Bank was then called). The defeat of that empire at the hands of the Maccabees is celebrated by Jews each year at Chanukah.*

And then came Rome. By 63 B.C.E., Judea was a client state (and, ultimately, a province) of the Roman Empire, which, a few decades later, set up Herod the Great as the "King of the Jews." Herod completed the building of the Second Temple in Jerusalem, and it is during this period of great turbulence and simmering discontent that Jesus enters the story. After his crucifixion in Jerusalem, a breakaway Jewish sect forged a new religion that became known as Christianity.

---

* This gave rise to one of the strange ironies of American Jewish life: In order to compete with Christmas for the hearts and minds of Jewish kids, assimilated American Jews elevated Chanukah, a relatively minor festival, to major holiday status—even though it celebrates a military victory by religious extremists over not only an occupying power, but also fellow Jews who had adopted non-Jewish customs (that is, who had assimilated). In other words, the Maccabees were given celebrity status in American Jewish life by people the Maccabees themselves would've probably put to the sword.

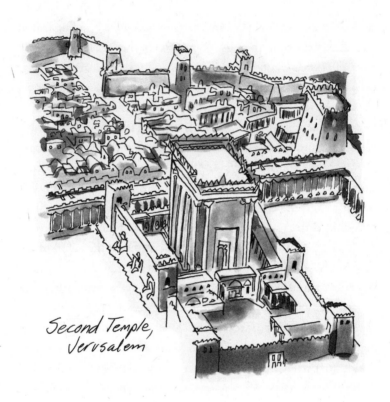

Second Temple,
Jerusalem

In 70 C.E., an unsuccessful Jewish revolt against Rome ended with the destruction of Jerusalem and of the Second Temple. (Today, the western and southern retaining walls of the hill on which the Temple was built are all that remain of the Herodian structure; the Western Wall is considered the holiest site in Judaism. This will be important later.) After the fall of Jerusalem, leading rabbis relocated to the town of Yavneh, near the Mediterranean coast. There, they began to transform Judaism from a local Judean religion based on animal sacrifices and pilgrimages to the Temple to the rabbinic Judaism we know today, based on laws, books, and prayer—and so, able to thrive anywhere. Meanwhile, under the emperor Hadrian, the Romans renamed Jerusalem "Aelia Capitolina" and banned Jewish rituals such as circumcision in order to crush any sense of Jewish independence. In response, another Jewish revolt broke out, and it, too, was crushed. Utterly defeated, the Jews were banned from entering Jerusalem, and large numbers of them were exiled. While there were always small communities of Jews living in the Land of Israel between 70 C.E. and the late nineteenth century, it would be almost two thousand years before they returned in significant numbers.

SCATTERED TO THE WINDS: DIASPORA AND THE RISE OF EUROPEAN JEWRY (70 C.E.–Mid-Nineteenth Century)

Following their expulsion from Israel, the Jews migrated across North Africa, through Asia Minor, and on into Europe. Wherever they went, they formed communities. Sometimes, such as during the "golden age" of Muslim Spain (which coincided with the not-so-golden Middle Ages in the rest of Europe), Jews were tolerated, and their communities flourished. Other times, such as during the long Christian reconquest of Spain, they were increasingly subjected to discrimination, forced conversion, physical violence, and finally, exile.

Over the centuries, two great cultures emerged among the exiled Jews, each with its own distinctive traditions, religious rituals, and languages. Sephardic Jews trace their origins back to the Iberian Peninsula—*Sepharad* means "Spain" in Hebrew—and they carried their culture with them after Spain's Catholic monarchs expelled them in 1492. Sephardic Jews settled throughout North Africa and the Middle East, southern Europe, and ultimately, South and then North America. The first Jewish residents of the Dutch settlement of New Amsterdam, on what we now call Manhattan, were Sephardic

Jews from Brazil.* Many Sephardic Jews spoke Ladino, a language related to Spanish (and also called Judaeo-Spanish). By virtue of geography, the Sephardic Jewish community was not subjected to the same level of violence and persecution in the critical nineteenth century as was the other major Jewish population, the Ashkenazi Jews.

Ashkenazi Jews trace their origins to Jewish communities that settled, in the Middle Ages, near the Rhine River in what is today France and Germany. Ashkenazi Jews lived throughout western Europe, but moved east over the centuries to escape persecution,

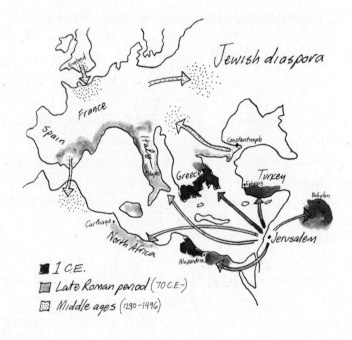

* Another name, "Mizrachi" (literally, "eastern"), describes Jews with origins in North Africa and the Middle East who immigrated to Israel in massive numbers in the 1950s and now make up the majority of the Jewish population of Israel. Just to confuse things, today "Sephardic" and "Mizrachi" are often used interchangeably, regardless of whether the Jews being referred to have any Iberian origins.

eventually settling in eastern Europe. These Jews spoke Yiddish (which, conveniently, means "Jewish" in Yiddish), a Germanic dialect that contains elements of Hebrew and other languages and is written in Hebrew script. By the eighteenth century, millions of Ashkenazi Jews lived in the territory of the Russian and Austro-Hungarian empires.

Life was rarely easy. Jews in Imperial Russia, ruled by the authoritarian monarchy of the tsar, were allowed to live only in the western territory of the empire, referred to as the "Pale of Settlement." The ancestors of most of today's American Jews once lived in the Pale, which included parts of western Russia, Belarus, parts of the Baltic states, and parts of Poland. This is the place where the musical and film *Fiddler on the Roof*, based on a story by the Yiddish writer Sholem Aleichem, takes place. It is the setting for many of Marc Chagall's greatest works. And it is also the place, as we shall soon see, that would become the hotbed and heartland of European Zionism.

Whether Sephardic or Ashkenazi, Jews were the ultimate outsiders, the "others," in Christian Europe, no matter how venerable their communities might have been. To the Catholic Church, the great European power of the Middle Ages, the Jews were a big theological problem. The Catholic Church considered Jews heretics who rejected the "one true faith." To justify this stance, the Church adopted a position of hostility toward Jews from its earliest days. One of its key components was the belief that the Jews had not only rejected Christ, but also actually killed him. This resulted in centuries of stereotyping (as embodied in Shakespeare's character Shylock, in *The Merchant of Venice*), persecution, and violence. Jews were permitted to engage in only certain professions (as moneylenders and merchants, for example) and were relegated to certain neighborhoods. In Venice, the neighborhood where the Jews were forced to reside was referred to by the Italian word for the iron foundry located there: *ghetto*. This was the original use of the term that is now synonymous with any part of a city where impoverished and marginalized minorities live.

Despite all this, Jewish communities grew and even flourished. A vibrant Yiddish culture emerged in the heavily Jewish areas of eastern Europe. The Enlightenment of the eighteenth century, the growing belief in science and rationality over faith, ushered in a new era of hope for the prospects of European Jews, at least those living in the western part of the continent. Ghetto walls came down, and many Jews began to see themselves not simply as Jews, but as French, German, or Dutch citizens who happened to be Jewish. In central and eastern Europe, the Haskalah movement, a sort of Jewish Enlightenment inspired by the broader European one, promoted the notion of integrating the Jewish community and culture into the broader society in which Jews lived, giving birth to Reform Judaism, today the largest denomination of Jews in the United States. The

Reform branch of Judaism (along with the other non-Orthodox branches) sought to allow Jews to accommodate, rather than separate themselves from, the wider society in which they lived and to adjust Jewish rules and practices accordingly.

THE JEWISH PREDICAMENT IN THE AGE OF NATIONALISM: WHAT IS TO BE DONE?
(Late Nineteenth Century)

By the end of the nineteenth century, it was increasingly clear to growing numbers of Jews that this dream of integration into European societies was not going to happen, certainly not in eastern Europe (Russia and Poland), where the masses of European Jewry lived. Across the Continent, old Church-based Jew hatred was morphing into an even uglier brand of prejudice, based on rising chauvinistic nationalism, xenophobia, tribalism, and pseudoscientific notions of racial purity and eugenics. This new form of hatred became known in 1879 as antisemitism. Russian authorities sanctioned, or at least tolerated, "pogroms," organized massacres of Jews by non-Jewish Russians. Young Jews were conscripted into the tsar's army for twenty-five-year terms of service. And the Russian secret police fabricated a document called *The Protocols of the Elders of Zion*, which purported to be a transcript of a secret global Jewish conspiracy.* The masses of eastern European Jews remained poor and persecuted, looking for some way out of the predicament of poverty, insecurity, and hostility.

Millions sought to immigrate to America, "die Goldene Medina" (the Golden Land). This is what my ancestors did, and each year on

---

* A century later, it's still out there, a toxic tract blaming the Jews for all the world's ills, warping the minds and fueling the perverse victimization fantasies of bigots, racists, and haters of all stripes.

the Fourth of July, a friend in Israel with a dark sense of humor sends me an email congratulating me for having had great-grandparents with the good sense to emigrate from eastern Europe to New York, as opposed to Palestine, as her family did.

Many more millions stayed behind, even as circumstances for the Jews in eastern Europe deteriorated. Some of them sought comfort in religion. Some turned to socialism and communism, in the hope that the problem of the Jews in Europe would be solved as part of a broader mass revolution that would lead to a more egalitarian society. A good number joined the General Jewish Labor Bund, a Yiddish-language socialist mass movement that rejected emigration and the salvation of religion and, instead, struggled for economic and political equality and, later, for communal autonomy, economic improvement, and some forms of self-governance.

And some Jews, in small numbers at first, turned to a new kind of secular faith. Convinced that the Jews of Europe would never be truly accepted, and thus never truly safe, they concluded that the only solution to the problem of the persecution of European Jewry in an age of rising nationalism was Jewish nationalism. Believing a catastrophe was brewing, they set their eyes on a new escape plan: immigration, and not to America. There was no guarantee of safety there, and the American melting pot held no appeal for them. In their view, there was only one thing that the Jews of Europe—never accepted, hounded for millennia, despised and suspected—could do to save themselves and build their future. There was only one place in which to express that self-determination. They had to go home.*

---

* To be sure, a "home" in which large numbers of Jews had not lived for a couple of thousand years.

CHAPTER 2

THE ZIONIST IDEA
Organizing, Immigrating, Building
(1860s–1917)

As I MENTIONED, even after the Roman exile, some Jews remained in the Land of Israel. By the nineteenth century, Palestine was a southern backwater in the crumbling Ottoman Empire. About twenty-five thousand Jews, overwhelmingly Sephardic and traditionally religious, lived there among the local Arab population, mostly in the four ancient holy cities of Safed, Tiberias, Hebron, and Jerusalem, reliant on charity from overseas Jewish communities. This philanthropy resulted in the founding, starting in the 1850s, of new Jewish neighborhoods and communities beyond the walls of the ancient cities.

In the 1880s, growing numbers of European Jews started to focus on immigration to Palestine as the answer to their persecution. They called themselves Hovevei Zion, Hebrew for "lovers of Zion"—Zion being both a hill in Jerusalem and a term referring to the Land of Israel itself—and they launched a movement for Jewish self-determination in the Land of Israel that soon became known by a simpler name: Zionism. At the time, most Jews rejected this philosophy out of hand as impractical, undesirable, and even absurd. Indeed, not until after the Holocaust (when the Zionists' analysis of the Jewish situation in Europe proved so horribly and unimaginably correct) would their idea be accepted by a majority of the Jews in the world.

Dreyfus

In 1894, the greatest legal spectacle and political scandal of the era rocked France, Europe, and Jews around the world. Alfred Dreyfus, a captain in the French Army, was accused of spying for Germany, convicted of treason, and sentenced to life imprisonment. The conviction was a cover-up; Dreyfus was innocent, but the conservative French political and military establishment needed a scapegoat after an embarrassing military defeat in 1871, and Dreyfus was a Jew, and thus a convenient target. What became known as the Dreyfus Affair divided France, with cultural celebrities such as the novelist Émile Zola—who believed in a France defined by liberty, equality, and fraternity, not by Catholicism, bloodline, or accident of birth—organizing on Dreyfus's behalf. Despite these noble efforts, and despite the fact that Dreyfus's conviction was ultimately overturned and the captain released from prison, many western European Jews were shocked by the affair. Their belief that they, enlightened European Jews, had finally been accepted in enlightened western Europe was shaken to the core by the framing, arrest, and trial of Alfred Dreyfus.

One of these Jews was a journalist from Budapest, Hungary (then part of the Austro-Hungarian Empire), who was covering the trial in Paris for the Viennese newspaper *Neue Freie Presse*. His name was Theodor Herzl. It was his time in Vienna and what he saw in Paris, he would later claim, that convinced him, a secular, cosmopolitan man, that the Jews of Europe had no future without a state of their own. He went on to write a pamphlet in 1896, *Der Judenstaat* (*The Jewish State*), advocating for his vision of Jewish self-determination, and he would devote the rest of his short life to organizing the various groups of "Lovers of Zion" into a movement, political Zionism, that would ultimately establish the State of Israel. Even though Herzl died in 1904, at age forty-four, decades before the State of Israel was founded, cities and streets and even hills throughout Israel are named for him. In fact, Herzl was somewhat less wedded than other early Zionists to the notion that the Jewish State be established in *Palestine*: the man often called the father of Zionism was willing to consider other locations, including Argentina and East Africa (in what is now Kenya).

In 1897, Herzl convened the First Zionist Congress in Basel, Switzerland. Hundreds of delegates from around the world gathered in a local opera house, formulated a Zionist platform, adopted "HaTikvah" ("The Hope") as the official Zionist anthem—it would later become the national anthem of the State of Israel—and launched the movement that would result, a half century later, in the creation of the State of Israel.

Herzl

A FEW QUICK WORDS ABOUT ZIONISM

Few terms are more loaded, misunderstood, or abused than *Zionism*. In a way, the word has come to stand for much more (or perhaps less) than its original definition. Depending on how you use it, it has become something of a political litmus test: a badge of pride or an insult. And how you use it, or if you use it at all, tends to indicate how you feel about Israel.

I'm often asked if I'm a Zionist. To ask the question now seems a bit strange: the goal of Zionism, the idea that the Jewish people are entitled to self-determination in their ancient homeland of Israel, was realized the day, in May 1948, when Israel was established. So, to ask if someone identifies as a Zionist or an anti-Zionist is a bit anachronistic, kind of like asking someone if they are "pro-Union" or "pro-Confederacy" 150 years after the end of the Civil War. Israel is a reality, so asking about someone's stance on the nineteenth-century movement that intended to create it doesn't seem particularly relevant. Of course, what that question is *really* usually meant to ask is "Where do you stand on Israel?" or "Do you support Israel's policies?" or "Do you believe Israel has a right to exist?" To try to clear up some of the confusion surrounding the Z-word, let's take a closer look at what it really means.

Zionism is an idea and a movement, both focused on reestablishing a Jewish homeland in Israel. Zionism was very much a product of the era of nationalism in which it was born. Nationalism can mean pride in one's country or xenophobia and a belief that one's country is better than all others. Zionism, like other nationalisms, has included elements of both. It was never monolithic. From its earliest days, there were numerous visions for what Zionism could be and how to achieve it, and a dizzying array of organizations in Palestine and around the world supported those visions.

Labor Zionists. Left-wing Labor Zionists advocated for a socialist society in a Jewish state. These Zionists dominated the pre-1948 era, the establishment of Israel, and the first three decades of Israel's existence. Labor Zionists pushed for the new state to guarantee health care to all, to pay all workers a decent wage, to create collectively owned farms (kibbutzim) that embodied the ideals of socialism in everyday life, and to encourage the emergence of a "new kind of Jew," one with a deep connection to the land and an ability to work and defend it.

Revisionist Zionists. Labor Zionists' primary ideological competitors, right-wing ("Revisionist") Zionists, preached a militant gospel of territorial expansion. Their early symbols included a map that showed a "Greater Land of Israel," purportedly based on the borders of a biblical Kingdom of Israel, encompassing all of what is today Israel, the West Bank and Gaza, parts of Lebanon, and all of what is now Jordan. The founder of this school of Zionism, Ze'ev Jabotinsky,

Kibbutz

argued in his essay "The Iron Wall (We and the Arabs)" that "the native populations, civilised or uncivilised, have always stubbornly resisted the colonists, irrespective of whether they were civilised or savage." Therefore, Zionists would have to build their new country in conflict, not cooperation, with the native Arabs, essentially beating them into submission (against his "Iron Wall"). Once that had happened, the Arabs would accept that the Jews were there to stay, and everyone could learn to live together.

Today, most right-wing Zionists would never describe Zionism as a colonialist movement; it doesn't serve their political talking points, or *hasbara* (public relations or, perhaps more accurately, propaganda) efforts.* They would also probably not feel comfortable with

---

* In Hebrew, *hasbara* means the act of explaining. It is used to refer to public relations and public diplomacy efforts aimed at portraying Israel and Israeli policies and actions in a positive light. Critics would argue that *hasbara* is often used to justify or "spin" problematic policies and actions. Today, it would be anathema to Israel's *hasbaraists* to say, as Jabotinsky

Jabotinsky's dedication to democratic principles, not to mention his vision for Israel. In 1934, he proposed a draft constitution for a future Zionist state that read, "In every Cabinet where the prime minister is a Jew, the vice-premiership shall be offered to an Arab, and vice-versa." It is difficult to imagine Israel's right-wing leaders, who claim to be Jabotinsky's political heirs, ever saying anything like this.

From Israel's founding in 1948 until 1977, the proponents of right-wing Zionism were in perpetual opposition, marginal to Israel's political life. But right-wing Zionists came to power in 1977, and leaders such as Menachem Begin, Yitzhak Shamir, and Benjamin Netanyahu have, with a few exceptions, dominated Israeli politics ever since.

Initially, both Labor and Revisionist Zionism were essentially secular movements. But in order to gain a majority in the Israeli parliament, called the Knesset, Zionist political parties found it necessary to work with ultra-Orthodox religious parties (whose leaders were interested in maintaining control over Jewish religious life and ensuring that their communities were well funded, but who were not particularly interested in other matters of state) to form coalition governments.

Religious Zionists. In addition to the two secular wings of Zionism and the ultra-Orthodox, there were the religious Zionists, who were motivated primarily by the belief that Jewish immigration to Israel was the fulfillment of theology and destiny. After the Six-Day War, religious Zionism, which had previously been relatively nonideological, took a hard-right, mystical, nationalist turn, becoming the creed of the settler movement—and one of the most powerful and influential groups in modern Israel.

---

did, that Zionism was a colonial endeavor. It doesn't fit the official narrative, suggesting as it does that people other than the Jews were indigenous to the land.

Cultural Zionists. Finally, there were the cultural Zionists, whose connection to the land and the language was predicated on their importance to Jewish culture and history. The cultural Zionist leaders believed that Jewish immigrants could and should share the land peacefully and fairly with its Arab inhabitants. The cultural Zionists influenced the academic, cultural, and intellectual life of Israel, but played little direct role in politics. They never established a political party of their own, and their bicultural vision remains the Zionist road not taken.

. . .

All these strains of Zionism—always competing, sometimes overlapping—shared a common vision: establishing a homeland and self-determination in Palestine for the beleaguered Jews of Europe.

So, am I a Zionist? Like I said earlier, it seems a somewhat silly question to ask in the twenty-first century. I consider myself a supporter of the liberal vision of Israel enshrined in the Declaration of the Establishment of the State of Israel (Israel's Declaration of Independence), the idea that Israel can be a home and a place of refuge for the long-persecuted Jewish people *and* a country that ensures complete equality for *all* its citizens. Whatever that is, that's what I am.

THE FIRST WAVE AND THE NEW YISHUV

Even before Herzl started his organizing, Jews were heading back to Palestine. Beginning in the 1880s, and against a backdrop of violent pogroms and rising antisemitism, Zionists had turned their idea into a movement, as waves of Jews, mostly young and mostly from eastern Europe, immigrated to Palestine. (Each wave was known as an *aliyah*, meaning "going up.") The earliest waves established rural collective communities and urban communities in towns built on land purchased from absentee Ottoman landlords. In the spirit of Zionism, Eliezer Ben-Yehuda and other linguists transformed Hebrew from a mostly liturgical and religious language into a daily spoken one.* By the early twentieth century, tens of thousands of idealistic, socialist-leaning Jews had emigrated from the Pale of Settlement to launch the collectivist farming kibbutz movement, start the first Jewish self-defense organizations, and build new institutions. One of these, which started out on a few sand dunes near the ancient port of Jaffa, would become the first great, bustling, culturally rich, politically liberal, Hebrew-speaking, modern, secular Jewish metropolis: the city of Tel Aviv.

Plenty of these early immigrants found life too difficult and returned home. There were few creature comforts, little in the way of communal infrastructure, and of course, a large native Arab

Founding of Tel Aviv,
1909

---

* Ben-Yehuda, who published the first modern Hebrew dictionary in 1908, had to invent words for all the things that weren't around two thousand years ago. One of my favorites is onomatopoeic: the word for "bottle," *bakbook*, sounds like water being poured from one.

population who quite understandably became more and more hostile to the increasing numbers of Jews. But many other pioneers stayed, founding and strengthening organizations and institutions that allowed the Zionist movement to establish new towns and kibbutzim, purchase more land, negotiate with the Ottoman authorities, and promote immigration into the growing Jewish community.

This community and its new institutions were known as the New Yishuv (the New Settlement), and they became the nucleus and then infrastructure of the state that would be established over half a century later. Perhaps the most important of these organizations was the Jewish Agency. Founded in 1929 to encourage Jews from around the world to move to Palestine, it served as the de facto pre-state government of the Jewish community there. An early chairman of the Jewish Agency, David Ben-Gurion, would become Israel's first prime minister.

IS ZIONISM JUSTIFIABLE?

A few years ago, I spent a week teaching about Israel at a liberal Jewish summer camp in the High Sierras of eastern California. I was there to help the camp's counselors (a mix of very progressive Bay Area Californians and young, post-army Israelis) wrestle with how to talk about Israel with their campers and one another.*

One day, a counselor asked me to spend the afternoon with his cabin of eleven-year-olds talking about the history of Israel. I wasn't sure how much the kids knew, or how much they would be able to understand and absorb, but I was game. I decided to begin at the beginning. For the next few hours, the kids and I took a fast zoom through thousands of years of Jewish history to get to the place where they could begin to understand what was going on in Israel today.

When we came to this part of the story—the part about the Zionists and the waves of Jewish immigration to Palestine—a kid named Brandon spoke up: "Okay, so, let me get this straight. It's kind of like I've lived in my home, on my land, all my life. My parents and my grandparents and my great-grandparents and their great-grandparents have all lived here, and they all farmed the land, just like me. We always paid some guy rent, but we always lived here. One day, I go out to my fields, and when I come home that evening, this guy"—here, he pointed to the kid sitting next to

---

* I use the word *wrestle* here for two reasons. First, I *do* think engaging with this issue and its complexities requires a certain amount of wrestling, for all of us. Second, the name "Israel" in Hebrew means "to wrestle (or struggle) with God." In the Book of Genesis, the biblical forefather Jacob does just this, wrestling with an angel through the night, until, at dawn, the angel blesses him and gives him a new name: "Israel."

him—"and his family are living in half my house. I say, 'Hey, what are you doing in my house?' And *he* says, 'My family and I got driven out of our town far away from here. People came and killed our neighbors and burned down our house. Now we have nowhere else to go—nowhere else will take us in. And so we came here, to the place where our great-great-great-grandparents lived long ago.' And so *both* guys are right, and neither one really has anywhere else to go. Is this kind of like what happened?"

I told Brandon that he had just reduced what some people see as the world's most complicated and intractable problem down to its essence, and that he understood the heart of the conflict better than 90 percent of the adults I'd spoken to.

In his masterpiece *In the Land of Israel*, the late Israeli author and peace activist Amos Oz writes that Zionism has "the justness of the drowning man who clings to the only plank he can. And the drowning man clinging to this plank is allowed, by all the rules of natural, objective, universal justice, to make room for himself on the plank, even if in doing so he must push others aside a little. Even if the others, sitting on that plank, leave him no alternative to force. But he has no natural right to push the others on the plank into the sea." Between Israel's greatest writer and an eleven-year-old kid from the East Bay, that's the whole problem in a nutshell.

. . .

So, who were the people living in the house Brandon described?

CHAPTER 3

WAIT, THERE WERE PEOPLE HERE

What About the Palestinians?

OF COURSE, THE history and catastrophe of European Jewry had nothing to do with the people living in Palestine when those nineteenth-century immigrants began to arrive. Nineteenth-century Zionists described the Palestine they aspired to "return" to as "a land without a people for a people without a land." The only problem with this famous saying was that it was wrong. Palestine was already populated by the people we now call the Palestinians. The traumatic, devastating loss of their homeland to the new arrivals remains an open wound, haunting the Palestinians, and the Israelis, to this day.

The origins of the Palestinian people are complicated, a bit murky, and like everything else having to do with this story, subject to controversy and disagreement. One school of thought has today's Palestinians descending directly from the biblical-era Canaanites and Philistines (which is where the name "Palestine" comes from). This theory provides some ammunition in the endless wrangling over whether Jews or Palestinians have the more "legitimate" claim to the land. If Palestinians descend from Canaanites, then by definition they've been in the land longer than the Jews, who the Bible says invaded and conquered the Canaanites. But some partisans of the Palestinian cause have criticized this theory, noting that it actually validates the Zionist narrative that Jews have an ancient connection to the land, rather than being a recent European colonial transplant to the region. In this way, the theory endorses an idea they reject: namely, that Jews and Palestinians have, essentially, been fighting it out for control of the country for thousands of years.

More recent and serious scholarship suggests that Palestinians descend from a mix of the various waves of peoples and civilizations that inhabited Palestine over the centuries—including some of those ancient biblical inhabitants. Over time, the people living in the land adopted the religions (paganism, Judaism, Christianity, and finally Islam) and languages (Hebrew, Aramaic, and finally Arabic) of the most dominant groups. As you may have noticed, there is an irony here: some of today's Palestinians may well have descended, at least in part, from the very people with whom they are in such conflict—Jews.

During the period the Christian Byzantine Empire ruled the territory, between the fourth and seventh centuries C.E., most inhabitants of Palestine became Christian. In 638 C.E., though, the new Muslim empire conquered Palestine, and by the nineteenth century, a majority of the inhabitants of the land had converted to Islam. Arabic was the primary language, and from that point onward, most inhabitants of Palestine saw themselves essentially as part of the larger Arab world.

Arab rulers allowed Jews, most of whom had been banned from Jerusalem during the centuries of Christian rule, to return to the city.

On the Temple Mount in the Old City, site of the Second Jewish Temple (which the Romans had destroyed and which Christian rulers had been using as a dump), Arab-Islamic conquerors built one of the most important, and stunningly beautiful, examples of early Islamic architecture in the world and perhaps the most recognizable symbol of Jerusalem to this day: the Dome of the Rock, completed in 692 C.E.

Dome of the Rock

The Dome is not actually a mosque. (The eighth-century Al-Aqsa Mosque is right next door.) Rather, it is a shrine. Jewish, Christian, and Muslim traditions hold that the rock beneath the Dome is the "Foundation Stone," one of the holiest sites in the world, the place where (variously) God created Adam, Abraham almost sacrificed his son Isaac, the Ark of the Covenant stood, and Muhammad ascended to heaven on his Night Journey. A lot of sacred activity for one small rock! Today, the image of the Dome of the Rock is used by Palestinians to signify their connection to Jerusalem. You can see it painted above the doors of Arab homes in the Muslim Quarter of Jerusalem's Old City.

By the sixteenth century, the mighty Turkish Ottoman Empire, with its capital in Constantinople (later called Istanbul), controlled most of the Arab world, including Palestine. The sultan Suleiman the Magnificent built the walls of Jerusalem's Old City that remain to this day. By the late nineteenth century, however, the Ottoman Empire had entered a state of rapid decline; Palestine, for its part, was an underdeveloped, lawless, provincial backwater. Its people were poor, literacy rates were low, and urban centers were few and far between. Jerusalem, the largest town, had only about twenty thousand people. Much of the land was owned by absentee landlords and worked by poor tenant farmers. A small elite, drawn from influential local Arab families, lorded over the impoverished masses. There wasn't much to speak of by way of a middle class. In 1880, just before the waves of Zionist immigration began, the whole of Palestine had just under six hundred thousand inhabitants, 95 percent of whom were Arab.

Conditions began to improve in Palestine as reform-minded Ottoman authorities tried desperately to modernize the empire, which had fallen far behind its European rivals. In the 1880s, the Ottomans cracked down on lawlessness in Palestine and built roads, rails, and other infrastructure. This enabled improvements in agriculture, which in turn led to increased food production, population growth, and an improved standard of living. Modernization efforts like the ones in Palestine were being carried out throughout the empire as it attempted to reverse decades of decline.

In fact, Ottoman modernization efforts actually contributed to this decline. Rising standards of living and the introduction of European ideas about how societies should be organized led to rising nationalist sentiment and a growing thirst for autonomy among the various countries ruled by the Ottomans. Greeks, Macedonians, Bulgars, and Albanians wanted the end of Ottoman dominance, and the Arab world, including Palestine, was no exception. Some

Palestinian Arabs joined the growing movement for a pan-Arab nationalism, the goal of which was a united Arab political entity. Others supported more localized versions. As these nationalist movements gained traction throughout its territory, the Ottoman Empire, already referred to as "the Sick Man of Europe," began to weaken further.

At the same time that they were developing their own nationalist ideas, Arabs in Palestine were coming into contact with the Zionist immigrants arriving on its shores. As they realized the extent of the Zionists' aspirations, Palestinian Arabs recognized that their Ottoman imperial overlords were not the only threat to their hopes; increasingly, Palestinian Arab nationalism was defined by its opposition to the Zionists, too, and their campaign of Jewish immigration and institution building. Like the Zionists, Palestinian Arab nationalists launched newspapers, founded political organizations and institutions, and held congresses to advance their cause. What all this amounts to is that, in yet another irony—this story is full of them—Palestinian Arab nationalism began to take shape in part as a result of and in response to Jewish nationalism, aka Zionism.

. . .

Up to this point, we have looked at the separate stories of how and why Jews and Palestinians became connected to the same place on the map. Now, these two stories come together. From here on out, the stories of the Jews and the Palestinians in the land become intertwined, inseperable, inextricable. The rest of this book reflects that reality.

CHAPTER 4

THE BRITISH ARE COMING

World War I, the Balfour Declaration, and the Establishment of the British Mandate (1917–39)

THE OUTBREAK OF World War I temporarily interrupted the waves of Jewish immigration to Palestine, and the world that emerged from the smoke and rubble of that conflict was a very different one for both the Zionists and the Palestinian Arabs to navigate. By 1917, the Russian Empire was overthrown by the Bolshevik Revolution, which led to the founding of the Soviet Union. While many Russian Jews remained, some taking leadership roles in the new Communist society, many others left, sparking new waves of immigration to Palestine. The Ottoman Empire, which ruled much of the Middle

East, including Palestine, shattered and split into a number of new nation-states. And in the wake of this collapse, the brand-new League of Nations (a predecessor to the United Nations) awarded the United Kingdom a mandate to govern Palestine and Transjordan (later Jordan), after the United Kingdom conquered the territory for the Western Allies during the war. The nations of the world had given the United Kingdom another colony to run, but one that would prove challenging to rule.

Balfour

This seemed like good news to the Zionists, who in 1917, in the midst of the war, had received an important boost from the British government. In response to years of lobbying by Zionists, Foreign Secretary Arthur James Balfour wrote a letter to the British Jewish leader Baron Lionel Walter Rothschild. The letter was short. Its central, substantive paragraph was just one sentence:

His Majesty's government view with favour the establishment in Palestine of a national home for the Jewish people, and will use their best endeavours to facilitate the achievement of this object, it being clearly understood that nothing shall be done which may prejudice the civil and religious rights of existing non-Jewish communities in Palestine, or the rights and political status enjoyed by Jews in any other country.

The Balfour Declaration, as it became known, did not go into detail about what, exactly, that national home ought to look like, what political form it ought to take, or whether it would be established in all or only some part of Palestine. The second part of the sentence was intended to reassure those who worried about what the establishment of a "national home for the Jewish people" might mean for the indigenous Arab residents of the country or for Jews living elsewhere. The Balfour Declaration made sense for the British, who looked forward to acquiring Palestine for the empire and establishing Britain's dominance in the Middle East. They saw support for a Jewish national home there as good international politics. They hoped, among other things, that the Declaration might reduce American Jewish opposition to the United States' entering World War I on the side of the Allies.*

For the Zionists, British support was a lifeline that gave their project legitimacy and, they hoped, the protection of the powerful state preparing to assume control of Palestine. But that support was soon tempered by the Palestinian Arab community's increasingly furious opposition to the Declaration and to Jewish immigration

---

* As strange as it is to think about now, the leadership of the American Jewish community in the first decades of the twentieth century was largely of German origins, while the masses of American Jewry were eastern Europeans who'd fled tsarist Russia. Neither group was eager for the United States to enter the war on the side of Russia, against Germany.

to the region. Over the course of the next three decades, the British faced a serious challenge in navigating between the two competing sides, Arab and Jewish, in Palestine. As a result, their positions on key issues—the establishment of a Jewish national home, Jewish immigration to Palestine, the relationship between Jewish and Arab residents of the land, and the ultimate disposition of the territory—would continually change. Their shifting positions confused and infuriated all sides, exacerbated mutual distrust, and increased tensions in an already fraught and fragile situation.

As it was for the Zionists, World War I proved to be a turning point for the Palestinian Arab nationalist movement. The Ottoman Empire entered the war as one of the Central Powers, along with Germany and the Austro-Hungarian Empire, fighting the Entente Powers, or Allies, Britain, France, and—until it dropped out of the fight due to the Bolshevik Revolution—Russia. The United States later joined the Allied side (as did Japan and Italy). During the war, as the Ottoman Empire was on its last legs, the British invaded Palestine on behalf of the Allies.

While the Balfour Declaration gave hope and encouragement to the Zionists, Palestinians and other Arabs took heart from an earlier set of letters: the Hussein–McMahon Correspondence, between British officials and Arab leaders from 1915 to 1916. Sir Henry McMahon was the British high commissioner to Egypt; Hussein bin Ali was the Sharif of Mecca. The letters between them promised British support for Arab independence (in a somewhat vaguely defined territory) in exchange for Arab support for the British against the Ottomans.

However, after the war, once the British received the mandate from the League of Nations to control Palestine, they claimed that the promise of Arab independence made in the Hussein–McMahon Correspondence didn't actually apply to Palestine; rather, they argued, it applied to other territories in the Middle East. Predictably,

Palestinian Arabs were furious and felt betrayed. The British continued to promise a lot of things where Palestine was concerned and then spent a lot of time reinterpreting and changing their minds about those promises.

To make matters worse, Russia (now "the Soviet Union"), having undergone its Communist revolution, decided to embarrass its two capitalist former allies, Britain and France, by making public a secret wartime agreement between the two countries. The so-called Sykes-Picot Agreement (named for the British and French officials who negotiated it) aimed to divide the Middle East into zones of French and British control after the war. Arab leaders saw this as a betrayal and a violation of the promises made in the Hussein–McMahon Correspondence.

Add to the mix the Balfour Declaration, and you can see why the Arabs were, by the end of the war, *extremely* skeptical about British intentions in the region. All this, understandably, led to a precipitous three-way rise in postwar tensions among the Arabs, the British, and the Zionists in Palestine.

It isn't hard to understand why Palestinian Arabs opposed the Zionist enterprise. They watched in trepidation as the Jewish community grew, acquired more land, established its institutions, and made clear its aspirations to build a new, independent Jewish state. All this seemed to come at the expense of the Arabs, who felt they were increasingly becoming displaced, disenfranchised, and marginalized in their own homeland—pushed off a plank into the sea. While some Palestinian Arabs and Jews did try to imagine what peaceful coexistence and a shared Arab-Jewish future in Palestine might look like, most people on both sides saw things more as a zero-sum game in which one side stood to win and one to lose.

In 1921, following an eruption of riots and attacks by Arabs on Jews in Jaffa, a main port town in Palestine and the point of arrival for many Jewish immigrants, the British issued a white paper (a

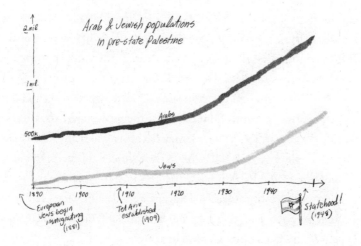

Arab & Jewish populations
in pre-state Palestine

government policy paper; the document's color indicated that it was intended for public release) authored by future prime minister Winston Churchill reiterating support for the idea of a Jewish national home, praising the industriousness and orderliness of the Yishuv, and supporting the notion of continued (although not unlimited) Jewish immigration to Palestine. At the same time, the Churchill White Paper, as it was known, attempted to assure the Arab side that the British had not thrown their weight fully behind the Zionist cause.

But violence between Jews and Arabs continued to flare, and the British authorities were unable (or unwilling) to contain it. To defend the Jewish communities scattered around the country from attack, the Jewish Agency created the Haganah (Hebrew for "Defense"), the most important of the pre-1948 paramilitary organizations. Its leadership and fighting ethos reflected the left-leaning Labor Zionism of the Yishuv's leadership. For example, it adhered, at least in theory, to the ideal of "purity of arms" (the notion that the Haganah would use its weapons only defensively and never against civilians) and to the policy of "restraint" (in which Yishuv leaders forbade counterattacks and reprisals against Arab attacks—again, limiting military action to defense). The Haganah evolved into the main military force of the Jewish community in Palestine and became, after independence in 1948, the core of the Israel Defense Forces (IDF).

The IDF inherited the concept of "purity of arms," which accounts for the oft heard claim that it is "the most moral army in the world." Of course, this sounds somewhat absurd to many non-Israeli ears, especially given the IDF's role as the enforcer of Israel's post-1967 occupation of the Palestinian territories and the disproportionate civilian casualty counts in Israel's repeated clashes with Hamas in Gaza in the twenty-first century. But in those early days, the Haganah perceived itself as a different kind of army.

In 1929, rumors flared that the Jews planned to seize control of the Temple Mount, the most precious site in the Old City of Jerusalem, which contained the Dome of the Rock and Al-Aqsa Mosque (the third-holiest site for Muslims) and the Western Wall (holy to the Jews), and, to this day, the single most dangerous flash point of the entire conflict. In response, Arab rioters began to rampage through Jerusalem, eventually reaching other locations in Palestine; almost seventy members of the ancient Jewish community of Hebron were murdered. The British authorities belatedly stepped in to stop the violence and evacuate the survivors.

In response to the growing violence, the British issued another white paper, one of whose recommendations was to restrict Jewish immigration to Palestine. This move prompted a group of right-wing Jewish activists to create a new paramilitary group called the Irgun ("the National Military Organization" in English). The Irgun did not feel constrained by the Haganah's goal of working with the British authorities, and it engaged in tactics that today we would describe as terrorism. For the next decade and a half, it competed and even clashed with the Haganah and attacked Arabs and British soldiers; at one point

in the mid-1940s, the Haganah even joined forces with the British against the Irgun. An Irgun leader, Menachem Begin, would go on to found the right-wing political party Herut, later renamed "Likud." In 1977, Begin would become Israel's first Likud prime minister.

THE ARAB REVOLT

Meanwhile, as Palestine was wracked by Arab-Jewish conflict, a new threat to the Jews of Europe, and indeed to Western civilization, was rising, one that only heightened the sense of urgency felt by the Zionists of the Yishuv. This threat would grow until it exploded, shattering the global status quo, proving the early Zionists horribly prescient, and changing the course of history. Fascism was on the march, and the fragile post–World War I order was teetering. In 1933, the antisemite and racist Adolf Hitler became chancellor of Germany. Hitler's immediate goal was to conquer all of Europe and to create Lebensraum (in English: "living space") for the German "master race," one that was devoid of

Jews, socialists, homosexuals, trade unionists, and other "undesirables."
As Hitler pursued his nightmare vision, war was once again approaching. The attempted destruction of European Jewry was almost at hand.

Hitler's ominous threat accelerated the pace of Jewish immigration to Palestine. Palestinian Arabs grew more alarmed, and in 1936, they launched a massive general strike to protest both Jewish immigration and British authority. Relations between Arabs and Jews in Palestine, never good, were worsening as the Jewish community in Palestine grew. Arabs saw the newcomers as invaders who were taking their land, exploiting their labor, and turning them into strangers in their own homeland. That the Jewish immigration to Palestine was the result of virulent antisemitism in Europe did not, in the eyes of Palestine's Arabs, justify the loss of their country.

In response to the rising unrest, a British commission of inquiry under Lord Robert Peel was convened to address the irreconcilable conflict between Jews and Arabs in Palestine. The Palestine Royal Commission, or Peel Commission, recommended for the first time the partition of the territory into two states, one Arab and one Jewish, and an eventual end to the British Mandate. Jewish leaders in Palestine didn't much like the Peel Commission's proposal—they wanted all of Palestine—but they recognized that, on balance, accepting it in principle, and being seen to accept it, was advantageous. Palestinian Arab leadership, for their part, rejected the idea of partition outright. What right did the British have to partition territory that rightfully belonged to its longtime Arab inhabitants? And so, with the Peel Report recommendations essentially dead on arrival, the Arab general strike turned into an armed revolt.

The Arab Revolt, which lasted from 1936 to 1939, likely hurt the Arab cause more than it helped, although it did contribute to the strengthening of an emergent Palestinian national consciousness and sense of identity. By the time they crushed the revolt, British forces had killed thousands of Arab fighters and confiscated many weapons, leaving Arab forces severely weakened. By contrast, the Haganah, after several years of coordination and cooperation with the British military and police to put down the revolt, emerged as a potent and formidable fighting force. The Irgun, meanwhile, carried out a series of bombing attacks against the Arab population that were condemned by Jewish leadership. These developments would have significant repercussions in the coming conflict between Arabs and Jews in Palestine.

The Arab Revolt did, however, have one other, arguably positive outcome for the Arab cause (or so it seemed at the time): it convinced the British that partition (separate countries for Jews and Arabs, as recommended by the Peel Commission) was unworkable. In 1939, on the eve of World War II, as disaster approached the Jews of Europe, the British issued yet another white paper reversing their position on partition and instead introducing a new policy that envisioned a Jewish national home—there were already almost half a million Jews in Palestine by this time, alongside around one million Arabs—as part of an independent Palestine governed jointly by Arabs and Jews, something like the "one-state solution" you hear people talk about today. The "White Paper of 1939" also imposed restrictions on Jewish land purchases in Palestine and, critically, announced severe limits on Jewish immigration to Palestine at perhaps the most dangerous and desperate moment in Jewish history, just before the beginning of the Nazi Holocaust, in which six million Jews would be murdered.

WORLD WAR ii, THE HOLOCAUST, AND THE RACE TO STATEHOOD (1940–49)

And so it was that, even as the Jews of Palestine volunteered to serve in the British Army to fight Nazism in Europe, the Jews of Europe were prohibited by Britain from finding refuge in Palestine. Recognizing the terrible irony of the predicament, Ben-Gurion announced that the Jewish community in Palestine would "aid the English in their war as if there were no White Paper [i.e., no British restrictions on immigration], and we must stand against the White Paper as if there were no war." But not all Palestinian Jews agreed. Toward the end of the war, in 1944, the militant Irgun (joined by another right-wing paramilitary organization, Lehi, which was also led by a future Israeli prime minister, Yitzhak Shamir) broke with the Jewish community leadership and declared a revolt against the British authorities. This began a period of intra-Jewish conflict, with the Haganah cooperating with the British to quell the militants' insurgency. Some version of this conflict continues to echo throughout Israeli history to this very day.

Like many in the Arab world, Palestinian Arabs resented the British and French for their colonial aspirations in the Middle East and for perceived British support of Zionism and the influx of Jewish immigrants—who, they feared, were displacing them in their own homeland. This led to some sympathy for the Axis powers (that is, Germany, Italy, and Japan). An extreme case was that of the Grand Mufti of Jerusalem (a position created by the British to administer Jerusalem's Muslim holy sites), Mohammed Amin al-Husseini, scion of one of the great Palestinian Arab families. Not only was al-Husseini militantly anti-British and anti-Zionist, but he also harbored deeply antisemitic sentiments. Fleeing Palestine to escape the British authorities, he ultimately washed up in Nazi Berlin, where he allied himself with Hitler.

World War II and the Holocaust changed everything, not least the trajectory of Zionism. As the extent of the near annihilation of European Jewry became clear, world sympathy swung toward the desperate survivors, hundreds of thousands of whom languished in displaced persons (DP) camps. This sympathy was no doubt increased by the guilt many in the West felt about the inaction of even the Allied nations (including the United States): restrictions on Jewish immigration had played a role in sealing the fate of millions of European Jews. In the wake of the Holocaust, global support for the Zionist project began to rise. Despite all this, the British, faced with Palestinian Arab fear, fury, and opposition, continued to prohibit mass immigration of Holocaust survivors to Palestine, even going so far as to enact a naval blockade to prevent ships bearing Holocaust victims from docking there.

In response, the Yishuv ramped up its efforts to bring Jews to Palestine. Ships, often crewed by volunteer American and Canadian World War II vets, ran the British blockade, bringing survivors to the Jewish community of Palestine, the only place in the world that wanted them.*

Often the ships were stopped and the survivors taken to internment camps in Palestine or Cyprus. Not surprisingly, this wasn't a good look for the British in the immediate postwar era. When one such ship, *Exodus 1947*, packed with more than 4,500 survivors, was stopped and boarded by British troops, passengers and crew members resisted. Several were killed in the ensuing clashes, and the survivors were taken to DP camps in Germany. The image of all this contributed to rising sympathies for the plight of the survivors desperately trying to reach Palestine. The incident also inspired the 1958 bestseller

---

* One of those volunteers was Leon Jick, one of my professors in college. Jick served in the U.S. Army Air Corps during the war and, later, went to the South of France, where he helped smuggle survivors to Palestine. He once told me about his adventures running the British blockade, and when he finished the story, he leaned back in his chair and said, "Those were heady times, Daniel. Heady times." It wasn't until I read his obituary, while researching this book, that I learned that Professor Jick, who was also an ordained rabbi, had also marched with Dr. Martin Luther King Jr. in Selma. Not bad for a kid from St. Louis. May his memory be for a blessing, as the Jews say.

Exodus, 1947

Exodus, by Leon Uris (which has served as a compelling, if extremely romanticized and rather biased, introduction to Israel for generations of Americans, including me), and the 1960 movie based on Uris's book (which starred Paul Newman as a very handsome Zionist agent and whose viewing has served as rainy afternoon activity for generations of American Jewish summer campers, also including me).

SALVATION AND DISPOSSESSION

After World War II, the British, diminished and depleted after six years of total war, were ready to pull out of Palestine. They faced rising resentment, violence, and revolt from Jews and Arabs alike and increasing criticism from around the world for their management of Palestine. Their attempts to put down various waves of resistance had failed, further inflaming anti-British sentiment on all sides.

In 1945, the Jewish paramilitary organizations put aside their differences momentarily and came together to wage a campaign of insurgency aimed at driving the British out of Palestine. The unified front didn't last long, with the Haganah rejecting the terrorist tactics of the right-wing groups. On July 22, 1946, the Irgun bombed the King David Hotel in Jerusalem, which housed British administrative headquarters, killing more than ninety people—Jews, Brits, and Arabs alike. The attack shocked both the British and the Jewish communities and ended the short-lived unity among the Jewish paramilitary groups. The Irgun claimed that it had phoned in a warning to the hotel prior to the attack, and so, responsibility for the carnage lay with the British authorities. But Ben-Gurion, head of the Jewish Agency and therefore de facto leader of the Jews of Palestine, condemned the bombing, urged Palestinian Jews to turn in Irgun fighters, and definitively broke with the militants.

By 1947, the population of Palestine was about 1.8 million people, one-third Jewish and two-thirds Arab, and they were at each other's throats. The British were ready to leave and to hand over responsibility for Palestine to the United Nations, which had been established in 1945. In one of its first acts, the United Nations authorized a Special Committee on Palestine, which recommended, as had the Peel Commission, the partition of Palestine into two states—one Arab and one Jewish. Because of its unique importance to the three monotheistic faith traditions (Judaism, Christianity, and Islam), the city of Jerusalem would have a special status and be administered by an international body. The new states would come into existence two months after the end of the mandate and the departure of the British.

And as with the Peel Report of a decade earlier, the leadership of Palestine's Jewish community—pragmatic, desperate to provide a haven for the survivors of the Holocaust languishing in DP camps in Europe, and eager to get on with the work of state building— accepted the plan. The Palestinian Arab leadership had fallen into a state of weakness and disorganization during World War II, but

King David Hotel
bombing

they joined with the governments of neighboring Arab countries in rejecting the proposal. They felt that they were being asked to pay for someone else's (Europe's) sins by relinquishing more than half the territory of Palestine, which they considered to be rightfully theirs.

Still, on November 29, 1947, the UN General Assembly voted 33 to 13 (with 10 abstentions) to support partition.* Palestinian Jews danced in the streets; Palestinian Arabs protested. But the UN partition plan was never implemented. Instead, Palestine descended into war.

---

* The British abstained; the United States, the major European powers, and the USSR all voted in favor.

CHAPTER 5

ISRAEL AND THE NAKBA

Independence and Catastrophe (1947-49)

ALMOST IMMEDIATELY, FIGHTING broke out between Arabs and Jews, the start of a two-phase conflict. The first phase, from November 1947 until May 1948, was essentially a civil war between the Jewish and Arab populations of Palestine. The Haganah clashed with loosely organized Palestinian Arab fighters and volunteers from nearby Arab states, who attacked kibbutzim and Jewish communities far from the main population centers. Arab fighters also tried to besiege the one hundred thousand Jewish residents of Jerusalem by cutting off the narrow mountain road that connected the city to the major Jewish population center of Tel Aviv and the coastal plain.

In February 1948, Palestinian Arab militants set off a series of car bombs on Ben Yehuda Street, in the heart of Jewish Jerusalem, killing around fifty civilians and injuring hundreds more. In April, as Haganah forces tried to break the siege of Jerusalem, militants from the ultraright Irgun and Lehi fighting organizations entered the Arab town of Deir Yassin, just outside Jerusalem. There, they massacred between 100 and 250 people, most of them women, children, and old men. Deir Yassin terrified the Palestinian Arabs and shocked the Yishuv—devoted as it was to the idea of "purity of arms." The massacre was roundly condemned by Ben-Gurion and the Jewish Agency. And it appalled the global Jewish community, which did not expect Jewish fighters to behave in this way. Prominent Jews in the United States, among them Nobel laureate Albert Einstein and the writer-philosopher Hannah Arendt, wrote a letter to the *New York Times* condemning Irgun leader (and future Israeli prime minister) Menachem Begin and urging American Jews not to support him or his militant organization.

Hannah Arendt

As Begin later bragged, there is little doubt that the massacre (or the *story* of the massacre, as he claimed, avoiding admission that it had actually occurred) encouraged other Palestinians to flee their villages in the face of approaching Jewish forces. What happened at Deir Yassin was big news at the time. Since then, though, it has been conveniently forgotten by many Israelis and in the global Jewish community. While it is included in every serious history of the conflict, it is largely unknown to many of Israel's supporters today, and some defenders of Israel's image deny that it even occurred. But for Palestinians, it is an important part of their history, an emotional scar that is as traumatic to them, and as essential to their perspective on Israelis and the conflict, as the massacres of Jews by Palestinians before and since are to Jews.*

THE STATE OF ISRAEL

On May 14, 1948, as fighting raged throughout Palestine and the British Mandate came to an end, David Ben-Gurion, leader of the Yishuv, gathered Zionist leaders at the Tel Aviv Museum to declare

---

* But, of course, sweeping things under the rug never really works; they tend to come back to bite you, sometimes in unexpected ways. Understandably, Deir Yassin isn't exactly something supporters of Israel like to talk about, if they are even aware of it. Most American Jewish kids aren't taught about what happened there as part of the Israeli history education they receive from Jewish community institutions. The fairly whitewashed version of Israel they learn about would *never* do such things. And so, when they go to college and encounter angry anti-Israel protesters talking about the Zionist atrocities at Deir Yassin, their first impulse is not to believe them. If they bother to do a bit of research and find out that the massacre there actually happened, they may immediately feel betrayed by the Jewish community institutions that gave them an incomplete and misleading history of Israel. Had their Israel education included Jewish terrorist groups and those Jewish institutions in the Yishuv that moved to crush their campaigns, young American Jews might be able to understand Deir Yassin in context, as uncomfortable and as upsetting as it is.

Israel's independence. U.S. president Harry S. Truman recognized the new country right away, and Jews around the world celebrated. As the *New York Times* reported:

> The declaration of the new state by David Ben-Gurion, chairman of the National Council and the first Premier of reborn Israel, was delivered during a simple and solemn ceremony at 4 P.M., and new life was instilled into his people, but from without there was the rumbling of guns, a flashback to other declarations of independence that had not been easily achieved.

Israel independence

Ben-Gurion read aloud the new Declaration of the Establishment of the State of Israel in its entirety and then announced, "We hereby declare the establishment of a Jewish state in Eretz-Israel [the Land of Israel], to be known as the State of Israel." The Declaration, Israel's founding document, announced that the new country would be devoted both to the "ingathering of the exiles"—that is, the Jewish people—and also to equality for all its citizens, regardless of religion or race. It's hard to overstate how powerful this moment was for the Jewish people. In the wake of the near eradication of European Jewry, there was, for the first time in two thousand years, a country established, built, and defended by Jews.

But this moment of promise for the Jewish people was one of catastrophe for the Arabs of Palestine: it was the moment their homeland disappeared. It was also a period of peril and anxiety for everyone in the region. The day after the Declaration of Independence was issued, the armies of Transjordan (today's Jordan), Syria, Egypt, and Iraq entered the territory of British Mandate Palestine with an objective to destroy the nascent State of Israel. The Israel Defense Forces (as the fighting forces of the Yishuv became known on May 14) attempted, ultimately successfully, to push them back and expand Jewish-controlled territory.

Phase two of the war followed Britain's withdrawal from Palestine and Ben-Gurion's declaration of Israel's independence. But the conflict wasn't limited to Arab versus Jew. Immediately after independence, the Haganah, Irgun, and Lehi were officially incorporated into the new Israel Defense Forces. But the militant groups were loath to give up their independence or moderate their hard-line ideology. They continued to make secret attempts to procure arms for their individual militant efforts. Ben-Gurion saw this as a direct challenge to the authority of the new Israeli government. In June 1948, he ordered one of his military commanders, a young officer named Yitzhak Rabin, to fire on a ship off the coast of Tel Aviv, the *Altalena*, which was secretly bearing weapons for the Irgun. Sixteen Irgun fighters and three IDF soldiers were killed in the confrontation, but the challenge of the militant groups to the new state's authority was halted. The threat of civil war between the Jewish factions was extinguished, and the IDF emerged as the sole military force of the new State of Israel. Ben-Gurion and other Israeli leaders, who viewed the Irgun and others as rogue Jewish terrorist groups that would undermine their efforts to defend the new state, realized that their effort to win their war and build their new state depended on having a monopoly on force, a united army firmly under the auspices of the new Israeli government.

The Altalena, 1948

Although Israeli Jews were united in their desire to secure and defend their new state, deep ideological fault lines within the Jewish community of Palestine never really disappeared. The pragmatic socialist school of Zionism exemplified by Ben-Gurion and his lieutenants could be tough, sometimes even ruthless, in pursuit of its ultimate goal of establishing a state. But this faction was also willing to compromise, to not let the perfect be the enemy of the good—for example, accepting every partition plan presented by the British and the United Nations. The pragmatists would continue to clash, sometimes violently, with the right-wing Zionists led by Begin, Shamir, and their ideological heirs.

In 1995, half a century after he fired on Irgun forces as a commander in the IDF, Yitzhak Rabin, now prime minister of Israel, would be assassinated by a right-wing extremist because of his attempts to reach a peaceful compromise between Israel and the Palestinians. While Rabin was no peacenik, he was heir to the early Labor Zionist and Israeli leaders' tough pragmatism. And for this, descendants of the opposite school—of a militant, expansionist Zionism—murdered him.

The First Arab-Israeli War ended on July 20, 1949, with the signing of an armistice agreement between the new State of Israel and the Arab states that had attacked it. When the fighting stopped, Israel, having successfully repulsed the invading Arab armies, held 78 percent of the territory of historic Palestine, more than half again as much as it had been allocated in the UN partition plan. Jordan held the West Bank and East Jerusalem (with the exception of an Israeli-held enclave at Mount Scopus, site of the Hebrew University campus); Egypt held Gaza. The Palestinians held nothing.

The victory came at a high cost: almost 6,400 Israelis were killed, about 1 percent of the population. Arab casualties were at least as high. About 700,000 Palestinians were expelled or fled from their homes in what is now Israel. Around 10,000 Jews were kicked out of or fled their homes in territories captured by Arab forces. The armistice line between Israeli and Arab forces was drawn with a green pen on the official map, hence its name: the Green Line. The Green Line became the internationally recognized border of Israel. Israelis call the Arab-Israeli War of 1947–48 the War of Independence. Palestinian Arabs call it the Nakba, the "catastrophe" of their dispossession from their land. Like so much else in this conflict, both narratives are true.

. . .

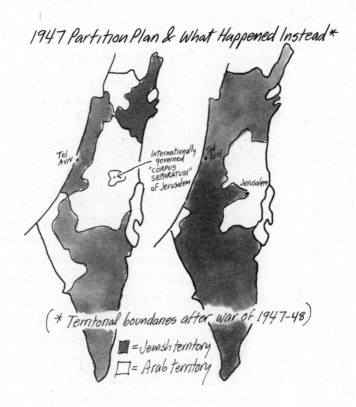

1947 Partition Plan & What Happened Instead*

Tel AVIV

Internationally governed "CORPUS SEPARATUM" of Jerusalem

Tel AVIV

Jerusalem

(* Territorial boundaries after war of 1947-48)

■ = Jewish territory
☐ = Arab territory

DOES THERE REALLY NEED TO BE A "JEWISH STATE"?

Don't Jews today live lives as secure and fulfilling in the United States and elsewhere as they do in Israel? Isn't the whole notion of a "Jewish State" a discriminatory anachronism in the twenty-first century? And was it maybe not the greatest idea in the world to put this "Jewish State" where Israel is, given its neighborhood and the demographics of the region? I hear these questions a lot, and I get it. I really do. From the perspective of a liberal American today, the rationale for Israel isn't always clear, especially if you don't really know the history.* But the fact is, as problematic and complicated as Israel's existence has been, as much as its creation has caused misery for innocent people, Israel was a good idea—or, at least, an idea born of a terrible and desperate necessity.

A few years ago, I visited the Anne Frank House in Amsterdam with my kids. Afterward, trying to make sense of it all, my daughter, then eleven, asked me why Anne and her family didn't just go to America, or Canada, or Australia, or "any of the good countries." I explained to her that even as it became clear that something terrible was happening in Europe, no country in the world was willing to accept the Jews of Europe. She was understandably incredulous and asked why there couldn't be just one country in the world where Jews could go to be safe. And right then and there, I witnessed the birth of a Zionist consciousness.

---

* My first response to these questions is usually to note that Israel actually already exists and isn't going anywhere and that time and energy is therefore probably better spent helping it be the best it can be than wondering if it was a good idea in the first place.

Because, of course, if just one country in the world had been willing to provide refuge to the masses of European Jewry in the years before the implementation of Hitler's "Final Solution," you probably wouldn't be reading this book. While the Holocaust isn't the reason the Zionist enterprise began, it was probably the reason it succeeded as it did. If any of the "good countries" had done what my daughter asked, the Yishuv, "the Settlement," deprived of both immigrants and a rationale for its existence, very well might have remained a tiny enclave that dried up and disappeared.

But that's not what happened. The Zionists were correct: nobody was going to look out for the Jews but themselves. Even today, the world is full of people who were alive and aware as Hitler tried to murder every single Jew in Europe. The rationale for Israel's existence isn't ancient history. It's living and breathing, right there next to you. Israel was a complicated and imperfect answer to a question of, literally, life and death. At the time of its founding, there wasn't a better one available to the Jewish people. It was the only available plank in the sea, the only life raft they had.

The Nakba

CHAPTER 6

THE DISPOSSESSED

THE POPULATION TRANSFERS that shaped the Arab-Israeli conflict have a terrible sort of symmetry, almost a choreography of expulsion and flight. Jews fleeing persecution in eastern Europe came to nineteenth- and early twentieth-century Palestine. They were followed by a major influx of Jews fleeing the Holocaust and the post-Holocaust Europe that had no home or future for them. This mass movement of people precipitated the mass expulsion and flight of Palestinian Arabs in 1947–48. And this was then followed by an equal number of Middle Eastern Jews who fled to Israel from their countries of origin—Iraq, Morocco, Tunisia, Egypt, etc.—after the establishment of the State of Israel led to rising antisemitism and hostility in the Arab world.

Accounts of these mass population transfers—what today many of us would call ethnic cleansing—are harrowing. In his memoir, former prime minister Yitzhak Rabin writes of being ordered by Ben-Gurion to force tens of thousands of Arab residents of the Arab town of Lydda (now the Israeli city of Lod and the location of Israel's international airport) to leave their homes during the fighting in

1948 and walk the eleven miles to cross the Jordanian lines into the West Bank.* (Interestingly, this incident appears only in editions of the memoir published after Rabin's assassination in 1995; in earlier editions, it was redacted by the military's censors.) In many instances, Arab villages and towns were razed and essentially disappeared from the map after their residents fled or were expelled. In others, new Israeli communities were built on the site of old Arab villages. Fleeing Arabs were not allowed to return to their homes.

In some cases, the long history of expulsions echoes down the years in the changing names of a particular place; a living palimpsest in which one period of history is erased and replaced by another. On a hill above the road to Jerusalem sits a beautiful kibbutz called Kibbutz Palmach Tzuba, built near the ruins of an Arab village destroyed in 1948. It is named for the Haganah strike force (the Palmach) that took the strategically located Arab town of Suba ("Tzuba" in Hebrew) during the fight to keep the Jerusalem–Tel Aviv road open. You can hike to the top of the hill and see the ruins of Suba, abandoned after its inhabitants fled and were prevented from coming back. Beneath these ruins are remnants of the Crusader fortress Belmont, built in the twelfth century to guard the western approach to Jerusalem. Belmont was built on the site of the ancient biblical Jewish village of, you guessed it, Tzuba, as mentioned in 2 Samuel. And so it goes.

---

* Rabin wrote that after he and another commander repeatedly asked Ben-Gurion what was to be done with the Arab population of Lydda, "B.G. waved his hand in a gesture which said, 'Drive them out!'" Rabin goes on to say, "'Driving out' is a term with a harsh ring. Psychologically, this was one of the most difficult actions we undertook. The population of Lod did not leave willingly. There was no way of avoiding the use of force and warning shots in order to make the inhabitants march the ten to fifteen miles to the point where they met up with the [Jordanian] legion. The inhabitants of Ramle [in Arabic: ar-Ramlah, a neighboring Arab town] watched and learned the lesson. Their leaders agreed to evacuate voluntarily" (*The Rabin Memoirs*, 383).

Ruins of Suba

It wasn't just Palestinians who were subjected to ethnic cleansing. Some ten thousand Jews were expelled by Arab soldiers from homes and communities that fell behind Jordanian lines, and another two thousand Jewish residents of the ancient Jewish Quarter of Jerusalem's Old City were expelled from their homes and forced to cross Israeli lines into West Jerusalem, after which the Jewish Quarter was largely destroyed.

Incidents of forced exile, flight, and destruction occurred throughout the country. This dispossession planted the seeds for the growth of a Palestinian diaspora in exile and that diaspora's demand to return to their homes in Israel. (To this day, old house keys remain powerful Palestinian symbols.) In one of the many painful ironies of the conflict, this situation is, of course, a mirror image of the Zionist demand that the Jewish people be allowed to return to their ancient home.

This being Israel and Palestine, even the factual history I've related here remains a subject of controversy. For years, the official

Israeli line was that Arabs were not forced out at all, but rather, left voluntarily in response to radio broadcasts from Damascus and Cairo urging them to clear out temporarily to let the invading Arab armies push the Jews into the sea. A variation of that argument has it that expulsions, as in places such as Lydda, were an unfortunate military necessity to eliminate the existential threat that the Arabs posed to the new state. By contrast, the official Arab line was that Zionist forces expelled Arab residents at gunpoint in order to rid the emerging state of all non-Jews.

The historical evidence suggests a more complicated story. For decades the claims about Syrian and Egyptian radio broadcasts were dismissed as Israeli propaganda, and indeed, no serious evidence has been found that such broadcasts were made. But in recent years, new evidence has come to light that, in fact, some Arab military leaders *did* tell local Palestinian Arabs to leave their homes and villages temporarily, although the extent to which this might have influenced the Arabs' decision to leave is unknown. At the same time, Zionist policy in the moment wasn't uniform, either. It is the case that in the mixed Arab-Jewish city of Haifa, the Jewish mayor implored terrified Arab residents not to flee and to remain in their homes. And Golda Meir, a high-ranking official and future prime minister, compared the plight of the Arabs of Palestine to that of the Jews of Nazi-occupied Europe.

It is certainly true that the leaders of the Yishuv, and of the fledgling State of Israel, viewed the presence of large numbers of Arabs within their new borders as a potential security threat. But historians are divided over whether there was a master plan for the forced transfer of the Arab population, or whether local military commanders were given the authority to make decisions and to take advantage of "opportunities" as they arose. Some Israeli historians argue that without the forced population transfers, Israel would not have emerged from the War of Independence as a cohesive geopolitical entity.

The Nakba

Whatever the case, the result was mass expulsion, the dispossession of hundreds of thousands of people, and a profound problem that vexes Israel and the Palestinians to this day.

Before we move on, a word about population transfer, ethnic cleansing, and context—because, as awful as all this is, it *does* have to be seen in context. The period from the 1920s through the early 1950s saw the greatest number of mass forced expulsions and population transfers in human history all around the world, as countries attempted to forcibly engineer more ethnically, racially, or nationally homogenous populations. Millions of ethnic Greeks and Turks were forced to leave their homes and cross the border to the "right" country in the 1920s. During World War II and its aftermath, not only Jews but also Russians, Poles, ethnic Germans, and tens of millions of others were forced from their homes and thrown out of their homelands for being the wrong ethnicity or nationality. Under Stalin's reign of terror, millions of Soviet citizens were forcibly transferred from their homes in one part of the country to another because of Stalin's monstrous, paranoid whims. During India's struggle for independence, millions of Hindus were forced to leave what would become Pakistan and Bangladesh, and millions of Muslims were ejected from India into those new neighbors.

All this is to say that what happened in Israel/Palestine in 1948 was awful but not unique. It happened all over the world during the terrible years of the early to mid-twentieth century. And during the decades since, for the most part, it has stopped. Today, ethnic cleansing—and, you guessed it (because this is Israel/Palestine we're talking about), some would argue that what happened to the Palestinians was *not* in fact ethnic cleansing, but then, you knew that was coming—is considered a crime against humanity, and when it occurs, it is met by serious international opprobrium. But it is difficult, if not impossible, to apply the standards of today to the 1940s, when the Jews of Palestine felt, quite reasonably, that they were, just five years after Auschwitz, once again on the brink of catastrophe.

Yet, even though it is tempting to relegate all that to the past, this is a luxury those of us who care about the future of Israelis and Palestinians cannot afford. Because when it comes to Israel and Palestine, it's like William Faulkner said: "The past is never dead. It's not even past." In fact, today, the specter of forced population transfer is not dead at all. It is alive and well in some corners of the hard right in Israel, including those in power, and indeed, it may be gaining currency in the ranks of Israel's ruling ultranationalists. And it is still very much alive in the rhetoric of some militant Palestinian-Islamist groups (not to mention in the language of their patrons in Iran and Hezbollah), who demand that the "cancer" of Israel be removed from the region and that "Palestine be free from the river to the sea."

. . .

So, what happened to the seven hundred thousand Palestinians who fled or were expelled from the new State of Israel? Most of them found their way to Transjordan (soon to be renamed Jordan), the

Transjordanian-controlled West Bank, Lebanon, Syria, Egypt, or Egyptian-controlled Gaza. Others made their way to neighboring Arab countries and beyond. In another ironic echo of Jewish history, the Palestinian diaspora—today numbering more than five million people who are the descendants of the "'48 refugees"—can, just like the Jewish diaspora, be found in countries around the world.

And as with the Jews, the experience of the Palestinians in exile has been anything but easy. In most of the Arab countries where they landed, Palestinians were housed in refugee camps—where many languish to this day, over seven decades later. The refugee camps were a way of dealing with the sudden influx of humanity while avoiding the potential risks of destabilization that state officials feared the Palestinians would bring. The camps also kept alive the issue of, and public anger over, the plight of the Palestinians. In the countries where they found themselves, Palestinians were unwanted, often despised, discriminated against, denied (in most instances) citizenship and (in many cases) basic rights, and used as a political football by their host countries in *their* conflicts with Israel and one another. It was, after all, useful for authoritarian Arab rulers to be able to remind their people of the twin specters of the Zionist invasion and the Nakba, both as a means of keeping the often oppressed masses angry and ready for the next round of conflict and also as a way of channeling the public outrage, anger, and dissatisfaction over these autocratic rulers and low standards of living outward, toward Israel, rather than inward, toward the regimes themselves.

In December 1948, at the end of the fighting between Israel and the Arab states, the United Nations passed Resolution 194, which stated that refugees from the 1948 war wishing to return to their homes to live peaceably with their neighbors should be allowed to do so as soon as possible. This is the basis for the claim to a Palestinian "right of return" to Israel *within* the Green Line—and one of the most challenging issues in the peace process. That's because if all the surviving 1948 refugees and, more important, their millions of descendants were allowed to come back to their homes in what is now Israel, their numbers, combined with the existing Arab population of the State of Israel and the occupied territories, could overwhelm those of the Israeli Jews living there now, ending Israel's Jewish majority. In short, the "right of return" could spell the end of the Jewish State.

In 1949, the United Nations created the UN Relief and Works Agency (UNRWA) to care for refugees and their descendants. Refugees who registered with UNRWA pass down, patrilineally, their refugee status to their children. Today, UNRWA operates in almost sixty refugee camps, housing 1.4 million people, in the West Bank, Gaza, Jordan, Lebanon, and Syria.

. . .

REFUGEES OF THE HOLY CITY

There is even a refugee camp in Jerusalem itself: Shuafat. Located a few kilometers away from the Old City, on the road to the Palestinian city of Ramallah, it began as a camp the Jordanians set up to house refugees from Jerusalem, Lydda, and elsewhere inside Israel. After Israel captured the West Bank and East Jerusalem in 1967, it expanded Jerusalem's borders to include land to the north and east, including Shuafat, and then annexed the newly enlarged East Jerusalem. Nobody recognized this annexation, but Israel built enormous new Jewish neighborhoods in the annexed territory, which now house more than two hundred thousand Israeli citizens. Thus, a 1948 West Bank refugee camp is, seventy years later, essentially a neighborhood of thirty-five thousand stateless people right smack in the middle of Israeli-annexed East Jerusalem, cheek by jowl with several large, post-1967 Israeli neighborhoods built on land confiscated by Israel (which non-Israelis would call settlements). Like most other Palestinian residents of East Jerusalem, the residents of Shuafat are not Israeli citizens, but rather, permanent residents.

According to Israel, the camp is inside the borders of the Municipality of Jerusalem, within the State of Israel, but make no mistake: Israelis simply do not go there. There is nothing remotely Israeli about Shuafat, even more so than most other parts of Arab East Jerusalem. Israeli police rarely enter the camp, but because it is "officially" in Jerusalem, Palestinian Authority police are forbidden from operating there. In fact, it is UNRWA, not the State of Israel or the Palestinian Authority, that provides most of the services to the people there. It's difficult to get building permits in Shuafat, so residents in the crowded neighborhood often build without them, and the Israeli authorities then sometimes demolish the structures. Meanwhile, the giant Israeli neighborhoods/settlements of Pisgat Ze'ev, Ramot Shlomo, and French Hill expand down the hills toward the refugee camp on three sides.

Shuafat

Shuafat is just the most extreme example of the way in which Jerusalem, in the most important ways, remains two cities, Arab and Jewish, under Israeli control. And the misery of Shuafat is largely invisible to non-Palestinians; you won't find an Israeli (other than a cop, soldier, or human rights activist) who has set foot in Shuafat, and you won't find a tourist or pilgrim to Jerusalem who knows a refugee camp is even there. This is not the Jerusalem you see on your trip to Israel.

. . .

At the end of the day, no less than the founding Israeli himself, David Ben-Gurion, well understood both the terrible predicament and the unending anger of the Arabs of Palestine, now Israel. He once said, "Sure, God promised it to us, but what does that matter to them? There has been antisemitism, the Nazis, Hitler, Auschwitz, but was that their fault? They only see one thing: We have come here and stolen their country."

CHAPTER 7

THE FIFTIES
State Building and Suez

AFTER 1948, ISRAEL turned to the work of building the state and forging a new national identity. In a sense, this process had been going on for decades, as the Yishuv built a foundation of infrastructure and institutions. But it was this period after the War of Independence that truly saw the emergence of a pioneering, collectivist Israeli society. The strong, independent, suntanned, and proud native-born Israeli was represented by the image of the "sabra," named for the fruit of a cactus that is prickly on the outside but sweet on the inside. This was the communitarian Israel that impressed so many in Europe and America and beyond: the scrappy little can-do start-up country that was taking care of its own after unthinkable tragedy, all the while growing Jaffa oranges and making the desert bloom.

Ben-Gurion knew that the State of Israel, made up of immigrants from all over and suffering from a kind of collective PTSD after the Holocaust, needed to come together as a country. His vehicle for accomplishing this was his concept of *mamlachtiut*, which

translates roughly to "statism." He saw the project of building Israel (rather than culture, religion, or ideology) as the center of everything and the engine for the renewal and rebuilding of the Jewish people. Loyalty to the state and to the Zionist enterprise was *the* primary societal value. Some of this was based in the early twentieth-century ethos of the kibbutz movement, in which personal interest was subordinated in favor of the common good.* The idea that everybody was working for the commonweal after the catastrophe that had befallen them—working to create a new future, a new Jewish people—was a powerful motivator.

This wasn't quite as North Korea as it may seem: early Israel was still a democracy, but individualism was less important than societal cohesion. This led to some silliness when, for example, in 1964, Israeli authorities banned the Beatles from touring in the country for fear that rock and roll's subversive messages might corrupt Israeli youth

---

* The kibbutz movement, always small in numbers, produced a disproportionate number of Israel's early leaders and had a huge impact on the initial character of Israel—including this focus on the collective over the individual.

and incite hysteria and riots. As a professor of history at Tel Aviv University put it, "Israel in the early 60s was afraid that from the west would come a bad wind of sex, alcohol and rock'n'roll."

But collectivism wasn't the only reason Ben-Gurion established *mamlachtiut* as the guiding principle of the new state. He was also intent on overcoming the ideological tensions, rivalries, and factionalism that had led to clashes among Zionist groups and that, he feared, could threaten the entire enterprise. The specter of the *Altalena*, the Irgun arms ship he'd ordered Rabin to fire on, haunted him. *Mamlachtiut* was a way for all new Israelis (the Jewish ones, anyway) to come together and rise above this divided history.

A top priority of Ben-Gurion's *mamlachtiut* was immigration into the country. Ben-Gurion took the "ingathering of the exiles" idea in the Declaration of Independence very seriously. In 1950, the Knesset passed the Law of Return, which declared that every Jew had the right to immigrate to and gain citizenship in Israel. Five years after the end of the Holocaust, there was a kind of legislative poetry to this.*

In the first decade of Israel's existence, its population grew by more than 2.5 times, to more than 2 million people. Hundreds of thousands of Holocaust survivors immigrated to Israel in the first years after independence. The ghosts of the death camps haunted early Israel. It was a topic that was simultaneously avoided—clashing as it did with the Israeli ideal of the tough, strong, self-sufficient "new Jew"—and ever present. Each day during the 1950s, Israeli radio broadcast programs listing the names of survivors who had reached the country, in the hope that family members could be reunited. And

---

* At least for Israel's Jewish citizens. For Arab citizens, many of whom had family members who'd fled in 1948 and were barred from returning to the country, the Law of Return represented something else entirely. It was a reminder that their status, while perhaps equal on paper, was not the same as that of Jewish Israelis.

Mamlachtiut

although thousands were, Holocaust survivors had trouble fitting in, and native-born Israelis had trouble knowing what to make of them.

Equally jarring to the sensibilities and self-image of the veteran sabras was the arrival of at least 750,000 Mizrachi (or "eastern") Jews fleeing their homes in the Middle East and North Africa because of rising antisemitism and intolerance in their countries related to the birth of Israel. These new immigrants didn't look or sound like the European Jews who had launched the Zionist movement and who, until this new wave of immigration, made up the majority of the new country. These new immigrants spoke Arabic, and their food, music, dress, and culture were products of the countries from which they came. Despite significant economic hardship, Israel absorbed these newcomers, creating almost a million new Israelis. But it did not always do so equitably, and the discrimination felt then by Mizrachi Jewish immigrants continues to color Israeli society and politics today.

Unlike European Jews, Mizrachi Jews were seen by the Ashkenazi, Labor Zionist establishment as primitives in need of reeducation and enlightenment in order to become civilized, productive citizens. That European Jews, historically treated as inferior, unsophisticated, and clannish by European non-Jews, would turn around and apply an analogous Jewish orientalism to Mizrachi Jews seeking refuge in Israel is not without irony.

Upon arrival, hundreds of thousands of Mizrachi immigrants were sent to transit camps, crowded tent cities with little in the way of modern amenities. Later, many were settled far from the relatively prosperous center of the country, in cities and towns on the periphery of the country or in dangerous or undesirable neighborhoods in Israel's big cities. So, even as Israel facilitated the emigration of Jews from Iraq, Morocco, Yemen, and elsewhere, often in dramatic airlifts, the country's establishment did not always welcome them as equals to the Ashkenazi Jewish majority. Mizrachi Israelis seethed at the treatment they received when they arrived. The 1950s saw civil unrest in Haifa and elsewhere, as Mizrachim demonstrated against brutal treatment by the police and discrimination in public housing.

Despite these challenges and their lingering legacies, the mass immigration of Mizrachim changed the character of the new country,

Israeli food?

introducing new sensibilities, new foods, and new folkways that define what Israel is today. Some claim that the reason hummus and falafel are considered the national dishes of Israel is because of the cultural appropriation that occurred when European Jews encountered Palestinian Arabs and their traditional foods. There is some truth to that, but it isn't the whole story; it is also because these are the foods Mizrachi Jews ate in Egypt, Lebanon, Syria, and elsewhere and brought with them to their new home. Jews with Mizrachi backgrounds now make up at least half the country's Jewish population, and decades of intermarriage with Ashkenazi Jews has resulted in a mix of Jewish cultures that is uniquely Israeli.

THE 1956 SUEZ CRISIS: THE WAR BETWEEN THE WARS

In the 1950s, as Israel was figuring out its identity, the Arab world was experiencing enormous changes. In 1952, a group of Egyptian Army officers led by the charismatic Gamal Abdel Nasser overthrew the Egyptian monarchy and took control of the country. Within two years, Nasser was president. An authoritarian and a fierce advocate of pan-Arab nationalism, Nasser was eager to see the British and French withdraw their forces from their bases around the region. He was also militantly anti-Israel, and he understood the potency of using Israel as a political tool to energize his base. He quickly became an iconic figure not just in Egypt but across the Arab world. He was young, modern, and secular, with an appeal that transcended borders. His provocative propaganda against Israel excited the Arab world, even as it distracted from his tyranny and mismanagement at home.

Nasser's propaganda ratcheted up anxiety in Israel. After Israeli forces raided Egyptian-held Gaza in response to Egyptian military intelligence's support for local anti-Israel militants, Nasser gave a green light to Gaza-based Palestinian terrorists to infiltrate Israel. He also turned to the Soviet Union to supply Egypt with arms, which began the long Cold War pattern of the Soviets funneling weapons to Egypt and Syria while the French and later the United States supplied arms to Israel.

As his status and stature grew, Nasser became the most powerful and admired leader in the Arab world. At the same time, he became public enemy number one for many others. The British saw him as threatening their interests in the Middle East, the French saw his pan-Arab nationalist appeal as fuel for the ongoing revolt against French rule in their North African colony of Algeria, and the Israelis saw him as the most powerful threat they faced. All three countries wanted him gone.

In July 1956, in the wake of Nasser's pivot to the USSR, Britain and the United States pulled their funding for Egypt's massive Aswan Dam project, an effort to contain and control the waters of the Nile and critical to Nasser's plans to modernize the country. In response, Nasser nationalized the Suez Canal, which connects the Mediterranean Sea to the Red Sea and, from there, the Indian Ocean. In so doing, he took control of the vital waterway from the British and French, who had built and now operated the canal. This move, along with Egypt's naval blockade on Israeli and Israel-bound shipping trying to reach the southern port of Eilat, further enhanced Nasser's hero status in the Arab world, but it also further panicked the British, the French, and the Israelis. Together, they decided it was time to stop him.

The three countries made a secret plan to invade the Sinai Peninsula in Egypt, take control of the Suez Canal to keep it open, and in the process, humiliate or even overthrow Nasser. For his part, Ben-Gurion hoped that the invasion would also lead to expanded Israeli borders, but his new friends weren't so interested in this. The

Americans, determined to resolve the crisis through diplomacy, were opposed to the idea of French and British involvement in such a dangerous scheme. So, the secret allies knew it had to look like the Israelis were acting on their own when invading the Sinai Peninsula. After they did, and once Nasser refused to stand down (as they expected he would), the two European nations would demand a cease-fire and enter the fray as "peacekeepers."

For a flimsy plan, it started off well enough for the secret allies. The Israelis invaded the Sinai on October 29, and the Egyptians (as expected) refused the Anglo-French call for a truce. The British then bombed Egyptian air bases, Nasser pulled his troops out of the Sinai, and the Israelis quickly reached the Suez Canal. On November 5, French and British forces invaded, too, but by then the jig was up. The supposedly secret alliance was revealed—it was pretty obvious to anyone watching that the three countries were in cahoots—and the world was outraged by the attempt by Israel and two fading colonial powers to play with fire in the Middle Eastern tinderbox. The United States, furious, pressured the British and French to end the campaign and led the condemnation of the attack in the United Nations.

At the end of the day, the secret allies accomplished little of what they'd hoped to. Yes, they achieved their military goals fairly quickly, but the victory was short-lived. Under strong U.S. pressure, Israel withdrew its troops from the Sinai. The Suez Crisis resulted in the humiliation and collapse of the British government and signaled the end of Britain's long role as a dominant power in the Middle East. And it didn't serve as the deterrent the French had hoped for—by 1962, the Algerians had kicked them out, and the country was independent.

For Nasser, the Suez war was a military defeat—Egyptian forces in the Sinai were quickly overwhelmed by the secret allies—but a massive political victory. He emerged from the crisis more popular than ever in the Arab world, seen as the hero who took on the combined might of France, Britain, and the Arab world's great nemesis, Israel. But Ben-Gurion extracted an important concession, one that would prove critical a decade later: the United Nations would provide a peacekeeping force in the Sinai, and if Egypt ever again blockaded Israeli shipping, Israel informed the world, it would consider this an act of war.

CHAPTER 8

THE BIG BANG
The 1967 War and the Reality It Created

STUMBLING TOWARD THE SIX-DAY WAR: A SERIES OF UNFORTUNATE EVENTS

Riding high after the Suez Crisis of 1956—despite the fact that, technically, Egypt had lost the war—Nasser moved to solidify his status as the leader of the Arab world. For the next ten years, a series of shifting alliances and rivalries consumed the Arab countries as they vied for influence and power. Global geopolitics was at play as well, as conservative Arab states like Jordan and Saudi Arabia moved closer to the United States (as did Israel), while more radical states like Syria and Iraq moved toward the USSR. The two superpowers saw these countries as useful Middle Eastern clients and proxies in their campaign for global primacy. Egypt, the largest and most important Arab player, flirted with both the United States and the USSR and attempted to assert its dominance over both the conservative and radical Arab camps.

In 1964, the Palestine Liberation Organization (PLO) was founded, with Nasser as its patron. The PLO sought to bring the plight of the Palestinians back to center stage and further roiled the waters of the Arab world by claiming that not only Israel but also Jordan, with its majority-Palestinian population, was destined to be part of the Palestinian state they aimed to establish. You can imagine how this went over with the Jordanian royal family.

Meanwhile, all the Arab players employed anti-Israel propaganda, still useful as a tool in energizing their populations and distracting them from the lack of freedom and opportunity at home. The propaganda also attempted to prove (rhetorically, anyway) how much tougher each Arab leader was compared to his rivals when it came to standing up to the "Zionist entity," a name they used to avoid having to actually say "Israel." Despite all this, the first years after Suez were relatively quiet as far as actual clashes between Israel and its neighbors were concerned. Soon, however, this began to change.

For years, Israel and Syria had exchanged fire near the demilitarized zone beneath the Golan Heights. These flare-ups increased in frequency and intensity in the 1960s. Israel also clashed with its neighbors over plans each side cooked up to divert the waters of the Jordan River and its tributaries to their advantage. Meanwhile, Palestinian militants from the new, radical, Syrian-backed Fatah organization began to launch operations into Israel. One of Fatah's founders was a young, Cairo-born son of Palestinian parents: Yasser Arafat.

Some of these incursions were aimed at military targets, but some were terrorist attacks aimed at civilians. The classic insurgency strategy behind Fatah's attacks was to provoke a disproportionate Israeli response. Such an overreaction, Fatah hoped, would then serve to unite the Arab countries against the Zionist enemy and, ultimately,

Arafat

usher in a war that would result in Israel's defeat and the liberation
of Palestine.

Egypt and Jordan were not fans of Fatah's tactics. They didn't
appreciate the idea of provoking Israel as a means to Fatah's end. But
Fatah's Syrian backers sought to use Nasser's vanity as leverage to get
him to do what they wanted. Syria mocked Nasser for his opposition
to Fatah's operations, accusing him of cowardice. They claimed he
was avoiding confrontation with Israel by hiding behind UNEF, the
United Nations Emergency Force, which, since the Suez Crisis, had
served as a "buffer" in Sinai between Israel and Egypt.

But things were changing fast in the Middle East, and by 1966, a
coup had replaced the Syrian leadership with one much friendlier toward Nasser in Egypt. The Egyptians and the Syrians began to encourage Palestinian militants to topple the more moderate King Hussein
of Jordan. The king found himself in a terrible predicament, wanting
to stay out of the increasing tumult in the region but caught between
the hard-liners in Syria and Egypt, the Palestinian militants using the
kingdom as a launching pad for their raids into Israel, and Israel itself.

Meanwhile, as Israel and Syria continued to clash near the Golan

Heights, Nasser declared that he aimed to liberate Palestine in a "revolutionary manner." Tensions were rising. In November 1966, in retaliation for Palestinian terrorist attacks launched from Jordanian territory, Israel conducted a major raid on a village deep in the West Bank, destroying homes and inflicting major losses. Jordanian forces, responding to the incursion, were badly beaten by the IDF. In order to maintain his legitimacy and credibility in the eyes of his Palestinian subjects (fully 60 percent of the population of the kingdom), the king had to talk tough—which he did by lashing out at Nasser with the now familiar accusation that he was a coward who blustered against Israel and then hid behind UNEF when Israel attacked Arabs. In return, Nasser and his Syrian allies excoriated the king for his refusal to accept their proposal to allow their forces into his kingdom to defend against Israel. Given the plots to topple him, who could blame him?

By early 1967, the situation in the region was deteriorating quickly. The Israeli prime minister, Levi Eshkol, was under increasing pressure from his military chiefs to respond forcefully to the Syrians.

Nasser

These officers represented a new generation of native-born Israelis—brash, tough, and blunt, a contrast to the more restrained European-born Eshkol. In early April, clashes between Israeli and Syrian forces escalated into an aerial dogfight in which Israeli fighter jets shot down six Syrian planes and then buzzed Damascus for good measure.

LIGHTING THE FUSE: ISRAEL AND ITS NEIGHBORS REACH THE POINT OF NO RETURN

Then the Russians decided to make a bad situation even worse. On May 13, with tensions already high, the Soviets informed the Egyptians that Israel was massing forces on the Syrian border in preparation for an attack. It wasn't true, but Nasser accepted it as such. It's still unclear why the Soviets did this—probably to stoke the atmosphere of crisis in a bid to enhance their status in the Arab world. Whatever the reason, it worked: Nasser mobilized the Egyptian Army and ordered his troops back into the Sinai.

Even now, Nasser didn't really want or expect war with Israel. He was engaging in brinksmanship, attempting to enhance his stature as the greatest leader in the Arab world, the one guy unafraid of the Israelis. And here we arrive at one of the inflection points of modern Middle Eastern history, a chain of events leading directly to the war that changed everything for both Israelis and Arabs: on May 16, Nasser requested that UNEF withdraw from its bases in the Sinai.

It is unclear whether Nasser really meant for the United Nations to pull out of the Sinai Peninsula completely. But U Thant, the UN secretary-general, immediately agreed to his request, noting that UN forces could remain on Egyptian territory only with Egyptian consent. He ordered all UN forces to pull out, and Egyptian troops moved into the abandoned UN positions. The United Nations then asked the Israelis if the departing UNEF troops could move into Israel's Negev Desert, next door to the Sinai. But the Israelis—worried that the presence of UN troops in their tiny country would hamper their ability to respond effectively in the event of a war, and perhaps sensing an opportunity to rid themselves of the threat at their borders—refused.

Nasser was playing with fire, but he still seems to have believed he could make bold moves that would give him yet another political victory without paying a significant price, impressing the Arab world while avoiding an actual war with Israel. He hadn't forgotten Ben-Gurion's pledge at the end of the Suez Crisis that Israel would consider any blockade of its shipping a casus belli, an act justifying war. And so, even as the Egyptian Army moved into the Sinai, Nasser did not send his troops to occupy the abandoned UN position in Sharm el-Sheikh, the strategic town overlooking the Straits of Tiran—the only way for ships to reach the southern Israeli port of Eilat. Unfortunately, this act of restraint provoked mockery from Jordan and Saudi Arabia, who accused Nasser of being a coward, afraid to occupy Sharm and close the Straits of Tiran. The taunting worked. On May 22, Nasser closed the straits to ships heading to or from Israel.

Nasser's generals told him Egypt's armed forces could handle any Israeli assault, and as the days went by without one, he seems to have thought the danger had passed. His troops dug in to their positions in the Sinai. His minister of war returned from a trip to Moscow with the fantastic news that the Soviets had pledged to back Egypt in the event of war with Israel—except that, almost unbelievably, he was lying. (It's still unclear why.) In fact, the Soviets had urged Egyptian restraint. Nasser then announced that Egypt wouldn't fire the first shot, but that if war with Israel came, the "pre-1948 situation" (i.e., no Israel) would be restored. On May 30, erstwhile rivals Egypt and Jordan reconciled when Nasser and King Hussein signed a joint defense pact. Not wanting to be left out of the increasingly bellicose tone coming out of the

Arab world, the head of the PLO declared that Israel was about to be destroyed and the Jews "thrown into the sea."

In those tense and heady days between late May and early June, Nasser appeared to have pulled it off. He was the unquestioned hero of the Arab street. He had outmaneuvered his Arab rivals and then seemingly united them. He had closed the Straits of Tiran, and the threatened Israeli response had not materialized.

In Israel, the political and military leadership initially considered Nasser's aggressive behavior a bluff. But with the withdrawal of the UNEF buffer, followed by the entry of Egyptian troops back into the Sinai and the closing of the Straits of Tiran, they began to think war was not only likely, but also necessary. They wanted the opportunity to destroy, once and for all, the enemy armies that threatened and surrounded them, to hit the Arabs so hard they would think twice before ever threatening Israel again. The Israeli military was confident

Six-Day War

in its ability to win any war with its neighbors. While the Soviets had equipped their Arab allies with huge quantities of arms, the weapons Israel had received from France and the United States were of much higher quality. But if the Israelis wanted to maintain the element of surprise, they had to move quickly. Military commanders urged the government to authorize a preemptive strike against the armies at Israel's borders.

Israel began preparing for war, mobilizing its forces and, after the closure of the straits, calling up the reserves. The army reserve force in Israel plays a critical role in augmenting the standing army in times of crisis. Most Jewish Israeli men participate in regular reserve duty for up to a month every year for decades after their active service is over, keeping the country fit, trained, and ready for war. But in 1967, Israel was a country of just 2.7 million people, and calling up tens of thousands of men in the prime of their lives from their jobs and families for an extended period of time put a huge strain on Israeli society.

If the military was confident of victory in the coming war, the Israeli public was less so. The news each day was oppressive. Israelis felt the strain of months of clashes with their neighbors, of terrorist incursions, and of the increasingly incessant drumbeat of hate speech and propaganda spewing from radio stations in Cairo and elsewhere in the Arab world. And now the massive call-up of the reserves made the situation feel untenable. To make matters worse, Prime Minister Eshkol seemed shaky and unsure. To address Israelis' growing concerns, he gave a speech, broadcast to the nation, during which he stammered and mumbled, hardly reassuring the jittery Israeli public. Meanwhile, the government urged citizens to donate blood, stockpiled coffins, and directed parks to be prepared for use as cemeteries. To many Israelis, unaware of the confidence of the IDF brass, it seemed that a new Holocaust might be at hand.

Even as pressure mounted for him to act, Prime Minister Eshkol hesitated. He did not want to go to war without the support of the Americans, and the Johnson administration was asking Israel to wait while the United States engaged in intensive diplomacy to convince Nasser to reopen the Straits of Tiran.

EXPLOSION: THE WORLD TURNED UPSIDE DOWN

On June 1, 1967, in a concession to his eager young military commanders, Eshkol appointed a new minister of defense: the hawkish war hero Moshe Dayan, famous for his eye patch. Eshkol also appointed, for the first time, the leader of the opposition, Menachem Begin (whom we last saw as leader of the militant right-wing, pre-state Irgun organization), as a minister without portfolio in an unprecedented national unity government, with a seat in Eshkol's emergency war cabinet.

By June 2, the Israelis were determined to act. They could not lose the opportunity to improve their position (by reopening the

Moshe Dayan

Paratroopers at the Wall

straits and teaching their hostile neighbors a lesson) that the crisis, provoked by their enemies, had provided them. When the war cabinet learned that Nasser had agreed to send his vice president to Washington, D.C., in an attempt to defuse the conflict and save face, Eshkol decided that the moment had come. Buoyed by reports that the Pentagon and CIA (if not the State Department) supported Israeli action, they made their move. On June 4, the war cabinet voted to approve a preemptive strike for the next morning.*

---

* The lone dissenting vote against going to war was cast by Yosef Burg, the leader of the dovish National Religious Party (Mafdal), the party of religious Zionists. The irony here is that in the decades after the 1967 war he voted to avoid, Burg's moderate party would be transformed into the political home of a new, national-religious community, one dominated by the militant settler movement. Mafdal ultimately disappeared as a party, replaced by new, even more ultraright-wing extreme national-religious parties advocating for the annexation to Israel of the land captured in 1967.

Early on June 5, two hundred Israeli fighter planes took off from their bases, racing south. Within hours of the early morning strike, virtually the entire Egyptian Air Force was wiped out. By the end of that first day, the Jordanian and Syrian air forces had met the same fate. Israeli tanks and troops stormed into the Sinai and Gaza, routed the Egyptians (who had no air cover in the vast open expanses of the desert), and reached the Suez Canal. In just a few days, the war with Egypt, Israel's most dangerous foe, was essentially over.

Meanwhile, Israel implored King Hussein of Jordan to stay out of the fighting. But the king was in a terrible situation. As he would say later, he knew that joining the war was a mistake. But he also feared that if he stayed out, his Palestinian subjects, and the broader Arab world, would never forgive him. And so, on June 5, Jordanian artillery began firing at Israeli West Jerusalem.

The Israelis were not about to lose the opportunity to take the Old City and its holy sites as well as the rest of East Jerusalem. On June 7, after fierce fighting through the narrow alleys of the Old City, Israeli troops reached the Western Wall and the Temple Mount, radioing to their commanders, "The Temple Mount is in our hands." In a famous photograph by David Rubinger from that day, tough paratroopers are overcome by emotion as they touch the wall, Judaism's most sacred site, for the first time.

Defense Minister Moshe Dayan, watching the scene through binoculars from a nearby hill, saw troops raise an Israeli flag over the Dome of the Rock, the third-holiest site in Islam. He immediately ordered the flag taken down, saying, "Do you want to set the Middle East on fire?" Shortly after the war, Dayan met with leaders of the Muslim Waqf, the religious authority that oversees Muslim holy sites, and agreed that while Israel would be responsible for security on the Temple Mount, the Waqf would remain the custodians of the site—and Jews would be allowed to visit, but not to pray there. This decision, taken by Dayan on his own, without consultation with the cabinet, was remarkably rational and thoughtful, given the emotions of the moment. It established a status quo that has eroded over time at one of the most potentially politically combustible places on earth.

In short order, the IDF conquered the rest of Arab East Jerusalem and drove deep into the Jordanian-held West Bank toward the Jordan River. The Jordanian Army collapsed, and the IDF captured the ancient cities of the West Bank, whose names evoke the biblical past: Hebron, Nablus ("Shechem," in Hebrew), Jericho. Israel now found itself in control of all of the almost mythical territory described in the Bible as the birthplace of the Jewish story.

As cease-fire talks intensified, the Israelis decided to go all out to eradicate the Syrian threat on the Golan. They did not want to miss the chance to destroy the military capability of the Arab country that had done so much to provoke the current crisis—because, despite

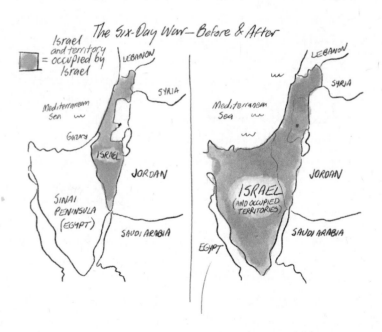

all the provocations, propaganda, and bluster, Syria had so far pretty much sat out the actual shooting war. On June 9, the Israelis attacked: tanks swept up the plateau, crushing the Syrian forces and, by June 10, pushing them out of the part of the Golan overlooking Israel and Lake Kinneret (the Sea of Galilee).

By the time the shooting had stopped, the Arab-Israeli conflict and the map of the Middle East had been entirely transformed. Tiny Israel was suddenly in control of Egypt's Sinai Peninsula, the Gaza Strip, the Golan Heights, the West Bank, and Jerusalem—including the one million Arabs who lived there. The combined military might of its enemies had been utterly shattered. Fears of annihilation were replaced by feelings of euphoria in Israel and throughout the Jewish world. Not only had Israel been saved, but it had also emerged from the crisis more powerful than anyone in the region could have imagined. For the first time in almost twenty years, Israelis were able to venture into the Old City, the markets of East Jerusalem, and the newly captured territories of the West Bank biblical heartland.

Almost immediately, Israeli leaders declared that Israel would trade at least some of (but not all) the land it had captured for peace with its Arab neighbors. In September, the Arab League (a regional organization of Arab states founded in 1945), meeting in Khartoum, Sudan, responded with "the Three Nos," also known as the Khartoum Resolution: no peace with Israel, no recognition of Israel, and no negotiations with Israel. But at the time, Israelis weren't worrying too much about that. They were too busy taking stock of their new situation. Like the rest of the world, they were astonished by the scope of their incredible victory.

. . .

EVERY PICTURE TELLS A STORY

Back in college, I found a copy of an old *Life* magazine cover in a bin at a used-book store. I was dazzled by it. The cover seemed to sum up something beautiful, hopeful, innocent—and even a little bit seductive—about Israel. The handsome soldier cooling off in Egyptian waters after winning the "astounding war" that Israel, as I understood it then, hadn't even wanted to fight. It made me feel a kind of pride in Israel and in the astonishing turn Jewish history had taken just a few decades after the Holocaust. It was inspiring and romantic. This was a country I wanted to cheer for and fall in love with. The magazine cover seemed to sum up all of that, and for years, it lived on my wall.

But as the years passed, I began to feel more ambivalent about the image. As I got older, taking any kind of pride or pleasure in war and violence, however justifiable or unavoidable, was something I just couldn't do anymore. It felt juvenile. Honestly, I felt kind of guilty for having felt those things in the first place.

Increasingly, that picture began to represent something very different to me. Because the moment right after that photo was snapped, the moment the war ended, was the moment that the occupation of the Palestinian territories began. Fifty-four years later, Israel continues to rule over millions of Palestinians who have no equality, no freedom of movement, no civil rights, and no vote for the Israeli governments that control their lives and fates. And all this primarily to safeguard and secure the settlements Israel has built throughout the West Bank in violation of international law.

Since 1967, Israel has sent its children to the IDF not only to serve as the guardians of the country against external threats, but also as the enforcers of a military occupation that is eroding Israel's democracy maybe even more: you can't deny millions of people their basic rights for more than half a century without permanently damaging your soul. Over the years, the picture began to mean the exact opposite of what it had meant to me when I first found it, and yet I could never quite bring myself to take it down. There was something about that image that continued to vex and discomfit, but also intrigue me. Instead of a snapshot of innocent Israel at the beginning of a new dawn, I now saw it as a snapshot of the end of Israel's innocence.

A few years ago, I got a visit from an Israeli friend, a prominent LGBTQ+ activist who runs a major human rights organization in Jerusalem. When he saw the magazine cover on my wall, he raised his eyebrows. He was familiar with the image, which had become almost iconic over the years, and he was surprised to find it hanging in my office. Why would I, of all people, have a picture glorifying both military might and an outdated notion of Israeli masculinity—especially given that I knew very well what happened immediately after that picture was taken? A bit embarrassed, I told him the story of my troubled relationship with the soldier on my wall.

A few weeks after my friend returned home, I got a package from Israel. In it was a note from him and a copy of a different

Adi Nes, soldiers

picture, one made by the prominent Israeli photographer Adi Nes. Nes, who is gay, is well known for a series of photographs called *Soldiers* that reimagines iconic images of Israeli military masculinity through a delightfully subversive homoerotic lens, and now he'd reimagined the image from the *Life* magazine cover.

The freedom implied by Nes's series is inherent in the original *Life* picture. Without the first image and all that it represents, Israel likely wouldn't be a country where the second image—representative of an Israeli desire to question, critique, and satirize the country's most sacred self-perceptions—was even allowed to exist. Nes's reimagining of the *Life* magazine cover photo provided me with a new way to understand and relate to it: as a uniquely Israeli image that now evokes a different kind of pride, not in Israel's military prowess, but in an Israeli culture that cultivates self-reflection, self-criticism, and satire, a culture that allows for multiple ways to be an Israeli.

A copy of Nes's version now hangs next to the original on my wall.

. . .

There were a few Israelis who saw warning signs in the midst of the triumph of 1967 and its aftermath. Amid the euphoria that swept the country in the wake of Israel's victory, an almost legendary figure emerged from self-imposed retirement to warn his fellow countrymen against being carried away by their miraculous victory. They could not, he said, keep the territories they had just conquered. Rather, they had to return them (except for East Jerusalem and the Golan) as quickly as possible, or risk the destruction of the country they had worked so hard to build. Even if peace were not then achievable, he said, they must give back the territory; otherwise, Israel could not go on being both a democratic and a Jewish state. Nobody paid much attention to him then. The country was too busy rejoicing.

If he said those things today, he would likely be branded a self-hater or a "beautiful soul" (Israeli for "snowflake") or even a traitor by hard-line Israelis—which would be awkward, because that prophetic voice belonged to none other than the country's most important and revered founding father, the George Washington of Israel, Israel's first prime minister, David Ben-Gurion.

What Ben-Gurion said then is still true today. After the Six-Day War, there were three main aspects to Israel's national identity, what I call "Ben-Gurion's Triangle": Israel was a majority-Jewish state; Israel was a democracy; Israel held all this new territory. Israelis could choose two of these points of identity, but not all three—and that choice would determine what kind of country Israel would be. If Israel annexed the new territories and made the Palestinians it now ruled full citizens, it risked losing its Jewish majority. If it formally incorporated the territories into Israel and denied the Palestinians citizenship, it would no longer be a democracy. The third choice, the only choice, as far as Ben-Gurion was concerned, was to remain a democracy and a Jewish state. And the only way to do that was to get rid of the territories.

Sadly, few Israelis in 1967 listened to what Ben-Gurion—"the Old Man," as he was known—was telling them. Within mere months of Israel's lightning victory in the Six-Day War, the first settlements were established in the West Bank. (We'll take a deeper look at what happened, and at the terrible conundrum Israel finds itself in as a result, in chapter 18.)

In November 1967, the UN Security Council issued Resolution 242, which reinforced the notion that a country could not acquire territory through war and stated that "establishment of a just and lasting peace in the Middle East" required the following:

> (i) Withdrawal of Israeli armed forces from territories occupied in the recent conflict;

> (ii) Termination of all claims or states of belligerency and respect for and acknowledgment of the sovereignty, territorial integrity and political independence of every State in the area and their right to live in peace within secure and recognized boundaries free from threats or acts of force.

In other words, give up land for peace. Eventually, all the parties to the conflict affirmed Resolution 242, although they continue to argue over its meaning. To this day, it remains the basis for virtually every round of Middle East peace negotiations. It sounds pretty simple, doesn't it? But if we've learned anything thus far, it's that nothing is simple when it comes to Israel.

The Six-Day War, more than any other Arab-Israeli war since Israel's founding, reshaped the landscape of the Middle East and altered the trajectories of Israel's politics, society, and future. It was the

Ben-Gurion

hinge on which history turned. Afterward, everything for Israel and its neighbors was different. Israel emerged from the war empowered and emboldened, in control of territory three times greater than its original size, the dominant power in the region. The Six-Day War instilled in Israelis and Jews around the world a new sense of pride: just over two decades after the near destruction of European Jewry, Israel was now a mighty military power, able to defend itself against overwhelming odds. But Israel's greatest victory also planted the seeds of perhaps its greatest challenge: an unresolved internal threat to itself more dangerous to its future as a democracy and Jewish homeland than any of its external enemies ever were.

For the Arabs, especially the Palestinians, 1967 was a second Nakba, a catastrophe. In time, Nasser, shattered and humiliated by the epic defeat, faded away, replaced by a new generation of regional autocrats. Their military forces in tatters, the Arab countries, especially Egypt, began to rethink their approach to the conflict with Israel. Almost a million Palestinians who'd fled their homes in 1948 for the relative safety of Gaza and the West Bank suddenly found themselves living under the control of the Israeli enemy they'd tried to escape from two decades earlier. And hundreds of thousands more fled the approaching Israelis into the less-than-friendly arms of neighboring Arab states.

Given its importance to the history of the region—indeed, of the world—it is puzzling and more than a little ironic that the Six-Day War was a conflict into which the participants stumbled largely blindly. This epoch-shattering war was the result, more than anything else, of a series of blunders, bluster, brinksmanship, and lies.

CHAPTER 9

ROLLER COASTER
From the Yom Kippur War to the First Intifada (1968–87)

THE SIX-DAY WAR was the beginning of the end for Egypt's Nasser. In March 1969, Nasser began what he called "the War of Attrition" against Israel, a grinding series of clashes and battles aimed at wearing down the Israelis, recapturing and crossing the Suez, and retaking the Sinai. During this period, the PLO launched attacks into Israel from Jordan, and the Israelis responded with reprisal raids against both PLO and Jordanian troops. In August 1970, after sixteen months of inconclusive fighting, Egypt, Jordan, and Israel agreed to a U.S.-brokered cease-fire. Despite the destruction and the thousands killed or injured, the situation at the end of the war was, for Egypt and Israel, pretty much what it had been at the beginning.

BLACK SEPTEMBER (1970)

Meanwhile, in Jordan, King Hussein faced a rising threat. During the Six-Day War, hundreds of thousands of new refugees fled to Jordan from the West Bank after it was captured by Israel.* The post-1967 influx of refugees created new instability and tensions in the kingdom, as militants from the PLO set up new bases of operations in Jordan for their attacks into Israel. These attacks led to Israeli reprisals into Jordan. Meanwhile, the PLO built a political, military, and social infrastructure that began to resemble a state within a state. (Remember: at least half the population of Jordan was already Palestinian.) PLO officials and militants flouted Jordanian concerns and laws, operating with relative impunity; some even called for the overthrow of the monarchy. PLO fighters clashed with the Jordanian Army, and several plots to assassinate the king were discovered.

In September 1970, Palestinian terrorists hijacked three commercial

Hijackings before Black September

---

* Palestinians remaining in the West Bank retained their Jordanian citizenship until 1988, when, in recognition of the PLO's claim to be the sole representative of the Palestinian people, King Hussein relinquished his claim over the West Bank and Jerusalem.

airliners and landed them in Jordan, taking the passengers hostage and blowing up the planes. This was the final straw for Hussein: the king ordered his army to uproot the PLO. In response, Syria moved to intervene in support of the PLO, sending infiltrators into Jordan and tanks toward the Jordanian border. King Hussein asked the United States for help, and President Nixon ordered the Sixth Fleet to the eastern Mediterranean. Meanwhile, the Israelis, with American approval, let the Jordanians (with whom they were officially at war) know that the Israeli Air Force would support them against the Syrians, if needed.

After months of heavy fighting, the PLO was defeated. PLO leadership and fighters fled across the border into Syria and then into Lebanon. (But more on that later.) In the wake of what came to be known as "Black September," the situation of Palestinians in Jordan deteriorated, and the tensions between the native population and Palestinian Jordanians became more pronounced. Meanwhile, the U.S.-Israeli alliance emerged from the Black September crisis much stronger, marking the start of the special relationship between the two countries we know today.

In September 1970, after exhausting himself working for a ceasefire between the Jordanians and the PLO, Egypt's president Gamal Abdel Nasser died of a heart attack. Despite the catastrophic Arab loss in the Six-Day War, he was honored as a hero: five million mourners marched in his funeral procession in Cairo.

THE RISE OF SADAT OF EGYPT AND THE YOM KIPPUR WAR (October 1973)

Nasser was replaced by his vice president, Anwar Sadat. Sadat surprised Egypt and the world by moving quickly to purge Nasser's followers from government and to move Egypt away from the Soviet Union and toward the United States, even ordering Soviet military advisers out of the country. He wanted to see the Sinai returned to Egypt, and he wanted to bring stability and prosperity to his country. To do this, he knew he needed an end to the endless wars with Israel.

So, he began, somewhat counterintuitively, to prepare the Egyptian military for a new major confrontation with Israel. Sadat believed that the Arab countries were unlikely to retake the conquered territories back from Israel by sheer force. But he thought a tremendous shock, one that forced the Israelis to reevaluate their Arab enemies, could convince Israel that it was time to come to the negotiating table. He reached out to Syria's new strongman, President Hafez al-Assad, who wanted the return of the Golan Heights to Syria as much as Sadat wanted the Sinai, and began to prepare his master plan.

Sadat wasn't wrong in his read of the Israelis. Still riding high after the Six-Day War, they were not particularly worried about war with their Arab neighbors, including Egypt. They were focused on the new territories they occupied and, more and more, concerned about terrorism. In 1972, Palestinian terrorists had murdered eleven Israeli athletes at the Munich Olympics. Despite this, though, Israelis were feeling bullish about regional geopolitics, and pressure was growing on Prime Minister Golda Meir and her government to walk back Israel's support for aspects of UN Resolution 242, which, you'll remember, called for Israel to give back the territories it had occupied in 1967 in exchange for peace and full recognition. For practical reasons (the greater strategic depth the West Bank afforded Israel and access to the oil fields of the Sinai and Suez Canal) and, increasingly, ideological ones (the captured territories, especially the West Bank, were the heartland of Jewish history, so how could Israel give them up?) many Israelis now felt the state should not be so quick to pledge to return the captured territories. In the West Bank, the Sinai, and the Golan, Israeli military bases were built, some of them developing into civilian settlements.

And so, as October 1973 rolled around, Israelis were busy preparing for the Jewish High Holidays, not for war. It is something of an Israeli tradition to go to the beach or the park for family barbeques on the first of these holidays, Rosh Hashanah, the Jewish New Year. But on Yom Kippur, the Day of Atonement, the holiest day of the year, the whole country shuts down; most Jewish Israelis, even secular ones, can be found at synagogue or at home. And that's where they were on October 6, 1973, Yom Kippur, when the sirens began to wail. The country was caught almost entirely unprepared by an Egyptian-Syrian surprise attack on Israeli positions in the Sinai and on the Golan Heights.

This was, in no small part, due to a failure of leadership in Israel. Days earlier, Israeli intelligence had reported that one of its spies in Egypt had warned that an attack was imminent, but the government dismissed the reports. Believe it or not, that spy was, allegedly, the son-in-law of the late president Nasser himself. (It sounds like the plot of a movie, and it is: *The Angel* came out in 2018.)

At first, things went well for the Arabs. Egyptian troops and armor surged across the Suez Canal, overrunning Israeli defenses and driving deep into the Sinai. Syrian forces pushed the Israelis back in the southern Golan. As the Israelis reeled from the initial attacks, the Soviets sent arms shipments to the Syrians and Egyptians. (Sadat had not yet orchestrated his full pivot away from the Soviets.)

But President Nixon authorized an airlift of arms to Israel, and Israelis began their counterattack. Within days, the Israelis had driven the Syrians back in the Golan. After one of the largest tank battles in history, they drove the Egyptians out of the Sinai once again and crossed the Suez Canal.

As the IDF got within striking distance of the Syrian and Egyptian capitals, the Soviets threatened to intervene; tensions rose between the USSR and the United States, sparking fears of a nuclear confrontation. Arab oil producers announced an oil embargo on Israel's allies. Finally, after UN Security Council Resolution 338, demanding a cease-fire and the implementation of Resolution 242, several rounds of shuttle diplomacy, and American pressure on Israel to accept a cease-fire, the war ended on October 26. Israel had won, conquering even more territory on the Golan and throwing the Egyptians back across the Suez Canal.

Despite this victory, the Israelis had been badly rattled by the Yom Kippur War. They had underestimated their enemy at great cost, with thousands dead and wounded, and soon after, Prime Minister Golda Meir resigned. The Americans, whose arms airlifts had helped turn the tide of the war for the Israelis, began to take more seriously Arab frustration over Israel's unwillingness to return the occupied territories. Sadat, despite his army's defeat, emerged from the war something of a hero. He declared the war a great Egyptian victory: he had crossed the Suez and delivered a terrible blow to the Israelis, restoring to the Arab world some of the pride lost in 1967. His plan had worked. As he turned away from Moscow and toward Washington, he was determined to leverage his newfound stature to get the Sinai back at the negotiating table.

Meir

TOWARD CAMP DAVID (1973–79)

In Israel, the shock, human cost, and near disaster of the Yom Kippur War rocked the establishment to its foundations. It created the conditions for a political earthquake that would change the face, future, and perhaps fate of the country. In May 1977, the Israeli political right, led by Menachem Begin and his Likud Party, defeated Ben-Gurion protégé Shimon Peres and his left-wing Alignment Party (precursor to Israel's Labor Party) in a general election. Alignment and its Labor Zionist predecessor parties had led Israel since its creation. But now Begin, the stubborn opponent of socialist Zionism and keeper of the hard-line flame, became Israel's first right-wing prime minister. In Israel, this election was known as the Mahapakh, or "the Upheaval." The Hebrew word for "upheaval" is closely related to the Hebrew word for "revolution," and the election of 1977 lived up to its nickname.

Begin's rise broke Labor Zionism's thirty-year monopoly on political power in Israel. (Actually, it was much longer, if you count its decades of dominance in the pre-state era.) And it wasn't just political power that the newly ascendant Likud was intent on claiming. Since the early waves of Jewish immigration to Palestine in the 1900s, the narrative of Zionism had been, essentially, a Labor Zionist, left-wing narrative. The Zionist enterprise was a socialist enterprise; as Jews returned to Israel to rebuild their homeland, they themselves would be rebuilt through their labor. For Begin, Labor Zionism's socialism was suspect, something to be uprooted and replaced. He and his fellow Likudniks were bourgeois capitalists and territorial maximalists, conservative nationalists who believed that Jews were the only rightful heirs to the Land of Israel. For them, "the Upheaval" represented the victory of Zionism's ultimate underdog and a chance not only to remake the character of the state, but also to change the story of Zionism itself. In the decades since Begin's initial victory, power has switched back and forth among parties of the left, center, and (increasingly) right. But starting in 1977, Labor Zionism's exclusive hold on Israel was broken for the foreseeable future.

Likud's win reflected the loss of faith in the ruling coalition, which many Israelis blamed for its perceived failure to adequately prepare for the war. But there was another major factor in the victory: Begin's triumph also represented a demographic changing of the guard. A critical component of his victory was Mizrachi voters: Jews with origins in Arab and Muslim countries, rebelling against the left-wing leadership they associated with their decades of shabby treatment at the hands of the state. Mizrachi Israelis had not forgotten the discrimination and paternalism they encountered from their fellow Israelis when they arrived from nearby Arab countries. They still resented the transit camps to which they (unlike European immigrants) had been sent when they arrived in the country and the desert towns and far-flung villages in which they (unlike European immigrants) were ultimately settled. Begin inveighed against the kibbutzniks as "millionaires lolling around their swimming pools," code for the Ashkenazi elite, and won the support of Israel's Mizrachim.

Indeed, Mizrachi Israeli resentment toward the "Ashkenazi leftist elite" still lingers. Mizrachi voters are an important component of Prime Minister Netanyahu's base today. And Netanyahu, an Ashkenazi Jew from an elite founding family who has long championed free-market economic policies that have benefited Israel's mostly Ashkenazi 1 percent, nevertheless makes a point to speak to their long-standing sense of grievance against perceived "Ashkenazi establishment elites" when election time rolls around. He always finds an enthusiastic audience. Mizrachi voters have remained fiercely loyal to the party that they helped bring to power. Thirty-plus years after "the Upheaval," in the labyrinthine produce markets of West Jerusalem, the stalls of Mizrachi vendors are still decorated with

Menachem Begin

pictures of venerated Sephardic rabbis and saints, Mizrachi pop singers, and a glowering, dark-suited Ashkenazi Jew from eastern Europe: Menachem Begin.

Begin's rise to power also marked a major change in the attitude of the Israeli government to the nascent settlement enterprise in the West Bank. Whereas a decade of Labor Zionist governments had toggled between ignoring and tolerating the settler movement's early efforts to build Jewish settlements in the occupied territories, Begin's right-wing coalition gave the settler movement its full blessing. The new government poured political and financial support into the settlements. For Begin, and for his successors on the Israeli right, keeping and settling the conquered territories was a top priority and an intentional policy, a central strategy in extending Israeli rule over as much of the biblical Land of Israel as possible. As for the Palestinians who lived on that territory, Begin saw them as local Arabs, not as a distinct Palestinian people. They deserved decent treatment, he believed, but—ironically, for a man who had devoted his entire life to the dream of realizing Jewish self-determination—not a state of their own.

But while Begin's brand of Jewish nationalism created a blind spot when it came to the aspirations of the Palestinian people, it enabled him to understand the aspirations of fellow nationalist leaders, like Israel's number one enemy, President Anwar Sadat of Egypt. Begin understood what Sadat wanted: the return of the Sinai Peninsula that Israel had captured in 1967. And while Begin was loath to give up the settlements Israel had built there in the decade following the war, he also understood that peace with Egypt would remove perhaps the single-greatest threat Israel faced. Begin saw himself as an Israeli Nixon: tough, shrewd, and uniquely qualified to go to China—or, in this case, negotiate with Egypt. As we shall see, this self-perception was a critical component of his response to the peace overtures Sadat would soon make.

Meanwhile, in the United States, the new administration (like so many before and after) made Middle East peace a priority. President Carter envisioned a grand regional peace plan, resolving Israel's disputes with its neighbors, especially Egypt, and also its conflict with the Palestinians. For Sadat, this represented the opportunity he'd been waiting for since the Yom Kippur War. In November 1977, he shocked the world and stunned Israelis by traveling to Jerusalem and addressing the Knesset—the first Arab leader to do so—offering Israelis peace in exchange for return of the occupied territories. After months of rocky negotiations and browbeating, Carter succeeded in getting Begin and Sadat to come to Camp David, the rustic presidential retreat in Catoctin Mountain Park, Maryland. There, they negotiated the peace treaty that would end the state of war between Israel and its largest Arab neighbor, return the Sinai to Egypt, and normalize relations between the two former enemies.

But Carter's grand plans to resolve the Palestinian issue didn't come to fruition at Camp David. Begin wanted peace with Egypt, but he was committed to thwarting any process that might lead to

Sadat, Carter & Begin

a Palestinian state in the West Bank, instead favoring some form of limited autonomy. And Sadat, as much as he wanted to champion the Palestinian cause, wasn't about to sacrifice his hard-won peace with Israel on the altar of Palestine. Carter had to settle for partial success.

In yet another irony—a particularly unfair one, in my opinion—Carter's compassion for the dispossessed Palestinian people made him suspect in the eyes of many Israelis and American Jews, despite the fact that his tireless diplomatic efforts resulted in peace between Israel and its most dangerous adversary. For almost half a century, no Israeli soldier has died fighting against Egypt. Just imagine what might have been if Carter's broader vision for a resolution of the Arab-Israeli conflict had been realized back in 1979.*

---

* In 2006, Carter published the book *Palestine: Peace, Not Apartheid*, arguing that Israel's settlement enterprise in the West Bank has been the main obstacle to a peaceful resolution of the conflict between Palestinians and Israelis. The book, and especially its title, provoked a storm of criticism from some American Jewish leaders. Many felt that Carter assigned too much blame to Israel for the lack of progress in achieving peace and for suggesting that Israeli rule in the West Bank was akin to apartheid. (For more on that particular question, see chapter 19.) Others defended the former U.S. president, arguing that he was only pointing

Begin and Sadat shared the Nobel Peace Prize in 1978 for ending their war. And while Carter was the U.S. president with perhaps the greatest amount of concern for the plight of the Palestinians, the failure to resolve the Palestinian question at Camp David actually served to further sideline the issue for the United States and paved the way for Israel to extend its control over the West Bank and Gaza.

In the years that followed, Israel did just that, continuing the pre-1967 Jordanian strategy of conquer and divide, keeping West Bank Palestinians from forming strong connections with Arab citizens of Israel while working to sublimate the West Bank economy to Israel's. All the while, Israel dramatically expanded settlement building in the West Bank and Gaza. A main proponent of the settlements was then Agriculture Minister (and future Prime Minister) Ariel Sharon. Sharon, a hawkish, canny former general, was a controversial figure. Nicknamed "the Bulldozer," he was a hero of both the Six-Day War and the Yom Kippur War, where he saved the day when his armored columns swept the Egyptians from the Sinai and actually crossed the Suez Canal into Egypt proper. But he also had a reputation for ruthlessness and for playing fast and loose with the facts when it suited his purposes. (His mentor Ben-Gurion once asked him, "Have you weaned yourself of your off-putting proclivity for not telling the truth?")

Begin knew this about the war hero, but he also felt that a settlement supporter like Sharon had the right credentials to lead the efforts to dismantle the Sinai settlements as Israel handed the territory back to Egypt. And so, Sharon the Bulldozer bulldozed the Sinai settlements even as he led the charge to expand settlement building

---

out an inconvenient and unpopular truth. But Carter's main point—that a two-state solution is preferable to permanent Israeli control of millions of disenfranchised Palestinians—sounds pretty reasonable to me.

in the West Bank and Gaza. There was a tidy process for this: Israeli military administrators of those territories acquired privately owned Palestinian land for "military purposes" and then transferred it over to Sharon's Ministry of Agriculture for settlement purposes. And so, the settlements grew and grew.

If the peace agreement with Egypt was wildly popular in Israel, it was somewhat less so in Egypt. In the Arab world, Sadat was condemned for shattering the united front against Israel, obliterating the legacy of Nasser and Egyptian leadership, and abandoning the Palestinians. Militants called him a traitor. In October 1981, while reviewing a military parade commemorating Egypt's crossing of the Suez Canal back in the 1973 war, Sadat was assassinated by members of the radical Egyptian Islamic Jihad organization. His vice president, Hosni Mubarak (wounded in the attack), took his place. Mubarak ruled Egypt for almost thirty years, until he was deposed, tried, and imprisoned during the Arab Spring in 2011.

Settlements

INTO LEBANON (1979–85)

As Israel and Egypt were moving toward peace, Lebanon was falling apart. After being expelled from Jordan in 1971, the PLO and other Palestinian factions established themselves in the south of Lebanon, alongside hundreds of thousands of Palestinian refugees who'd fled from their homes during the Six-Day War in 1967 and Israel's founding in 1948. There, as they'd done in Jordan, Palestinian leadership began to build what was essentially a state within a state. Palestinian factions competed over strategies and goals, as Yasser Arafat sought to consolidate control under his PLO, whose charter officially called for the defeat of Israel and its replacement with a secular democratic state. The power to speak on behalf of West Bank Palestinians shifted from the king of Jordan to the PLO, and militant Palestinian groups launched terror attacks from the new base in Southern Lebanon across the border into Israel.

The PLO became a powerful player in Lebanon, involving itself in the bewildering and complex internecine struggles for power among Lebanon's sectarian communities: Christians, Sunni Muslims, Shia Muslims, and Druze.* Lebanon's fragile political balance—which, since independence from France in 1946, held that a Christian would serve as president, a Sunni as prime minister, and a Shia as Speaker of the Parliament—began to crumble.** Each of

---

* Sunni and Shia constitute the two largest Muslim denominations. The vast majority of the world's 1.8 billion Muslims are Sunni (about 80–85 percent), with Shia making up most of the others. In Lebanon, there are roughly equal numbers of Sunni and Shia. In Iran and Iraq, Shia are the majority. There are also large Shia communities in some of the Gulf States, India, and Pakistan.

** Today, it is estimated that the Lebanese population is 61 percent Muslim (30.5 percent Sunni, 30.5 percent Shia), 34 percent Christian (mostly Maronites, a sect of the Catholic Church), and 5 percent Druze ("World Factbook: Lebanon," CIA, https://www.cia.gov/the-world-factbook/countries/lebanon/).

the sectarian communities had powerful backers by the mid-1970s. The PLO allied itself with the Lebanese Sunni community, which was also supported by Iraq and Libya. Syria and (especially after the 1979 Islamic Revolution) Iran supported the Shia, and Israel backed the Christians.

Leaders of the Christian community, in particular, saw the Palestinian presence in Lebanon as a threat both to their own power and to the stability of the country. A weak Lebanese government in Beirut essentially ceded control of the south to the PLO and Shia militias, who sometimes viewed each other as allies but more often as rivals. In 1975, the attempted assassination of a powerful Christian militia leader led to his militiamen ambushing a bus full of Palestinians and murdering dozens. Fighting erupted between Christian and Palestinian militants in Beirut, and soon other sectarian groups joined in. Alliances shifted and changed, fighting intensified, and the country slid toward a full-scale, multifaceted civil war.

In 1976, with the blessing of the Arab League, tens of thousands of Syrian troops crossed the border into Lebanon, ostensibly as peacekeepers. In fact, they were there to maintain Syrian influence over their smaller neighbor and to prevent the country from descending into even greater chaos. But fighting, bombings, assassinations, and shifting alliances soon resumed, with Syria now a full player in the war. Palestinian militants increased their attacks on northern Israel. In March 1978, terrorists slipped across the border, hijacked buses, and fired at cars on Israel's northern coastal road, murdering thirty-seven people. Days later, the IDF launched a full-scale invasion of Southern Lebanon to pummel the PLO in the area. Israeli forces soon withdrew, but the IDF established a twelve-mile-wide "security zone" running north from the Israeli border, patrolled by an Israeli-supported, Christian-dominated—some Shia were also involved—militia called the South Lebanon Army (SLA). (I told you it was bewildering.)

In 1981, Begin was reelected as prime minister; he appointed Ariel Sharon as defense minister, traditionally the second-most-important job in Israeli government. Begin and Sharon moved to replace the Israeli military administration in the West Bank with a civil administration, in the hope that this would be perceived by Palestinians and the rest of the world as a move toward providing greater autonomy for West Bank Palestinians. In fact, the IDF remained in charge of the civil administration, and the move served to further expand Israeli control over the territory without providing any benefits to the Palestinians there. Palestinian frustrations and resentments increased, and in response, Israeli rule became even more heavy-handed. Tensions in the occupied territories began to rise.

Meanwhile, north of the border, the Lebanese Civil War raged on. American mediators came and went, calming the situation down until the next round of bloodshed erupted among the various competing sides. The PLO and its rival factions fought with one another even as they continued to launch attacks on Israel.

In Israel, the new defense minister, Sharon, began to craft a plan to achieve three major goals. If his plan succeeded, he would (a) break the growing power and influence of the PLO on the West Bank Palestinians under Israel's control; (b) rid Israel, once and for all, of the PLO threat from Lebanon; and (c) end Syrian influence in Lebanon and install a friendly Christian government in Beirut. Sharon sought to transform Lebanon from a chaotic source of threat and danger on the northern border to a stable and friendly Israeli ally. It was an audacious, even outrageous, plan. And there was only one way that he knew of to accomplish it: a full-scale invasion. The First Lebanon War would be for Israel both a decisive military victory against the PLO and a spectacular and costly disaster. For Lebanon, and especially for the civilians caught in the crossfire, it would be another chapter in a long book of tragedy.

In classic fashion—remember the Ben-Gurion quote on Sharon's mendacity?—Sharon was less than candid about his intentions with Begin, the rest of the Israeli cabinet, and Israel's most important patron and ally, the United States. He portrayed his objective as a limited invasion to stop PLO attacks on Israel, like the one in 1978, focusing only on the south of the country. In fact, he'd drawn up plans to send Israeli forces all the way to the capital, Beirut. When Americans signaled that any invasion would be unacceptable without provocation, Israel, as pretext, seized on the attempted assassination on June 3, 1982, of the Israeli ambassador to the United Kingdom by Palestinian terrorists. But the military incursion that Prime Minister Begin and the Israeli cabinet approved (a limited invasion twenty-five miles into Lebanon with the aim of routing the PLO from its bases in the region) was not the one Sharon planned to carry out.

On June 6, Sharon sent the IDF racing toward Beirut. Giving new meaning to the old saying "It's better to ask for forgiveness than for permission," Sharon deliberately misinformed Begin and the cabinet about the extent of his plans, misled them about his objectives, and attacked Syrian forces when he was instructed not to, in order to provoke them into a fight. By the middle of the month, the IDF was just outside Beirut. For the first time in history, Israeli forces had essentially besieged an Arab capital city. Sharon sent in ground troops and ordered air strikes and artillery attacks on PLO strongholds and neighborhoods in the city, which resulted in heavy civilian and PLO casualties. The elegant city once known as "the Paris of the Middle East," already devastated by years of civil war, was pummeled further by the ferocious Israeli assault.

Eager to find a way to end the fighting, the United States pressured the badly mauled PLO to withdraw all its forces from Lebanon. By the end of June, it agreed to do so. Under pressure from his own cabinet and the Americans, Sharon (who much preferred destroying the PLO to allowing it to escape) reluctantly agreed to a truce, and a multinational peacekeeping force arrived to ensure the safe departure of Palestinian forces from the country. By September, the PLO was gone, setting up its new base of operations in Tunis. The threat of Palestinian attacks on Israel from Southern Lebanon was substantially reduced. The war between Israel and the PLO in Lebanon was over.

With the PLO out of the picture, Sharon turned his attention to setting up the Israel-friendly Christian government he dreamed of installing in Beirut. But on September 14, the Christian militia leader who was meant to be the president of Sharon's new Lebanon was assassinated by a Syrian nationalist. The next day, Sharon ordered IDF ground troops surrounding the capital to enter and occupy West Beirut. Once again, he did not seek or receive cabinet approval for the move. On the evening of September 16, with Israel in control of the city, hundreds of fighters from the assassinated leader's militia made their way toward two Palestinian refugee camps, Sabra and Shatila, on the outskirts of Beirut, where it was believed a number of PLO fighters remained in hiding. With Israel's approval, as IDF troops surrounded the refugee camps and fired flares so that the militiamen could see, the Christian militia fighters entered Sabra and Shatila. Once inside, they massacred the inhabitants. By the time they left the camps on September 19, at least eight hundred men, women, and children were dead. Virtually all were civilians; no PLO fighters appeared to have been killed. Even as the massacre was being perpetrated, Israeli soldiers, journalists, and others just outside the camps informed IDF senior commanders about what was happening. Senior government officials in Jerusalem were also informed. But no Israeli action was taken to stop the marauding Christian militiamen from their three-day murder spree.

Israel's international profile, already tarnished by the destruction the IDF left in its wake as it moved north through Lebanon to Beirut, was further sullied as news of what had happened in Sabra and Shatila spread around the world. In Israel itself, news of the massacre sparked the largest protests in the history of the country. On September 26, four hundred thousand outraged Israelis rallied in Tel Aviv, demanding that Israeli officials responsible for what had happened be held accountable. Under pressure, Prime Minister Begin set up a commission of inquiry helmed by the chief justice of the High Court of Justice (Israel's Supreme Court), Yitzhak Kahan. The Kahan Commission released its report in February 1983, finding that even though the Israeli military did not bear direct responsibility for the massacre, Israeli military and political leaders were aware of, and thus bore responsibility for, what happened at Sabra and Shatila. Sharon, in particular, was held personally responsible for not acting

Sept. 26, 1982
Tel Aviv

to prevent or stop the atrocities. The commission recommended that he resign, and Sharon stepped down as defense minister—but he remained in the cabinet.

The Israeli public, once largely supportive of the invasion of Lebanon, which they were told was meant to bring peace and quiet to Israel's North, was now overwhelmingly against it, shocked at what had happened at Sabra and Shatila and furious at the government that had dragged them into the maelstrom of Lebanon's civil war. Hundreds of Israeli soldiers had been killed in the fighting, as well as many thousands of Lebanese and Palestinian civilians. For the first time, Israelis felt (perhaps conveniently forgetting the Suez Campaign of 1956) that their country had initiated a war of choice as opposed to necessity. The traditional faith Israelis had had in their government and institutions, especially the IDF, was badly shaken. By September 1983, Begin, broken and depressed, resigned as prime minister in the midst of his term and withdrew from public life. He was replaced by the foreign minister, Yitzhak Shamir, another Likud hawk whom we last saw as the leader of the ultramilitant pre-state Lehi organization, which had participated, along with Begin's Irgun, in the massacre at Deir Yassin in April 1948.

Israeli troops began to pull back from Beirut and other occupied areas in Lebanon amid continued fighting and bloodshed. By 1985, the IDF had largely withdrawn to the security zone it had established in Southern Lebanon. (It would remain there until 2000.) The PLO had been roundly defeated and removed as a threat, but now Syria, Israel's most dangerous enemy, stepped more firmly into the power vacuum created by the invasion and withdrawal, strengthening its hold over bleeding Lebanon. And, in a stark example of the law of unintended consequences, the PLO threat in Southern Lebanon was soon replaced by a new one. With the PLO gone, a powerful, heavily armed, Iranian-backed fundamentalist Shia militant organization

Troops rolling home from Lebanon

began to rise. It soon became one of the dominant military and political powers in the country and, ultimately, one of Israel's most tenacious adversaries. From the start, it saw Israel as its number one enemy, and it vowed to resist the continuing Israeli occupation of the South of the country by taking the fight to the IDF—and into Israel itself. It was called the Party of God: Hezbollah.

In Israel, political divisions exacerbated by the unpopular Lebanon War were reflected in an inconclusive election in 1984, with neither of the two major parties able to form a coalition. This led to the formation of a "national unity government" between Shimon Peres's Labor Party and Shamir's Likud. (The same thing would happen four years later, after another inconclusive election in 1988.) Peres would serve as prime minister and Shamir as foreign minister for the first eighteen months, before the two traded jobs. Peres's longtime rival for Labor leadership, Yitzhak Rabin (hero of the Six-Day War), would serve as defense minister.

. . .

OPERATION MOSES

In the mid-1980s, a horrific famine ravaged Ethiopia, ultimately resulting in 1.2 million deaths. Images of the suffering shocked the world, including teenaged me. I was one of 1.9 billion people around the globe who watched the 1985 Live Aid concert and who donated what they could to try to end the suffering. (Still, in my opinion, the greatest act of musical social justice of all time, the concert raised tens of millions of dollars for famine relief, and Queen, in particular, put on a show for the ages.) Strange as it sounds, the famine in Ethiopia also played a significant role in my love affair with Israel. That's because my first trips there, in 1984 and 1985, coincided with one of the greatest Jewish rescue stories of them all.

In 1984, as the famine in Ethiopia worsened, members of the ancient Jewish community in the northern regions of that country began to trickle into Israel, having made the unthinkably arduous journey from Ethiopia—through deserts, over mountains, across borders—on foot. The origins of the Jewish community of Ethiopia are murky, but it's been around for thousands of years. Ethiopian Jews, who call themselves Beta Israel (House of Israel), believe they are descended from the biblical Tribe of Dan, one of the ten "lost tribes of Israel" that legend says were kicked out of the region sometime around 700 B.C.E. Ethiopian Jews practice a pre-rabbinic form of Judaism—meaning their origins in Africa pre-date the writing of the Talmud—and for centuries, they thought they were the only Jews left in the world. They made contact with the rest of the Jewish world only in the nineteenth century. It's an incredible story.

After the establishment of Israel, many Ethiopian Jews, facing political instability, poverty, and discrimination at home, wanted to emigrate. In the 1970s, the Israeli government declared that the

Law of Return applied to them, meaning they could become citizens. But because their Jewish practice was so different from that of other Jewish communities (to say nothing of the fact that they also happened to have Black skin), it was some time before Israel's official rabbinate approved their status as Jews under Israeli law, eventually declaring them the "official" lost Tribe of Dan. (Well, whatever works.)

Aliyah from Ethiopia

But as famine gripped Ethiopia, and as Jews stumbling across the border into Israel warned about the threat of imminent starvation facing the Jewish community there, Israel's intelligence agency, Mossad, devised a plan to rescue them. With the cooperation of the CIA, Israel airlifted more than eight thousand Jews from Ethiopia to Israel. It was called "Operation Moses," and on those early trips to Israel, I visited "Absorption Centers," where Ethiopian Jews (many of whom had never seen electric lights or indoor plumbing) learned Hebrew and prepared for lives in Israel. I met and talked to young Ethiopian Jews, kids my age, who told me about their lives, their dreams of coming to Israel, the terrors of war and famine, and their arrival in the airlifts. It seemed to me then, and it still does now, that Operation Moses was a beautiful example of the whole rationale for Israel in the first place. Nobody else was going to rescue these people. Nobody else was going to help them. In the midst of a terrible famine, they were doubly damned because they were "other"—they were Jews. And then, out of the blue, Israeli planes swept down to carry them away to safety. Throughout the 1990s, thousands more Ethiopian Jews were brought to Israel in similar airlifts. And at end of the day, that's why Israel was created: so that being Jewish wouldn't equal a death sentence.

Today, there are about 125,000 Jews from Ethiopia or of Ethiopian descent living in Israel. It hasn't been easy for them. As with dark-skinned Mizrachi Jews, who came to Israel from Arab countries a generation earlier, the absorption process was flawed, patronizing, and often insensitive, not respectful of the ancient customs, traditions, and culture of the community. Ethiopian Jews in Israel are at the bottom of the economic ladder, and they often face discrimination and racism of the sort that Black Americans face today. In 2019, protests erupted over police brutality against Black Israelis. Today, Ethiopian Israeli civil rights activists organize and advocate in a long campaign demanding justice and equality for their community. And yet: when Ethiopian Jews faced discrimination and death, when they wanted more than anything to find safety in Israel, those Israeli planes swept down from the skies to save them.

. . .

In the hope of coming to some resolution over the West Bank without the participation of the PLO, Peres, supported by the United States, made peace overtures to King Hussein of Jordan. Both Israel and the United States considered the PLO a terrorist organization and refused to negotiate with it (even as much of the rest of the world recognized it as the legitimate voice of the Palestinian people). They much preferred dealing with Jordan, which, you'll remember, had ruled the West Bank from 1948 to 1967. Foreign Minister Shamir, however, opposed these diplomatic moves, not wanting to relinquish any Israeli control over the occupied territories. The so-called national unity government was not, on some of the biggest issues of the day, particularly unified.

The king of Jordan, for his part, reached out to his old enemy, the PLO's Arafat, in an attempt to regain some control over his lost West Bank territories. Arafat and the PLO leadership agreed to talk: the leadership may have succeeded in positioning themselves as the sole representative of the Palestinian people in the eyes of the international community, but they were in Tunis, far away from Palestine, and fast becoming irrelevant in the everyday lives of the millions of Palestinians actually *living* in the Israeli-occupied West Bank. Arafat and the king discussed a plan calling for a Palestinian state in the West Bank, with East Jerusalem as its capital, in confederation with Jordan, which would then make peace with Israel in exchange for Israeli withdrawal from the West Bank—but this never came to fruition. In fact, none of this frantic diplomatic activity in the mid-1980s amounted to much. There was too much animosity and distrust, too much intransigence, and too many players on all sides who opposed any compromise at all.

In 1986, Shamir became prime minister, in line with the rotation agreement he'd made with Peres (who became foreign minister). True to form, he quickly increased settlement building in the West Bank.

The Reagan administration frowned on this; Reagan (like all other U.S. presidents, with the exception of Donald Trump) considered the settlements a bad idea: a violation of international law and an obstacle to peace. But the strong relationship between the two countries was not significantly weakened. The Cold Warrior president was more concerned with Israel's role as a buffer against Soviet interests in the Middle East than he was with its policy in the West Bank. And so, with Israeli troops mostly withdrawn to the security zone in Southern Lebanon, a renewed commitment to the settlement enterprise, and the diplomatic efforts that he opposed petering out, things appeared to be proceeding just as Prime Minister Shamir might have hoped. That was all about to change.

CHAPTER 10

SHAKING IT OFF
The First Intifada

ISRAEL MOVED TO tighten its control over the occupied territories during the 1980s. With Likud's ascent to power in 1977, settlement building had increased exponentially. Palestinians watched as land near Palestinian villages was expropriated and handed over to Israeli settlers. New, Jewish-only settlements began to proliferate throughout the West Bank and Gaza, separating Palestinian towns and villages from one another and eating up arable land. Israeli control of the aquifers beneath the West Bank meant that water, the region's rarest and most precious commodity, was disproportionately allocated to these new Israeli settlements, rather than to Palestinians. More and more, it was clear to both Palestinians and Israelis that, twenty years after the Six-Day War, the Israeli occupation of the West Bank was anything but temporary.

Palestinians' frustration and resentment grew as they suffered daily humiliations, discrimination (both in the West Bank and Gaza and also in Israel itself, where thousands of Palestinians traveled to work each day as low-paid manual laborers), and violence at the hands of Israeli settlers and the soldiers who patrolled the territories to protect them. Palestinian protests, demonstrations, and violence against Israelis in the occupied territories grew. In response, the IDF arrested hundreds of young protesters and rioters. Serving time in an Israeli prison became a badge of honor for young Palestinian activists, a university of sorts, where they learned doctrines of Palestinian nationalism and liberation. Israel brought back the old British Mandate–era practice of punitive home demolitions to punish the families of rioters and militants, a form of collective punishment banned by the Geneva Conventions. By 1987, despite Israel's increasingly heavy-handed rule and the increasingly angry Palestinian response, the West Bank was still relatively quiet. But it was starting to smolder.

And if the West Bank was smoldering, Gaza was beginning to

Punitive home demolitions

burn. Crammed into a narrow strip of land the size of Detroit, 1.8 million Palestinians watched as Israeli troops patrolled their cities and as tidy, red-roofed Israeli settlements sprang up, devouring their agricultural land. Gaza, always poorer and more religious, conservative, and militant than the West Bank, was a tinderbox, seething with anger, hopelessness, and resentment.

On December 8, 1987, an IDF tank-transport truck crashed into a van filled with Palestinian day laborers heading home to Gaza. Four were killed. Rumors that the collision had been deliberate spread like wildfire, and that night, the funerals of the workers turned into massive demonstrations against the occupation. Israeli troops shot and killed several protesters, and within days, Gaza and the West Bank were consumed by mass protests. Soon, civil disobedience, a general strike, and riots spread throughout the occupied territories. Tens of thousands of Palestinians took to the streets. They were shaking off the military rule, daily humiliations, and endless expropriations of the occupation—and that's what they called their mass uprising: the *intifada*, Arabic for "the shaking off."

Soon the unrest spread to East Jerusalem, forcing Israelis within the Green Line to pay attention to what was happening in the occupied territories. Israelis who'd started to believe, in the years since 1967, their government's oft repeated proclamation that Jerusalem was the "eternal and undivided capital" of Israel quickly saw that it simply was not so: Jerusalem was a divided city. The demonstrations, burning tires, and hurled stones made this abundantly, violently clear. Jewish Jerusalemites stopped visiting the markets in the Old City's Christian and Muslim quarters; they stopped eating at the Arab restaurants in East Jerusalem. In fact, the vast majority avoided the Arab parts of the city entirely. Thirty years later, they still do.

. . .

MENTAL MAPS

Just what *do* Israeli Jews think about Jerusalem? In 1999, I spent time in the city researching Israeli "mental maps" of Jerusalem. By mental maps, I mean the ways in which Israeli Jews actually perceive, understand, and experience the city—as opposed to the ways "official" Israel talks about the city. I wanted to know what these mental maps might mean for the potential for and possibility of compromise with Palestinians on one of the thorniest issues to be resolved in any peace negotiation there: the status of Jerusalem. It seemed to me then (as it does to me still) that in the context of a negotiated settlement, Israelis might be more likely to give up parts of the city they didn't feel connected to or didn't "use" and might never have even been to. I wanted to understand how Israelis understood Jerusalem.

Since Israel's capture and unilateral annexation of the eastern half of the city in 1967, and then its expansion of the municipal borders to include wide swaths of land in the occupied West Bank,

JERUSALEM
■ Israeli areas (including settlements)
☐ Palestinian areas
⬚ "Green Line"

Shu'afat refugee camp

Knesset

Old City

Jewish Israelis have mostly voiced support for their government's mantra about an "eternal and undivided capital of Israel." But given that Palestinians claim Arab East Jerusalem as the capital of any Palestinian state, the problem of Jerusalem appeared insoluble. Still I wondered: Did average Israeli Jews experience the city that way? Did they really relate to Jerusalem as an undivided city?

This certainly wasn't my experience when I lived in Jerusalem in the mid-1990s. Israeli friends thought I was nuts for exploring the eastern part of the city. (Their loss: The best hummus in Jerusalem is found at Abu Shukri, in the Muslim Quarter of the Old City. Lina, in the Christian Quarter, is a runner-up. And don't even get me started on the *knafeh*, a highly addictive Palestinian warm sweet cheese pastry that is much better than that description makes it sound, at Jaffar and Sons, near the Damascus Gate.) After the unrest of the intifada and the terror attacks of the 1990s, they simply stopped going to the markets and restaurants in the Palestinian parts of the city. I rarely saw Jewish Israelis in East Jerusalem beyond the Jewish Quarter of the Old City, now populated almost exclusively by Orthodox and ultra-Orthodox Jews and full of yeshivas, archaeological sites, and tourist shops.

Actually, with the exception of the Old City, it wasn't so easy to get from West to East Jerusalem—and that was deliberate. On the "seam" between what used to be Israeli West Jerusalem and Jordanian East Jerusalem, where the border once ran, was now a busy six-lane road, pratically a highway, not exactly the easiest barrier to cross. (It's even harder now: a new light-rail train runs along the same route as well.) It wasn't put there by accident: as in other divided cities around the world, highways and train lines are convenient ways to keep antagonistic populations apart.

To try to get a sense of how Israelis thought about the city, I looked at a series of surveys taken during the 1990s, in which

The Old City

Jewish Israelis were asked to rank the various parts of Jerusalem in order of importance. Perhaps not surprisingly, the western, Jewish neighborhoods; the Jewish Quarter of the Old City (including holy sites like the Western Wall); and the oldest and most developed of the "post-'67" neighborhoods were ranked highest. The Arab neighborhoods of the eastern part of the city, including the Arab Quarters of the Old City, were not seen as integral or terribly important to the Jerusalem that Israeli Jews experienced and thought about. In fact, the "unified Jerusalem" Israelis felt so strongly about appeared to be, in reality, "unified Jewish areas of Jerusalem."

This perception, or lack of perception, was reflected and reinforced by perhaps the most common visual representation of the city Israelis saw every day: the route maps on display at bus stops throughout the city. The main Israeli bus company, Egged, had extensive routes throughout West Jerusalem, but it did not serve most of the neighborhoods of Arab East Jerusalem.

Those neighborhoods were served only by private Palestinian bus companies.

As a result, the maps Jewish Jerusalemites saw every time they waited to catch the bus showed a complicated network of streets and bus routes jammed into the western (Jewish) part of the city. But the farther east you looked, the more the map resembled an undeveloped empty space, with few neighborhoods and fewer bus stops. The maps didn't even attempt to capture the crowded, bustling network of streets and neighborhoods in which more than 330,000 Arab Jerusalemites lived and worked. These skewed, incomplete maps in turn helped shape the way Jewish Israelis felt about and envisioned the city. As far as their daily lives were concerned, and in terms of how they understood and experienced the city, East Jerusalem might not have existed at all.

It didn't seem like too much of a stretch, then, to imagine that in a serious peace process with the Palestinians, Israelis might be willing to compromise over territory they rarely visited, didn't deem important, and barely knew. Those Arab neighborhoods—entirely discounted by Jewish Israelis even as they were intrinsic to the Palestinian experience and identity—could then, in theory, form the core of the capital that Palestinians demanded in East Jerusalem. One person's empty bus map is another person's bustling hometown. Just make the official map match the mental map, and both parties could be satisfied. Indeed, the idea of dividing Jerusalem along these lines was presented by the Clinton administration in its last major round of U.S.-brokered Israeli-Palestinian negotiations and accepted in principle by Israeli prime minister Ehud Barak.

But those negotiations ended when Barak left office, and what seemed possible then seems far less so now. Over the last several decades, Israel has built tens of thousands of homes for hundreds of thousands of Jewish Israelis in new neighborhoods in

East Jerusalem, neighborhoods that ring the traditional Palestinian neighborhoods closer to the urban core. Now Arab East Jerusalem, once the cultural and economic focus of West Bank Palestinian life, is largely cut off from the rest of the West Bank by the new Jewish neighborhoods. It stands to reason that this politically motivated urban planning has succeeded in changing those Israeli Jewish mental maps of the city, perhaps making any creative compromise over Jerusalem that much less likely—and, ironically, guaranteeing that "undivided Jerusalem" remains divided.

. . .

The 1987 uprising began as spontaneous protests with no centralized leadership, but soon an underground group of representatives of the various Palestinian factions began coordinating. The goals of the intifada, the coordinators said, were an end to settlement building, an end to land confiscation, and an end to special taxes and restrictions that applied only to Palestinians. They called for the establishment of an independent Palestinian state under PLO leadership, and they aimed to exert economic pressure on Israel by calling general strikes, closing shops, refusing to pay taxes, and boycotting Israeli goods. Tourists walking through the twisting alleys of the Old City's normally crowded Arab souks (markets) encountered a sad and empty vista of silent, shuttered stores. The intifada's coordinators disavowed the use of knives and guns—this was to be an uprising of civil disobedience and stones.* And in Tunis and Jerusalem, Palestinian and Israeli leaders took note. They were worried.

---

* It wasn't always, though. Increasingly, in the later years, Molotov cocktails and firearms were also used against Israeli forces.

Intifada

Israel responded to the uprising with predictably overwhelming force. Then Defense Minister Rabin is said to have ordered IDF troops to "break the bones" of Palestinian stone throwers. Israel punished West Bank residents by shutting down schools and universities, putting towns under twenty-four-hour curfew, cutting off electricity and water, uprooting olive trees, and arresting thousands of young Palestinians. Israel's international image, already badly bruised by the debacle in Lebanon, was further damaged as images of heavily armed IDF soldiers beating unarmed teenagers in T-shirts were beamed around the world. And the world was watching.

. . .

"A JEW WALKS INTO A BAR IN BELFAST . . ."

Along with everyone else, I was watching Israel's response to the 1987 uprising, too. Remember when I told you that my brother once said I took the *New York Times* personally? Well, this was when he said it. As I sat in my college dorm room, images on the evening news of what was happening on the streets of the West Bank haunted me. Israeli soldiers—guys my age I'd venerated for their courage and commitment to the Jewish people—were firing tear gas, rubber bullets, and sometimes live ammunition. But they weren't firing at other soldiers. They were firing at civilians burning tires and throwing stones—or not throwing stones; some were just protesting and chanting. They were firing at teenagers.

It felt as if the world had turned upside down. This wasn't the Israel I thought I knew, that I'd visited, that I'd staked so much of my own identity on, that I'd been raised to believe in. I couldn't sleep. And I kept thinking back to what I'd seen the year before, in Belfast.

In 1986, during spring break of my freshman year of college, a buddy of mine and I took a backpacking trip throughout Ireland. I fell madly in love with the place, and have remained so, returning many times; my Irish American friend thought it was a nice place to visit, and never went back. Go figure. Anyway, at a youth hostel in Dublin, we decided to take the bus up to Northern Ireland. It was during the height of the Troubles in the North, and I wanted to see for myself what was going on.

Belfast was bewildering to me. It looked like a typical handsome, slightly shabby, somewhat somber city, homey and bustling, the kind you can find throughout the British Isles. But it felt like a city under some kind of military occupation.

In Catholic republican and nationalist neighborhoods, where opposition to a divided Ireland was strong, armored vehicles of the

Royal Ulster Constabulary, the police force of Northern Ireland in the days of the Troubles, patrolled the streets, accompanied by armored vehicles of the British Army. Soldiers in battle gear scanned the crowded streets, sweeping their guns back and forth as kids played soccer and moms walked to the shops along the Falls Road, the main thoroughfare. The civilians mostly ignored the soldiers pointing guns at them, but I was shocked. What the hell were combat soldiers doing patrolling the market street of a neighborhood in which they were clearly not wanted, as the pro-IRA murals and Irish tricolors painted on every curb made clear?

Belfast

This didn't look like a police force; it looked an occupying army. It sure didn't seem like the soldiers were there to uphold the peace or thwart potential terrorists, at least not primarily. It seemed they were there to intimidate the local population, to display power, to ensure that the privileges and advantages enjoyed by the Protestant Unionist community were neither threatened nor challenged. I couldn't believe that this was still going on; that in the mid-1980s, a "civilized" country like the United Kingdom could treat its own citizens like this. In a West Belfast pub, a guy told me that as teenagers, he and his friends had thrown stones at the patrols, and the soldiers had chased them down and beaten them.

And there I was, just a year later, in 1987, watching similar scenes—let's be honest: even more upsetting ones—play out on the streets of Bethlehem, Ramallah, and East Jerusalem. I tried to rationalize the differences. But if I felt it was wrong for heavily armed security forces to uphold, through intimidation and the ever-present threat of violence, an inequitable arrangement and systemic discrimination in Northern Ireland, how could I justify a similar situation in the Israeli-occupied territories? The question tormented me for a few bad and sleepless weeks, and when the answer finally came, it was simple: I couldn't.

By the way, that guy at that West Belfast pub also told me a joke that managed to condense into one little package the absurd interchangeability of territorial conflicts and, whether he knew it or not, the absurdity of being a Jew in the world—never safe, not even in the midst of someone else's conflict. Hearing my American accent, he had leaned over and asked me where my "people were from." Cincinnati, I told him. "No," he said. "I mean way back: Where in *Ireland* did they come from?" I explained to him that, way back, they came from Belarus and Latvia; that I was Jewish, not Irish. To my surprise, his face lit up. "Ach, you're Jewish? Do you know the story of your man the Jew on the Falls Road? Well, your man the Jew is walking down the Falls Road at midnight, and suddenly he feels a gun in his back. A voice says, 'Be you Protestant or be you Catholic?' Your man sighs in relief. 'Neither,' he says. 'I'm a Jew.' And the voice answers, 'Ah, right! Then I'm the luckiest Palestinian in all of Ireland.'"

. . .

Meanwhile, as the intifada raged on in Israel and the occupied territories, the world outside was changing fast. In 1989, the Berlin Wall fell, and the Soviet Union began to teeter. In August 1990, Saddam Hussein's Iraq invaded its smaller, oil-rich neighbor Kuwait. Led by the United States, a global coalition, including Arab countries, drove the Iraqis out in the First Gulf War. Hussein tried to shatter the Western-Arab alliance arrayed against him by firing Scud missiles at Israel, hoping to prompt an Israeli response. But the United States urged restraint, and Israel didn't take the bait.

By 1991, the Soviet Union was in final collapse, Kuwait was free, and the United States stood as the unparalleled global superpower. President George H. W. Bush decided to try to use some of America's extraordinary power and influence in the region to resolve, once and for all, the Middle East conflict and, in particular, the Israeli-Palestinian conflict. He convened a peace conference. Prime Minister Shamir didn't want to attend, but what could he do? The initial meetings were held in Madrid and attended by Israeli, Palestinian, Syrian, Jordanian, and Lebanese representatives, as well as American mediators. And while those talks were soon superseded by the Oslo peace process, Madrid marked the end of the First Intifada and the beginning of what now looks like a golden decade of attempts to resolve this seemingly intractable conflict.

But while the uprising was over, its ramifications were only beginning to be felt. The intifada had shaken Israel's sense of itself in a way that perhaps only the near loss of the Yom Kippur War and the disaster of the Lebanon War had previously. It forced Israelis to confront, for the first time, the costs of occupation, both to Israel's society and to its standing in the world. It gave Palestinians on the ground in the West Bank and Gaza a new sense of power and agency. In Gaza,

Intifada

in particular, the intifada raised the profile of a militant, hard-line Islamic organization called Islamic Jihad.

Soon, though, another militant Islamic organization, the Islamic Resistance Movement, emerged in Gaza. Known by its Arabic initials, Hamas quickly superseded Islamic Jihad as the more popular group. Despite the fact that Hamas called for armed struggle against Israel, including terror attacks against civilians, Israel initially viewed Hamas's rise as a useful counter to the PLO. Hamas's goal was the creation of an Islamic state in all of historic Palestine—and that meant Israel, too. Hamas was critical of, even hostile to, secular Palestinian leaders of the intifada and the PLO for what it saw as their willingness to compromise with Israel. For the time being, though, it was willing to coordinate with rival Palestinian groups in the common struggle against the occupation. Hamas provided not only protesters and fighters for the struggle, but also social services and support for the embattled, beleaguered population of Gaza. In this way, it rose in popularity and soon became a dominant force in Palestinian politics, a counterweight to the PLO.

As for the PLO, the intifada shocked the old guard in their

Tunisian exile into realizing that they were at risk of irrelevance. Yasser Arafat determined that in order to reassert the PLO's primacy, he would have to work with the emerging local leaders in the occupied territories. He would follow their lead in demanding not the end of Israel, but the creation of an independent Palestinian state in the West Bank and Gaza. In December 1988, Arafat announced that the PLO had "accepted the existence of Israel as a state in the region" and renounced terrorism. "We accept two states, the Palestine state and the Jewish state of Israel," he said. The Israeli government dismissed this, but something was clearly changing. After the Israeli elections of 1992, the world would find out just how much.

CHAPTER 11

ISRAEL IS WAITING FOR RABIN

Shalom, Chaver. Goodbye, my friend.

—PRESIDENT BILL CLINTON, NOVEMBER 6, 1995

NINETEEN NINETY-TWO WAS an election year in both Israel and the United States. By the time the Israeli election rolled around in June, tensions between Prime Minister Shamir and President Bush were high. Shamir, upset at being pressured to participate in the Madrid Peace Conference, intensified settlement building in the occupied territories. This in turn served to increase Palestinian despair and violence as well as anger in the Arab world. In response, a furious President Bush leveled sanctions on Israel: the United States would reduce the amount of its loan guarantees to Israel commensurate with what Israel spent on the settlements.* This rift between Israel and its

---

* With loan guarantees, the United States essentially cosigns for Israel, giving banks

Rabin

greatest supporter and ally was deeply unsettling to the Israeli electorate, and soon they rendered their verdict on Shamir's intransigence
and lack of concern for American opinion.* The left-of-center Labor
Party, now led by former defense minister Yitzhak Rabin, broke the

---

reassurance that it will not default on the loans. In 1992, Israel requested $10 billion in loan
guarantees, mostly to help resettle Jews arriving from the former Soviet Union, and the Bush
threat would have reduced that amount by about $400 million. To be clear: loan guarantees
were, and are, only a small part of the annual U.S. aid package to Israel. Israel is the largest
recipient of U.S. aid, receiving more than $140 billion since 1948. The current aid package
amounts to $38 billion in military assistance over ten years.

* Today, it's hard to imagine a U.S. president—let alone a Republican one—pressuring Israel
over its settlement policy like this. But that kind of tough love also worked at Camp David,
when Jimmy Carter told Menachem Begin that if he refused to sign a peace treaty with Egypt
over the issue of the Sinai settlements Begin didn't want to evacuate, he, Carter, would call
a press conference, let the world know what Begin had done and why, and recommend that
Congress reconsider its aid package to Israel. Begin couldn't withstand the pressure of a determined American president, and he backed down. In return, he got the greatest diplomatic
coup in Israeli history: total peace with Egypt, Israel's largest and most dangerous foe (Thrall,
The Only Language They Understand, 25–26).

political stalemate of the previous eight years with a convincing victory over Shamir's Likud.

Rabin cut a unique figure on the Israeli political scene. A gruff, taciturn, straight-talking, chain-smoking, whisky-drinking ex-soldier with a reputation for toughness, he was the first Israeli prime minister born in pre-state Palestine. He had tremendous experience, having served in a number of key jobs: a young military commander in Israel's War of Independence, IDF chief of staff during the stunning victory of 1967, ambassador to the United States and a turn at prime minister in the 1970s,* defense minister in the 1980s—and now, at age seventy, prime minister once again. He had a deep connection with the Israeli public, and his campaign slogan reflected it: *Yisrael Mechakah le Rabin*, "Israel Is Waiting for Rabin."** For many, he was the embodiment of the most cherished Israeli institution: the IDF. When it came to issues of war and peace, regular Israelis trusted him more than any other leader.

Rabin quickly formed a Labor-led government with the left-wing Meretz Party and the ultra-Orthodox Mizrachi Shas Party.*** He

---

* Rabin served as prime minister from 1974 to 1977, after Golda Meir stepped down in the wake of the 1973 Yom Kippur War.

** An Israeli friend of mine, explaining why his family had voted for Rabin in 1992, once said this to me, "We aren't a Labor Party family, and we're not a Likud Party family. We are a Rabin Party family." Rabin wasn't a traditionally charismatic politician, but his connection with regular Israelis was profound, even emotional. Once, in the winter of 1994, a time when the country felt increasingly fractured by the furious debates over the peace moves Rabin was making, another Israeli friend and I found ourselves walking by the prime minister's official residence on Balfour Street, in Jerusalem. Just then, we saw the flashing lights and motorcycle cops of the prime minister's motorcade pull up to the gate. As armed guards held their hands up for us to stop, we watched as Rabin's black car slowly pulled into the compound. We could see him in the backseat, exhausted, cigarette in his hand, looking down. My friend gasped at the sight of him. "Oh, he looks so tired," she murmured, and her eyes filled with tears.

*** While it may seem strange for an ultra-Orthodox party to join a center-left government, appointed as foreign minister Shimon Peres, his perennial rival for leadership of the Labor Party. He kept the Defense Ministry portfolio for himself. (A prime minister serving simultaneously as defense minister is not uncommon in Israel.)

In the wake of the 1990 Gulf War and the fall of the Soviet Union—and the new era those events suggested—and after years of a grinding intifada, increasing numbers of Israelis were concluding that holding on to the occupied territories might not be worth the trouble. They were buoyed by the arrival of hundreds of thousands of Jews from the former Soviet Union and what appeared to be the triumph of Western-style liberal democracy over totalitarianism. New possibilities for peace seemed to be opening up.

New arrivals

---

keep in mind three things: First, in 1992, Shas was somewhat more moderate on issues of war and peace than its rival Ashkenazi ultra-Orthodox party. Second, almost every Israeli ruling coalition—right, left, or center—has included at least one Orthodox party. This makes more sense than it may seem at first. In Israeli politics, big parties need little parties to build governing coalitions, and the smaller, ultra-Orthodox parties were, traditionally, more concerned with receiving state funding and maintaining their areas of control in Israeli society than they were with issues of war and peace. So, deals could be and were made. Third, as we shall soon see, Shas didn't last long in Rabin's coalition.

. . .

THE RUSSIANS ARE COMING

B etween 1989, when the last Soviet leader, Mikhail Gorbachev, announced that they were free to leave, and 1995, more than 623,000 Jews from the former Soviet Union (FSU) immigrated to Israel. Hundreds of thousands more arrived in the following years. For the most part, the new arrivals, most of whom were Ashkenazi Jews, were accepted and integrated into Israeli society. But unlike the Russian Jews who'd moved to Israel a century earlier, the Jews from the former Soviet Union were not idealistic socialists, let alone Labor Zionists. They were products of a monstrously autocratic political system built on repression, corruption, and fear. They had little or no experience with liberal democracy, but they were quite familiar with the culture of the authoritarian strongman. They distrusted Israel's Arab neighbors and were suspicious of liberals calling for compromise and negotiation. After the election of 1992 (when they, like so many other voters, rejected Shamir for Rabin), they gravitated toward the hard-line political parties of the right and even started their own. In time, FSU Jews would become an essential part of the coalition of the political right in Israel.

That said, they differed in some significant ways from the other parts of that coalition. Most FSU immigrants were secular, and many of them, while qualifying for Israeli citizenship under the Law of Return, were not considered properly Jewish (according to Jewish law, or halacha) in the eyes of Israeli religious authorities. As a result, they faced restrictions on whom they could marry, where they could be buried, and the Jewish status of their children (and thus whom *they* could marry, etc.)—all issues that come under the purview of Israel's official state rabbinate. FSU immigrants resented this and chafed at the power of the rabbinate to influence their lives, limit or ban public transportation, and require that stores close on Saturdays, the Jewish Sabbath. They found plenty of workarounds. When I lived in Jerusalem, it was an open secret that you could go to one of the markets owned by FSU immigrants to buy *basar lavon*, "white meat," aka pork, forbidden to religious Jews and Muslims and, so, not easily found in the Holy City.

In recent years, a generation of young Israelis born to immigrants from the FSU has come of age. Their views, politics, and voting patterns tend to track with those of other Israelis in their age cohort rather than of their immigrant parents. More and more, the children of immigrants from the FSU look less like a distinct group in Israel and more like other Israelis. Still, the massive waves of immigration over the last thirty years have had a huge impact on Israel, strengthening the economy, altering the demographic landscape, and remaking the social fabric and traditional political alliances of the country—and not always in predictable ways.

In early 2020, Tel Aviv and some surrounding municipalities finally instituted public transportation on the Jewish Sabbath. There was a predictable outcry from the political right, with representatives of the ultra-Orthodox and national-religious settler parties decrying the move. Not so the Russian community, nor the most important politician from the FSU, Avigdor Lieberman, a former defense minister and foreign minister and leader of the right-wing Yisrael Beiteinu (Israel Our Home) Party. He was happy enough to incite against Arab citizens of Israel and deride leftists as weak and traitorous, but when it came to public transportation on Shabbat, he was all for it. He called the move by Tel Aviv's liberal city government "a ray of light" and "an important step which is needed in our days."

OSLO

Rabin sensed that a moment of tremendous opportunity for Israel had arrived. On the day he announced the formation of his government, he made his intentions clear: "In the current reality there are only two options: either a serious effort will be made to make peace with security . . . or we will forever live by the sword." Rabin believed that Israel could not continue to rule indefinitely over the lives of millions of Palestinians, and he believed that the only way to secure the country's future was through peace. He came to power ready to pursue this vision, but he needed help. He knew that the ultra-Orthodox Shas Party, with 5 seats, might well balk at a deal with the Palestinians and leave the coalition. Between them, Labor and Meretz had 56 seats.* A powerful pro-peace block for sure, but if Shas left, they'd be 5 seats short of a governing majority. But Rabin knew where to look for 5 more seats: that was the exact number held by Israel's two Arab parties.

It had never been done before. There was (and still is) a taboo in Israeli politics against including Arab-dominated parties in governing coalitions, ostensibly because the Arab parties (understandably enough) did not describe themselves as "Zionist." But the fact that ultra-Orthodox parties that *also* didn't describe themselves as Zionist were regularly included in ruling coalitions suggested the real reason: Israeli politicians assumed that the Jewish public would not accept the idea of majority-Arab parties sharing power in government. For their part, majority-Arab parties were reluctant to join coalition governments (not that they'd ever been asked to) that, by definition, were responsible for overseeing the military administration and settlement enterprise in the occupied territories, policies the Arab parties opposed.

---

* Just to give you a sense of the tremendous changes in the Israeli political landscape over the past quarter century: in the election of March 2020, Labor and Meretz won a combined 7 seats.

Rabin was ready to break with that tradition. While he didn't invite the Arab parties to join the government, he did the next best thing: he told them of his intention to jump-start the peace process and invited them to work in alliance and coordination with the ruling coalition. The Arab parties accepted. They would serve as a so-called blocking coalition, ensuring that, so long as he was pursuing peace, Rabin's government wouldn't fall.* Equally important, he would treat them like partners.

And he did. Between 1992 and 1995, government spending on infrastructure, education, health care, and affirmative action programs for Israel's Arab citizens increased exponentially. For the first time, the Arab parties wielded real power: when they insisted that the government abandon plans to confiscate Palestinian-owned land in Jerusalem to build a new police station, Rabin called an emergency cabinet meeting and announced that he would halt the move. For a brief and shining moment, Jewish and Arab parties worked together for a shared future.

Soon after he took office, Rabin ordered a freeze on settlement building in the occupied territories. This sent a clear signal of intent both to the Bush administration, which quickly agreed to sign the loan guarantees it had frozen under Shamir (enabling Israel to build housing for new immigrants from the FSU), and to the Palestinians and the wider Arab world.

Rabin was committed to pursuing peace, but he didn't think the multilateral Madrid talks were the best way to do that. He wanted to approach the Arab parties directly. Supported by the Americans, he made an initial peace overture to Syria, and while this seemed promising at first, it didn't amount to much; the Syrians weren't willing to take the risk.

---

* They would be needed: in 1993, Shas quit the government in protest of the peace process.

Then, in January 1993, Rabin gave official approval for a back-channel process of direct negotiations with Palestinians representing the PLO. Until that moment, Israeli leaders had refused to speak to, let alone recognize the legitimacy of, the PLO. But Rabin, as much as he distrusted and despised Arafat, whom he thought a liar and a terrorist, knew that Arafat and the PLO were the only ones capable of negotiating on behalf of the Palestinians and actually delivering peace. As he told an American diplomat, "What can we do? Peace you don't make with your friends, but with your very unsympathetic enemies." Because of the extraordinary sensitivity of the talks, they were to be held in secret, far from the prying eyes and expectations of press, politicians, and the public. To keep them under wraps, they held the talks not in the Middle East, but on the other side of the world, in the city that would forever be associated with them: Oslo.

In fact, the negotiations had been under way for a while, even before Rabin approved them. In 1992, Norwegian officials offered to open a back channel for negotiations between Israelis and Palestinians. Both sides were interested. Because Israeli law forbade official contact with the PLO, Israeli academics with close ties to foreign ministry officials were tapped to meet secretly with a leading PLO representative in Oslo. Foreign Minister Peres kept a close eye on the developments, and in early 1993, he informed Rabin, who gave his approval. The talks were still secret, but now they were official.

The Oslo negotiators agreed to work toward a Declaration of Principles (DOP) that would create a framework for Palestinian interim self-government, a Palestinian Authority (PA) in the West Bank and Gaza for a limited period, which would end with a full-scale peace treaty and a resolution of all outstanding issues. Israel would draw down its military presence in the occupied territories, starting by pulling out of Gaza—it would leave settlements there for the interim period—and the ancient city of Jericho, in the West Bank. The occupied territories would be divided into three areas: A, B, and C, each with a different arrangement of Palestinian and Israeli control.* The idea was that this interim period of five years would serve as a testing ground for coexistence, a time in which to build the trust that would be required to tackle the big and thorny "permanent status" issues (Jerusalem, borders, the fate of Palestinian refugees) that would need to be resolved in a final peace treaty.

Underlying the entire process, although not stated explicitly in the DOP, was an understanding between the negotiators about what the ultimate aim of Oslo really was: Israelis would get security and a permanent end to the conflict with their neighbors, and the

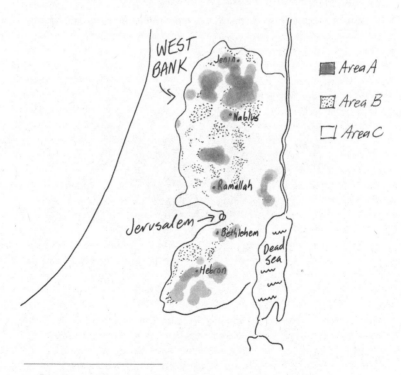

---

* Definitely a good time to check the lexicon for details.

Palestinians would get an independent state of their own. The goal of the peace process that began at Oslo was a two-state solution.*

In order to achieve all this, however, Israel and the PLO would first have to agree to mutual recognition, with Israel formally recognizing the PLO as the official representative of the Palestinian people—remember: until this point, it was illegal for Israelis even to *talk* to the PLO—and the PLO formally recognizing Israel and renouncing violence and terrorism. And so, on September 9, 1993, PLO chairman Arafat and Israeli prime minister Rabin exchanged letters doing just that. They had crossed the Rubicon.

Four days later, Arafat and Rabin stood next to President Bill Clinton on the White House Lawn to sign the agreement. Rabin, his face reflecting both distaste and determination, reached out and

Rabin, Clinton & Arafat

---

* The very idea of a two-state solution was, up until this point, seen as a radically left-wing, totally unrealistic position in Israel. After Oslo, it became, and remains today, the official position of the State of Israel (not to mention the Palestinian Authority, the Arab League, the United States, the European Union, and the United Nations). Even right-wing leaders like Benjamin Netanyahu express support, however disingenuously, for two states.

shook hands with his old adversary Arafat.* It's hard to overstate the power of that moment. In one sense, the handshake felt very much of the times—another step in an ongoing global march toward sanity and progress in a decade that also saw the crumbling of the apartheid regime in South Africa, the fall of the Soviet Union, and the end of the conflict in Northern Ireland. But the handshake on the White House Lawn also felt like a miracle. It seemed to signify the end of one of the last, most intractable problems in the world: the hundred-year conflict between Arabs and Jews in the Holy Land. I remember listening to the ceremony on NPR and saying to myself, *I have to go there.* A few months later, I did.

Negotiations now focused on the creation of the Palestinian Authority, which was to assume control of Gaza and Jericho from Israel, but they were interrupted, and almost derailed, by the first in a long string of terrorist assaults from extremists on both sides who shared a burning desire to stop the peace process. On February 25, 1994, a fanatically right-wing Jewish settler, wearing his IDF reservist uniform and carrying his army-issue M16 assault rifle, walked into the Ibrahimi Mosque in the Cave of the Patriarchs, in Hebron. Jewish and Muslim traditions hold that the cave contains the tombs of the biblical patriarchs and matriarchs Abraham and Sarah, Isaac and Rebecca, and Jacob and Leah; it is a holy site for both religions. It was Ramadan, the Muslim holy month, and the mosque was full of Palestinian Muslims at prayer. Once inside, the gunman, a doctor who had immigrated to Israel from Brooklyn, opened fire on the worshippers, killing twenty-nine and injuring more than a hundred before being beaten to death by the survivors.

The murders were roundly condemned by Israel. Addressing

---

* After he'd shaken Arafat's hand, Rabin turned to Peres, grimacing, and said, "Your turn now" (Ephron, *Killing a King*, 30).

the militant settler community from which the murderer had come, Rabin said, "I am shamed over the disgrace imposed upon us by a degenerate murderer."* Israelis were horrified at the massacre, but Palestinians were furious, and they took to the streets. The demonstrations grew violent, and in response, Israel imposed a curfew—which infuriated Palestinians further. The PLO demanded that the issue of the removal of West Bank settlements like the one the murderer had come from be addressed immediately, not in two years, as the DOP called for. Israel said no.

For a terrible moment it seemed as though everything were unraveling and that the entire peace process stood on the brink of collapse. But frantic American diplomatic efforts pulled the two sides back to the negotiating table. The talks continued. Finally, on May 4, 1994, Israel and the PLO signed the agreement resulting in the creation of the Palestinian Authority and the withdrawal of the Israel Defense Forces from Gaza and Jericho. The Israelis began handing over control of Palestinian towns and cities to the PA and the Palestinian police force. Yasser Arafat returned to Palestine, set up his headquarters in Gaza City, was elected president of the Palestinian Authority, and triumphantly visited Palestinian cities and towns as Israel withdrew from them. The negotiating teams prepared to move toward discussing permanent-status issues. A few months later, Rabin, Peres, and Arafat won the Nobel Peace Prize.

But the attacks on the peace process would pick up pace. Just like the militant Jewish settlers, the fundamentalist Palestinian groups

---

* Rabin continued: "You are not part of the community of Israel, you are not part of the national democratic camp which we all belong to in this house, and many of the people despise you. You are not partners in the Zionist enterprise. You are a foreign implant. You are an errant weed. Sensible Judaism spits you out. You placed yourself outside the wall of Jewish law. You are a shame on Zionism and an embarrassment to Judaism."

Hamas and Islamic Jihad wanted to murder the Oslo process. Over the next few months, they carried out a series of terror attacks on buses and shopping malls in Israel that killed scores of civilians and wounded hundreds. Rabin held firm: "We must fight terrorism as if there's no peace process, and work to achieve peace as if there's no terror," he said.* Despite the mounting violence, things were back on track—for now.

AMMAN CALLING

I, Military I.D. No. 30743, Retired General in the Israeli Defense Forces, consider myself to be a soldier in the army of peace today.

I, who served my country for 27 years as a soldier, I say to you, Your Majesty, the King of Jordan, and I say to you, our American friends:

Today we are embarking on a battle which has no dead and no wounded, no blood and no anguish. This is the only battle which is a pleasure to wage: the battle of peace.

—*Prime Minister Yitzhak Rabin, address to joint session of U.S. Congress, July 26, 1994*

The two Semitic people, the Arabs and the Jews, have endured bitter trials and tribulations during the journey of history. Let us resolve to end this suffering forever and to fulfill our responsibilities as leaders of our peoples and our duty as human beings towards mankind.

I come before you today fully conscious of the need to

---

* Sharp-eyed readers will note that this was a direct echo of Rabin's political mentor David Ben-Gurion. If you need a refresher, flip back to page 50.

secure a peace for all the children of Abraham. Our land is the
birthplace of the divine faiths and the cradle of the heavenly
messages to all humanity.

I also come before you today as a soldier who seeks to bear
arms solely in the defense of his homeland, a man who under-
stands the fears of his neighbors and who wishes only to live
in peace with them, a man who wishes to secure democracy,
political pluralism and human rights for his nation.

—*King Hussein, address to joint session of U.S. Congress,
July 26, 1994*

Since before the establishment of the State of Israel, the Jordanian
royal family and the Jewish leadership in Palestine had maintained a
useful, if covert, relationship. Even when Jordan and Israel clashed—
as they did in 1948 and 1967—lines of communication and sometimes
even cooperation remained open. The Jordanian monarchy, said to be
descended from the Prophet Muhammad, still maintained close ties
to the West Bank it lost to Israel in the Six-Day War and, especially, to
East Jerusalem. In the late 1980s, under pressure from the Arab world,
King Hussein had renounced his claim to the West Bank in the PLO's
favor. But Jordanian and Israeli leaders continued to talk; both sides
wanted to end the official state of war that had existed between the
two countries since 1948.

More moderate than its larger, radical Arab neighbors, with a
Palestinian population that was at least as big as the Bedouin population that made up the royal family's base, little Jordan had to steer
a careful and cautious path in a very difficult neighborhood. By the
early 1990s, King Hussein was ready for an official peace with Israel,
but the fragile demographic balance of Jordan made him cautious.
He did not want to get too far out ahead of the Palestinians, now
negotiating with Israel.

King Hussein

So it was that, the very day after the handshake on the White House Lawn, Israeli and Jordanian negotiators began work on an agreement between the two countries. Just over a year later, on October 26, 1994, all eyes were once again on the White House Lawn as President Clinton, King Hussein, and Prime Minister Rabin signed the peace treaty. Israel was now formally at peace with two of its frontline neighbors, Jordan and Egypt, and was working toward an arrangement with the Palestinians. Rabin's U.S.-supported overtures to President Assad of Syria hadn't gotten anywhere yet, but that seemed to be only a matter of time. And peace with Syria would almost certainly mean peace with Syria-controlled Lebanon. It felt like a new day was dawning in the Middle East.

. . .

WELCOME TO THE NEW MIDDLE EAST?

In 1995, a few months after the Israeli-Jordanian peace treaty was announced, I grabbed my backpack and took a bus south into the desert. I was living in Jerusalem during those halcyon days of the Oslo peace process and the hope it generated, and as soon as travel from Israel into Jordan was permitted, I decided to go there on my own to see what I could see.

I crossed the border at a desolate frontier post in the middle of the desert, just north of the southernmost Israeli city, Eilat. It was completely empty. The soldier at the Israeli guard booth asked me what I was planning to do in Jordan, and I told him I wanted to visit the city of Petra, one of the wonders of the ancient world (and a setting in an Indiana Jones movie). "Good luck getting there," he told me, shaking his head and looking at me like I was nuts as I set off across the dusty strip of no-man's-land to the Jordanian guard post on the other side. The Jordanian guard didn't inspire much confidence, either. "There is no *bus*," he said, "only sometimes taxi."

And so, passport stamped, I crossed the border into Jordan and proceeded to sit on a curb by the side of a lonely desert road until, after a little while, a rattletrap taxi pulled up. I told the driver where I wanted to go, and he looked horrified. "But that will cost you too much!" he told me. I asked how much, and he said it would be the equivalent of about twenty dollars. Even as a broke twentysomething, I could afford that.

The driver, Omar, was a nice guy, and he felt so bad about how much the ride would cost me that he insisted we stop at his home on the way to Petra. There, he and his family set up an amazing spread of food and treated me to a beautiful meal. It was an extraordinary example of a tradition of hospitality and welcome, and I was moved. Because they didn't get many (by which I mean *any*) visitors from abroad in their tiny town, pretty soon Omar's neighbors started showing up to meet me. They asked me where I was from, and I told them the United States. "But you are Israeli?" they asked. Wary, given that a state of war had existed between Jordan and Israel until just a few months ago, I told them I wasn't—I was an American, not an Israeli citizen. "But you are *living* in Israel?" they insisted. I finally admitted that I was, indeed, living in Israel. That was the answer they were looking for. "You are most welcome, our Israeli brother! Finally, there is peace between us. We have so much in common!" Relieved and moved, I agreed that we did. "Yes," they said. "We are both Children of Abraham! We both want peace, and we both want to live our lives and raise our families and be happy! And we both *hate* the filthy Palestinians!"

I was shocked. To this day, I'm ashamed that I didn't say *something* in response. But that was the moment when I realized that resolving this conflict was going to be a lot harder, and a lot more complicated, than I'd ever imagined.

. . .

THE ASSASSINATION

While many Israelis and much of the world rejoiced at what seemed to be the inexorable move toward peace in the Middle East, the enemies of peace were doing their best to stop it. That they would succeed seemed impossible. That they *did* succeed is one of the great tragedies of our times.

From the beginning, there were powerful groups on both sides who opposed the peace process. Some, like the conservative leaders of Israel's Likud Party and their nationalist counterparts in the ranks of the Palestinian liberation movement, had strong ideological objections to the process under way. Likud leaders opposed Israeli withdrawal from any part of the occupied territories and the dismantling of the Jewish settlements there. Palestinian hard-liners opposed Palestinian concessions. Yes, they said, peace was important, but peace on *our* terms. This process was flawed and dangerous, they argued; it gave away too much. They organized in their respective courts of public opinion, warning that those in power were making a mistake, couldn't be trusted, and were leading the people toward a disaster.

But others objected to the very idea of *any* peaceful resolution at all. The fundamentalists of Hamas and Islamic Jihad opposed any compromise with Israel. They felt that the PLO had no right to negotiate away the Palestinian birthright: possession of all of historic Palestine. Israel was a cancer that had to be destroyed. Palestine, as the chant went, would be "free from the river to the sea."

Meanwhile, militant settlers from the national-religious camp and their supporters were a Jewish mirror image of the Palestinian extremists. They saw Rabin and Peres as traitors for their willingness to compromise over any part of the Greater Land of Israel—land that God had promised the Children of Israel and that no secular leader had the right to surrender to Israel's enemies. Extremist rabbis even issued fatwah-like religious rulings declaring that Rabin was a *rodef* (a "pursuer")—in Jewish law, one who is pursuing another in order to kill him, and thus, a legitimate target for death. Israeli security forces, divided over the magnitude of the threat, didn't initially pay too much attention to these fringe rabbis. But others did.

The extremists on both sides saw the conflict as a zero-sum game that not only couldn't be resolved, but also *shouldn't* be resolved. It was a fight to the finish, and each side was certain that they would win it. Each knew for sure that God was on their side. The rejectionists relied on the old terrorist's playbook of shock, violence, and fear. They knew that it is far easier to destroy trust than to build it and that the best way to do that is through murder and mayhem. Once the process collapsed, they could get back to their endless holy war, and eventual triumph.

From the beginning of his renewed push for peace, Rabin knew that there would be fierce, even violent, backlash from those opposed to the goals of Oslo. He was prepared not only for an increase in terrorism from Hamas and Islamic Jihad, but also for pushback from Israelis who disagreed with him. He knew he was hated by many religious settlers and their supporters, who saw peace with the Palestinians as the end of the settlement enterprise. He was certain, however, that Israeli security forces could handle it. But increasingly, Israel's security forces were worried.

Throughout 1994 and 1995, right-wingers protested against the peace process. The tone of these protests grew increasingly dark and extreme. Demonstrators held signs with pictures of Rabin and Peres in kaffiyehs (traditional Palestinian headdress) or Nazi SS helmets. They waved placards with Rabin's face in the center of a gun's sights. They passed around pamphlets calling Rabin a traitor, declaring that he had blood on his hands.

Some Likud leaders seemed to contribute to, or at least tolerate, the rising atmosphere of incitement. In March 1994, opposition leader Benjamin Netanyahu led an anti-Oslo march in which protesters carried a mock coffin bearing the inscription RABIN WILL BURY ZIONISM. At a massive rally in the center of Jerusalem in October 1995, Netanyahu presided from a balcony as supporters burned pictures of Rabin, waved signs reading, IN BLOOD AND FIRE WE WILL EXPEL RABIN, and chanted "Death to Rabin!"* Netanyahu said noth-

---

* For years, Netanyahu has rejected the notion that he bears any responsibility for contributing to the atmosphere of incitement in the months leading up to Rabin's assassination. He has pointed to statements he made during that time in which he disagreed with the notion that Rabin was a traitor. But while he may not have *intended* to incite, the things leaders say, and

ing. Israeli security officials were concerned about the atmosphere and Rabin's safety. They'd gotten reports about potential plots on his life. They urged him to wear a bulletproof vest, but Rabin, the old soldier, rejected this out of hand. He had helped build this country, and he felt safe in it.

The increasingly vituperative public discourse around Oslo, the threats and incitement, and the spike in acts of terror aimed at derailing the peace process were taking their toll. The ultra-Orthodox Shas Party had quit the ruling coalition back in 1993, in protest over the direction of the peace negotiations, and Rabin now presided over a minority government, reliant on the blocking coalition of Arab parties to stay in power. Whereas the Knesset had overwhelmingly endorsed the initial Oslo Agreement, a subsequent phase barely passed with parliamentary approval. The peace process was moving toward the "permanent status" negotiations phase, and Rabin knew it would be tough going. Feeling the need to shore up the pro-peace community and generate enthusiasm for the process, he agreed to speak at a massive rally in Tel Aviv in support of Oslo. It was scheduled for November 4, 1995.

The rally took place in a huge plaza called Kings of Israel Square, in front of Tel Aviv's city hall. More than one hundred thousand Israelis showed up, a major show of support, far more than at any anti-Oslo demonstration the country had seen. Onstage, Rabin was visibly moved by the turnout. Ever a man of few words, he told the

---

don't say, do matter. In a *New York Times* op-ed on September 5, 1993, Netanyahu wrote that Oslo was a "mortal threat to Israel" and compared Rabin's negotiations with Arafat to Neville Chamberlin's appeasement of Hitler. And at those anti-Rabin rallies, Netanyahu didn't urge his followers to stop portraying Rabin as a Nazi or to stop calling for his death. After the rally in which protesters carried the mock coffin, the head of Israel's internal security services, Carmi Gillon, met with Netanyahu to ask him to tone down his anti-Rabin rhetoric. Netanyahu refused to do so (Savir, *The Process*, 255).

Rabin sings "Shir La Shalom"

crowd, "I was a military man for twenty-seven years. I fought as long
as there were no prospects for peace. Today I believe that there are
prospects for peace, great prospects. We must take advantage of this
for the sake of those standing here—and for the sake of those not
standing here." He then joined the other leaders and celebrities onstage in singing the unofficial Israeli peace anthem, "Shir la Shalom"
("A Song of Peace"). Then he walked off the stage and, accompanied
by his bodyguards, headed down the stairs to the parking lot, where
his motorcade awaited him.

Yigal Amir, a twenty-five-year-old law student at a religious
university, was waiting for Rabin in the parking lot. Amir was a
right-wing extremist opposed to Oslo and to any compromise with
the Palestinians. He had taken seriously the rabbis' rulings that Rabin
posed a threat to Israel and the Jewish people, and he had decided that
it was his duty to stop him. As Rabin approached the open door of
his car, Amir fired three shots, two of which hit Rabin in the back.
As police tackled Amir, Rabin's bodyguards pushed him into the car,
and it sped off toward the hospital.

In Rabin's pocket...

Rabin died on the operating table. In his jacket pocket was a pack of Parliaments and a sheet with the lyrics to "Shir la Shalom." It was soaked in his blood.

A visibly shaken Shimon Peres, who had attended the rally with Rabin, quickly assumed the prime ministership, pledging to continue along the path he and Rabin had forged. Two days after the assassination, hundreds of dignitaries, including two former U.S. presidents, the president of Egypt, and eighty other heads of state, attended Rabin's funeral. Eulogies were given by King Hussein and President Bill Clinton. Clinton admired and respected the gruff old war hero. He recounted how Rabin, the quintessential Israeli, had not known how to wear a tie: "The last time we were together, not two weeks ago, he showed up for a black-tie event on time but without the black tie. And so he borrowed a tie, and I was privileged to straighten it for him. It is a moment I will cherish as long as I live." Clinton concluded his eulogy with words from the Kaddish, the Jewish prayer of mourning. And finally, "*Shalom chaver.* Good-bye, my friend."

. . .

EULOGY

Without question, Rabin's assassination was my "JFK moment." I had gotten home to the United States from Israel to start law school just a few weeks earlier. I'll always remember where I was and what I was doing when I heard the news. I remember pulling my car over to the side of the road; I couldn't drive. Later, I spoke with my cousin in Israel, who told me he was taking his young sons to watch Rabin's hearse pass by their kibbutz on the way from Tel Aviv to Jerusalem.

I watched the funeral, stunned and devastated. Perhaps the most powerful eulogy, for me, was the one delivered by Rabin's granddaughter, Noa, just eighteen years old. She said in part, "Forgive me for not wanting to talk about peace. I want to speak about my grandfather . . . Others, greater than I, have already eulogized you. But none of them had my good fortune to feel the caress of your warm, soft hands and the warm embrace that was reserved only for us. Or to see that half smile of yours, which always meant so much to me, that smile that is no more, frozen with you. I have no feelings of revenge because my pain and my loss are so big, too big. The ground has slipped away from under our feet, and we are trying somehow to sit in this empty space that has been left behind, but so far without much success . . ."

I was so moved by her words, and it turned out, so, too, was the woman who a few years later I would meet and end up marrying. One day, the topic of Rabin's funeral came up, and we decided right then and there that if we were ever to have kids together, and if one of them was a girl, we would name her Noa. And that's exactly what we did. Our Noa is now eighteen.

Warned by Israeli internal security officials that they were worried about his safety, Yasser Arafat did not attend the funeral. But he did pay a quiet condolence call on Rabin's widow, Leah. It was reported that when he heard the news of the assassination, he wept.

Rabin's assassination shocked the Israeli public like nothing before or since. Israelis flocked to Kings of Israel Square—now renamed Rabin Square—which became a makeshift memorial, almost a shrine to the fallen prime minister. Leaders promised a national soul searching, a reckoning with the horrific intercommunal hatred and violence that had burrowed its way into the soul of Israel. For a while, it seemed like the country would pull together and, having learned a terrible lesson, chart a new way forward. But that's not how it turned out.

CHAPTER 12

AS THE CLEVER HOPES EXPIRE
The End of Oslo

SOON AFTER THE assassination, Prime Minister Peres tried to move forward on the Syrian peace track, but to no avail. He decided to call for early elections in May 1996, in order to take advantage of the sense of remorse and mourning that had shaken Israel to its foundations. He felt the Israeli public would give him a vote of confidence to move Rabin's peace process forward. But once again, the enemies of peace intervened with brutal effectiveness. Hamas and Islamic Jihad terrorists carried out a series of horrific suicide bombings over the course of a week and a half, killing scores of Israelis. One of the attacks was at a big shopping mall in Tel Aviv, where crowds of children had gathered in costume to celebrate the Jewish holiday of Purim. Israel, already reeling from the assassination, was further unnerved.

Then, in April, in the midst of the campaign, the cease-fire that had held since 1993 between Israel and Hezbollah in Southern Lebanon broke down. Over several weeks of fighting, hundreds of thousands of Lebanese were forced to flee their homes in the south as Israel launched air raids and artillery barrages to pressure Hezbollah into stopping its rocket attacks into northern Israel. On April 18, IDF artillery fired on a UN compound near the village of Qana, in Southern Lebanon, where hundreds of Lebanese civilians had sought shelter from the fighting. More than one hundred were killed. The fighting soon ended, but Israel, and Peres, had suffered yet another major reputational blow. And many of Peres's potential supporters in Israel's Arab community—traditionally part of Labor's base—felt considerably deflated after the debacle in Lebanon, less passionate about getting out the vote for Labor.

Peres and Labor ran a lackluster campaign, assuming that victory was assured because of the national trauma that still gripped the country. But Peres's rival, Likud leader Benjamin Netanyahu, ran a campaign aimed at manipulating the anxieties of a nervous public and stoking fears. Peres, a Likud campaign slogan claimed, would "divide Jerusalem." Only Bibi (Netanyahu's ubiquitous nickname) could keep Israelis safe. As it does so often in so many countries around the world, the appeals to fear and tribalism worked. Although Peres led in the polls throughout the campaign, on Election Day, Bibi pulled off a razor-thin victory. Peres was toppled, Rabin was dead, and Oslo, it seemed, was over.

ENTER BIBI

Still, as Bibi became prime minister for the first time, international support for Oslo, and Israeli support for peace negotiations, remained strong. President Clinton was willing to apply pressure on the new prime minister to commit to and continue the peace talks he had so roundly criticized and, indeed, campaigned against. It worked, to a point. Soon, Netanyahu and Arafat were meeting, and in July 1997, Israel and the Palestinian Authority signed the "Hebron Protocol," which led to the redeployment of most IDF troops from the largest Palestinian city and the handing over of civilian authority to the PA. Throughout much of Area A of the West Bank and Gaza, the PA was now in charge of daily administration, and PA security forces kept the peace. In 1998, Clinton hosted Arafat and Netanyahu in Wye River, Maryland, in an attempt to get peace negotiations back on track. In the resulting Wye River Memorandum, the two Middle East leaders renewed the interim agreement that Rabin and Arafat had signed in 1995.

Netanyahu was in a way Israel's first "American-style" politician. Telegenic, media-savvy, and hubristic, he exuded confidence and a certain kind of charisma. He even spoke great English and felt he knew America well: as a teenager, he had attended high school in Philadelphia while his father, a disciple of Ze'ev Jabotinsky, the founder of right-wing Zionism, taught college in the city. Bibi attended MIT, then headed home to Israel to launch his political career. He was a rising star in the Likud Party, with a great résumé, one burnished by an extraordinary family story: Not only had his dad served as Jabotinsky's secretary, but also his brother, Yonatan, was a national hero. In 1976, when an Air France flight was hijacked and almost one hundred Israeli and Jewish passengers were held captive in Entebbe, Uganda, Yoni Netanyahu was killed in action commanding the Israeli raid that successfully rescued the hostages and spirited them safely home.

But for a guy who has completely dominated Israeli politics in the second decade of the twenty-first century (becoming, in 2020, the longest-serving prime minister in Israeli history), Benjamin Netanyahu was not a particularly successful first-term leader. He was in a tough spot. He did manage to increase settlement building and implement free-market economic policies that further dismantled the

Israeli social welfare state, but most Israelis, even in his base, didn't trust him. He faced massive opposition from the Israeli left for his role in creating the toxic atmosphere before Rabin's assassination and, now, for his foot-dragging on the peace process. Despite being overwhelmingly approved by the Knesset, the Wye River agreement was going nowhere.

At the same time, his own base of supporters on the right began to lose faith in him because of his decision, albeit reluctant and grudging, to continue along the path set by the Oslo Accords, handing over administrative authority in Area A to the PA. Here was the same Netanyahu who had attacked Rabin and Peres for negotiating with Arafat ... now negotiating with Arafat. Meanwhile, terrorist attacks continued, as did the grinding violence between Hezbollah and the IDF in Southern Lebanon. In addition, Bibi was plagued, just as he would be upon his return to power over twenty years later, by a series of corruption charges and various political scandals.

ENTER BARAK

In May 1999, after a vote of no confidence in Netanyahu's government, Israelis returned to the polls. Running against Bibi this time was Labor Party leader Ehud Barak, who had served as foreign minister in Peres's government after the assassination. Barak was brilliant and cerebral, an accomplished classical pianist with a reputation for aloofness, even arrogance. But he was also, like Rabin, a military hero and former chief of staff of the IDF, and the most decorated soldier in Israeli history. And, in an interesting twist of fate, he had been Netanyahu's commander in an elite commando unit back in their army days.

Barak ran on a campaign promising a return to, and completion of, the peace process—a fulfillment of Rabin's legacy. He also promised to pull IDF troops out of the security zone in Southern Lebanon

Ehud Barak

they'd occupied for twenty-two years. Like Rabin, he was a leader whom Israelis felt they could trust to keep them safe *and* negotiate peace. He blew out Netanyahu in a landslide.

Soon after his election, Barak met with Arafat, King Abdullah of Jordan (the son of King Hussein, who had died in February 1999), and President Mubarak of Egypt, signaling that a resumption of the peace process was a priority. Hopes for peace began to rise. It seemed that, just maybe, the horror of Rabin's assassination and Bibi's brief right-wing premiership were major bumps on the road to peace, but not the end of the line.

Once in office, Barak moved quickly. Like Rabin before him, he was enthusiastic about the potential for peace with Syria. This would be a game changer: a treaty with Syria would bring peace with Syrian-controlled Lebanon, meaning there would be no enemy states on Israel's borders. Barak was willing to hand most of the Golan back to Syria in order to achieve such a deal. But once again, despite high hopes and intensive American facilitation, the negotiations did not result in a breakthrough; the two sides just couldn't come to an agreement. Still, in May 2000, Barak kept his campaign promise, withdrawing the IDF from Southern Lebanon.

When it came to the Palestinians, Barak was critical of the incrementalist, step-by-step approach at the heart of Oslo. He favored a comprehensive, bold move to final status talks. He believed the window for peace was not open indefinitely; he knew Bibi's years in office had damaged Israel's credibility with the Palestinians, and he was worried about Israeli public opinion, which he knew was extremely susceptible to the inevitable violence perpetrated by the enemies of peace. In September 1999, Israeli and Palestinian negotiators met in Egypt and hammered out an agreement to put the peace talks back on track. The two sides were to resume permanent-status negotiations that month and to reach a settlement in one year, by September 2000.

Despite the jump-start, talks with the Palestinians proceeded slowly. Barak was focused on the Syrian track, and he worried that the Israeli public wouldn't be able to stomach too much change, or too many concessions, too quickly. This frustrated the Palestinians, who felt sidelined and who did not appreciate playing second fiddle to the Syrians. Once the Syrian talks foundered, Barak turned his attention back to the Palestinian track. But these talks, too, soon bogged down over disagreements on details, damaged trust, and missed time lines.

Barak's impatience with an incremental approach was based on his concern that the gradual concessions of Oslo would result in an erosion of Israeli public support for the process. But his dismissal of several interim steps Israel had committed to in previous rounds of talks eroded faith in his intentions on the Palestinian side. Barak's approach raised questions for the Palestinians about his priorities, his trustworthiness, and his ability to deliver a final deal. Barak was frustrated. Arafat felt played. The parties were at a stalemate.

There was a terrible danger here. If Palestinians came to believe the talks were going nowhere after seven years, that there was no Palestinian state on the horizon and that the occupation would continue indefinitely, the result might be a resumption of massive unrest and violence in the occupied territories. If that happened, the Israeli public, already shaky, could quickly lose its stomach for an agreement with the Palestinians and turn against the peace process entirely.

CAMP DAVID, 2000

Recognizing these dangers, and aware that his premiership was at risk if the peace process failed, Barak pushed hard for a summit meeting to finish the final status talks once and for all—an "all-or-nothing" peace conference. The Palestinians, wary of Barak's impetuousness, burned by his treatment of the Palestinian track as a secondary priority, and unsure of his intentions, did not want to go. They didn't feel ready, nor that the time for such a summit was ripe.

In the end, though, they had no choice. Clinton, fast approaching the end of his second term, intent on cementing his legacy as a peacemaker, and eager to support Barak politically, invited the parties to Camp David for a summit meeting to be held in July 2000. Aware of Arafat's concerns, Clinton promised him that he would not be blamed, regardless of what happened. At Camp David the parties would deal with the big, permanent-status issues identified in the Declaration of Principles back in 1993: Jerusalem, borders, Palestinian refugees, security, the settlements, and the end of all claims. Then, the plan went, they would sign an agreement leading to a treaty ending the conflict for good.

Barak, Arafat, Clinton, and their negotiation teams spent two weeks in the Maryland woods trying to get to a final status agreement. Israel offered the Palestinians the most ambitious proposal yet, including a state in Gaza, 92 percent of the West Bank, and parts of

East Jerusalem. In the end, however, major gaps remained on every issue, particularly on Jerusalem, refugees, and borders. The United States was simply unable to bridge the divide between the parties.

In the twenty years since Camp David, much has been written and argued about who is to blame for the failure to come to an agreement. It's a tricky exercise, given that the proposals were not written down; we have only the representations of the participants as to what actually happened. The Israeli and American narrative is that Barak offered the Palestinians the most far-reaching and generous offer they could've reasonably hoped for, and the Palestinians turned it down without even a counteroffer. Arafat, this line of reasoning goes, was simply unwilling to close the deal. Barak stated, famously, that Camp David proved that Israel had no true partner for peace. Some even argue that Arafat's intention all along was to sabotage the process by insisting on an unrestricted right of return for Palestinian refugees, which Israel could never accept—as the argument goes, this would fundamentally alter the demographic balance of the state—and then launch a violent uprising to defeat Israel.

The counternarrative put forward both by Palestinian negotiators and also some key American (and even Israeli) players is that Barak's proposals, while groundbreaking, were simply not sufficient to address Palestinian needs on territory. Egypt received 100 percent of the Sinai and the dismantling of all Israelis settlements there in exchange for peace. Barak had offered to return 99.9 percent of the Golan Heights to the Syrians. For the Palestinians, the territorial proposal, as bold as it was, was highly problematic. First, 92 percent of the West Bank really meant 92 percent of 22 percent of historical Palestine (given that Israel comprised the other 78 percent). As some Palestinians observed, they were being asked to accept a further compromise on a compromise. Worst of all, from the Palestinians' perspective, the Israeli proposal did not adequately recognize Palestinian claims to East Jerusalem as a future capital, or to the Muslim and Christian holy sites of the Old City. This was at the heart of the matter. Moreover, the Americans only consulted with and involved key Arab states on the issue of Jerusalem midway through the summit; to imagine that Arafat could accept compromises on Jerusalem without the backing of the broader Arab world was, to say the least, unrealistic.

As is the case with most aspects of this conflict, there is truth to all sides of the story. But even though a deal wasn't signed, Camp David was not quite the end of the line for the peace process. The parties departed the summit with a public commitment to keep plugging away at negotiations, despite the failure to come to a final status deal. And they did, with small groups of negotiators meeting to keep the talks going. But then, on September 28, 2000, Israel's new opposition leader decided to pay a visit to the Temple Mount in Jerusalem. It was a visit that would change everything.

THE BULLDOZER RETURNS

After his crushing defeat by Barak in the 1999 election, Netanyahu had been replaced as Likud leader by a formidable and familiar face. Ariel Sharon, who had served as Bibi's foreign minister, had now fully returned from the political wilderness in which he'd wandered for a few years after the debacle in Lebanon and the disgrace of the massacres at Sabra and Shatila. The Bulldozer was back.

True to form, Sharon—godfather of the settlement movement, architect of the invasion of Lebanon—deeply disapproved of Barak's peace initiative and the negotiations at Camp David. He opposed territorial compromise and decided to demonstrate this by asserting Israeli sovereignty over the single most controversial spot on the map of the Israeli-Palestinian conflict: the Haram al-Sharif (Noble Sanctuary)/Har ha-Bayit (Temple Mount) in the Old City of

Jerusalem.* In fact, disagreement over who got to control the Temple Mount—site of the Dome of the Rock, Al-Aqsa Mosque, and the Western Wall—was one of the main issues still unresolved after Camp David.** Sharon knew that visiting the Temple Mount now would be the political equivalent of lighting a match next to a pile of dry kindling. But he had a point to make—and a prime minister to challenge.

Sharon was no stranger to the powder-keg politics of Jerusalem; in fact, he'd contributed to them. He owned a house, bedecked by huge Israeli flags and guarded 24/7, smack in the middle of the Muslim Quarter of the Old City, the heart of Arab Jerusalem, which the Palestinians claimed as part of their future capital. The location of the house was a statement about Israeli control over the Arab areas of the city and an act, some might say, of intentional provocation, given Sharon's reputation as Israel's most prominent right-wing, pro-settlement hard-liner. It was inconceivable that the Palestinians would not perceive a visit to the Temple Mount, given its extraordinary importance to Muslims and to the Palestinian cause—remember when Moshe Dayan ordered the Israeli flag taken down from the Dome of the Rock after that site's capture in the Six-Day War, lest it ignite World War III?—as an even *bigger* provocation, given who Sharon was. It was predictable that the reaction would be furious and violent. But again: making a provocative gesture was the point of the thing.

---

* He was also interested in beating back any potential Netanyahu challenge for Likud leadership and ginning up his right-wing base for a run against Barak in the next election.

** Just as a reminder: Israel captured East Jerusalem—including the Temple Mount, which is in the Old City—in the 1967 Six-Day War. The Temple Mount is the giant platform on which the Jewish Temple once stood. The western retaining wall of the ancient platform is the Western Wall, holy to Jews. The Dome of the Rock and the Al-Aqsa Mosque stand on the Temple Mount today, making it the third-holiest site in Islam. Even as Israel claims sovereignty over the Temple Mount, it has allowed Palestinian Muslim religious authorities to control and administer the Muslim holy sites there.

Ariel Sharon's house

On September 28, 2000, surrounded by close to a thousand Israeli security personnel and with IDF helicopters clattering above, Sharon and his entourage entered the Temple Mount plaza through the gate used by tourists, which ascends from the Western Wall plaza below. He declared that he was there to defend the right of Jews to visit the site (although they were already allowed to under the agreement between Israel and the Muslim administrators of the Temple Mount) and to reaffirm that the Temple Mount would remain under permanent Israeli sovereignty (an assertion, argued a major Palestinian leader in Jerusalem, belied by Sharon's need for such a massive security presence even to visit the site*). Israeli police held protesters back, but stones were thrown, and rubber bullets were fired

---

* That leader, Faisal Husseini, said, "Israel has no sovereignty here. They have military might, they have the power of occupation, but not sovereignty."

in response. Within hours, rioting had spread through East Jerusalem. The Israeli response was predictably harsh, and soon, protests and riots spread across the West Bank and Gaza. Frustrated by the failure at Camp David after thirty-three years of occupation and settlement building, furious at Sharon's provocative visit, enraged by the hard-handed Israeli response, and egged on by Palestinian militants, the Palestinian streets were about to explode.

THE SECOND INTIFADA

As Palestinian demonstrations and rioting intensified, so, too, did Israel's harsh response. (We've seen this movie before.) Within the first weeks of unrest, scores of Palestinians were shot dead by the IDF, and thousands more were wounded. Palestinians and Israelis alike began referring to a new intifada, or uprising: Israelis called it the Second Intifada; Palestinians, the Al-Aqsa Intifada, because of Sharon's visit to the Temple Mount, which had lit the fuse. While early demonstrations were largely limited to chanting and stone throwing, as in the First Intifada, increasingly, Palestinian militant groups engaged Israeli security forces in gun battles. The uprising became an armed conflict. One of the most harrowing images from the beginning of the unrest, filmed by news cameras, was the fatal shooting of a terrified twelve-year-old Palestinian child crouching behind his father as the two tried desperately to take shelter in a Gaza street during a clash between the IDF and militants.*

---

* The IDF took responsibility for the death of the boy, Muhammad al-Durrah, later retract-ing it, however, after some questioned whether the fatal bullets had been fired by the Israelis or by Palestinian militants. Whatever the case, these are some of the most upsetting images from this period (William A. Orme Jr., "Israeli Army Says Palestinians May Have Shot Gaza Boy," *New York Times*, Nov. 28, 2000, https://www.nytimes.com/2000/11/28/world/israeli -army-says-palestinians-may-have-shot-gaza-boy.html).

The images of the shooting of the child and the broader harsh IDF response to demonstrations in the occupied territories provoked condemnation from around the world and sparked angry protests in Israel's Arab community. In early October, Israeli police clashed with unarmed Arab Israeli citizens, shooting twelve of them dead. (A thirteenth protester, a Palestinian from Gaza, also unarmed, was killed, too.) Arab Israelis noted, correctly, that such an incident would've been unthinkable if the unarmed protesters had been Jewish. An Israeli governmental commission later found that there was no justification for the use of live fire, but no Israeli police official was ever punished for what happened.

In mid-October, two IDF reservists took a wrong turn and ended up in the middle of the Palestinian city of Ramallah, just a few kilometers from Jerusalem. They were arrested by PA police, but a crowd stormed the police station in which they were being held and murdered them. The image of one of the murderers holding up his bloody hands in triumph was captured by news cameras and beamed around the world: another horrific sign of the times. In response to the killings, Israel launched air strikes against PA facilities in the West Bank and Gaza. The violence continued to increase throughout the autumn. Things were spiraling out of control.

TABA

Despite the escalating violence, peace talks continued. After the failure of the Camp David summit, the Clinton administration had prepared its own proposal for a final status agreement, but postponed releasing it after the outbreak of the intifada. On December 23, 2000, a month before he was set to leave office, Clinton presented it to Israeli and Palestinian negotiators in Washington, D.C. At the meeting, the outgoing president read aloud his plan to a rapt room full of

American, Palestinian, and Israeli negotiators. He made it clear the proposal would no longer be valid when he left office.

The Clinton Parameters, as the plan was known, proposed the establishment of a Palestinian state in Gaza and 97 percent of the West Bank. Israel would annex West Bank territory containing 80 percent of the settler population, and in return, it would give the new Palestinian state a commensurate amount of territory. The new state would be contiguous. The "broad principle," as Clinton put it, for Jerusalem was Palestinian sovereignty over Arab parts of East Jerusalem (including the Temple Mount) and Israeli sovereignty over Jewish parts of East Jerusalem (including the Western Wall). The new Palestinian state would be demilitarized. Israel would get "early warning stations" in the West Bank, and an international force would ensure border security. As for refugees, the Palestinians would waive their claim of right of return to Israel, and Israel would acknowledge the suffering it had caused the Palestinian people in 1948 and would contribute to an international fund to compensate refugees. The new Palestinian state would welcome all Palestinian refugees who wanted to move there. And both sides would declare all relevant UN Security Council Resolutions fulfilled and the conflict over.

The Israelis accepted the Clinton Parameters with minor reservations.* Arafat equivocated; he wasn't ready to say yes, but he didn't want to say no.** In the end, Arafat finally accepted the parameters with reservations, but unlike the Israeli reservations, the Palestinian

---

* In diplomatic terms, this means, "Yes, *but* . . ."

** Arafat and the Palestinians may have believed that the incoming George W. Bush administration, like the administration of the new president's father, George H. W. Bush, would be more amenable to the Palestinan position, and more willing to pressure Israel to compromise. If this was the reason for Arafat's equivocation, former U.S. peace negotiator Aaron David Miller argues, it was a fundamental miscalculation of the second President Bush's priorities (Aaron David Miller, conversation with the author, Mar. 2021).

ones were clearly "outside the parameters Clinton offered" (for example, Arafat rejected Clinton's proposal that the Western Wall remain under Israeli sovereignty, as well as the proposal on resolving the refugee issue).

Still, the peace negotiators kept trying. The negotiating teams met in the resort town of Taba, Egypt, near the Israeli border, in late January 2001. By all accounts, the sessions were positive and productive, and the Israeli and Palestinian negotiators made significant progress toward a final status agreement based on (and even going beyond) the Clinton Parameters. But by then, Israel was heading toward elections in February and Clinton was out of office. At the end of the Taba Summit, the negotiators issued a joint statement: "The sides declare that they have never been closer to reaching an agreement and it is thus our shared belief that the remaining gaps could be bridged with the resumption of negotiations following the Israeli elections." It would be the last time the negotiating teams met.

Taba

. . .

HOW DO YOU MURDER A PEACE PROCESS?

Since its creation in 1948, Israel has fought a major war (or a series of vicious smaller ones) in every single decade of its existence except for one: the 1990s. That's no coincidence. The roughly ten years from the Madrid Peace Conference in 1991 to the end of the line at Taba in late 2000 represent the golden age of peace negotiations between Israelis and Palestinians and the broader Arab world, a time during which all sides focused on resolving, rather than winning, the conflict. In addition to Oslo, this period also saw the signing of the peace treaty between Israel and Jordan, attempts to make peace with Syria, and the beginning of a process normalizing Israel's presence in the wider Middle East, reflected by the initiation of official contacts between Israel and countries like Morocco, Qatar, and others. (Those early seeds of contact grew, several decades later, into the formal recognition of Israel in 2020 by some of those Arab states.) And even though a few genuine efforts to get back to the negotiating table have taken place in the years since the 1990s, they haven't generated the momentum of the Oslo decade.

There are many reasonable critiques of the Oslo process, and there is no guarantee that it would eventually have resulted in a final agreement. But we'll never know. At the end of the day, Oslo didn't fail because the process was flawed, or because the endgame, a two-state solution, was unachievable. In fact, Oslo didn't fail; it was never given the chance to fail. Instead, it was murdered.

The assassination of Yitzhak Rabin may prove to be that rarest of modern political murders: one that actually achieved its goal. The assassination of Martin Luther King Jr. didn't stop the march toward civil rights in America. The assassination of Anwar Sadat didn't destroy the peace between Egypt and Israel. But the assassination of Rabin took from the field the one Israeli leader who might have been able to close the deal with the Palestinians while bringing his country along with him. That we will never know what could have been only compounds the tragedy of the loss.

And it wasn't just the assassin: As if in concert, Rabin's murderer, the Jewish terrorist of Hebron, and the militant movement that spawned them essentially worked together with the suicide bombers of Hamas, Islamic Jihad, and the other violent enemies of peace. Aided and abetted by the rejectionists on both sides, they successfully killed the peace process. Together, they changed history.

War, terrorism, increasing tribalism, and a half century of corrosive occupation have hardened hearts on both sides. Still, the basic contours of a peaceful resolution remain. The major obstacle to the vision that shimmered at Taba isn't a lack of political imagination; it is, as I write earlier in this book, a lack of political will. That said, the "status quo" between Israelis and Palestinians is anything but. As the reality on the ground changes, so, too, do Israeli and Palestinian mental maps of the conflict. As the rhetoric of demonization and the rounds of violence continue, hearts harden further. As the settlements continue to grow, the chances of achieving a viable two-state solution become more and more remote. The question is: If and when the political will to end the conflict is ever rediscovered by Israeli and Palestinian leaders, will it be too late?

CHAPTER 13

THE BULLDOZER'S LAST SURPRISE

ON FEBRUARY 6, 2001, Israelis went to the polls again. Barak—weakened politically by the collapse at Camp David, the worsening violence of the Second Intifada, and the shooting of the unarmed Arab Israeli protesters in October (which sank his support in the Arab community)—lost to Sharon in a landslide. The Bulldozer was now the prime minister of Israel. Oslo was over.

Throughout 2001 and 2002, violence in the occupied territories escalated, with the IDF killing Palestinian militants and demonstrators and with Palestinian militants targeting Israeli soldiers and civilians—many of whom were settlers in the West Bank and Gaza. Hamas, Islamic Jihad, and other militant Palestinian factions, including groups linked to Arafat's Fatah Party, carried out armed attacks with greater frequency. As for Arafat, he and the Palestinian Authority did little to prevent these attacks. Rather, they attempted to use the unrest to improve their bargaining position, to

Ariel Sharon

demonstrate to Israel that the Palestinians would not be taken for granted. They made no serious attempts at de-escalation. Instead, they tried to ride the tiger. And that rarely ends well. If Sharon had lit the fuse of the Second Intifada with his visit to the Temple Mount, Arafat poured gasoline on the flames with his refusal to try to stop the growing violence.

On May 19, 2002, a suicide bomber attacked a mall in the Israeli city of Netanya, killing six. While suicide bombers had targeted Israeli civilians before, Netanya was the start of a horrific string of suicide bombings within Israel targeting civilians. Over the course of the intifada, hundreds of Israelis were murdered on buses, at train stations, and in pizza parlors and restaurants and shopping malls. In one particularly nightmarish terror attack, thirty people were killed by a suicide bomber who detonated himself at a Passover seder being held at a seaside hotel. Going to school or grabbing a falafel suddenly felt like a high-risk activity. Every Israeli knew someone who had been affected by the violence. Altogether, more than seven hundred Israeli civilians were killed in suicide bombings and other terror attacks over the course of the Second Intifada.

Sharon's response to the wave of suicide bombings was "Operation Defensive Shield," a full-scale reoccupation of the West Bank. Once again, IDF troops patrolled the streets of Nablus, Jenin, Hebron, and other Palestinian cities. Israeli soldiers battled Palestinian militants throughout the occupied territories, but the highest price was paid by Palestinian civilians. Around 2,200 Palestinian noncombatants were killed by Israeli security forces during the uprising.* Israel began construction of a separation barrier (running roughly along the Israel–West Bank border, but making deep incursions into the occupied territories) aimed, in part, at preventing terrorists from attacking Israelis. Sharon blamed Arafat for the violence and ordered the IDF to lay siege to his Palestinian Authority headquarters in Ramallah. Arafat had moved there from Gaza City in 1996. He would remain there, as Israeli security forces destroyed many of the compound's buildings, until he was evacuated to a French hospital in October 2004, after falling seriously ill. He died the next month.

---

* The Israeli human rights organization B'Tselem reported that 719 Israeli civilians and 334 Israeli security force members were killed by Palestinians in the Second Intifada. B'Tselem reported that 2,204 Palestinian civilians "who did not take part in the hostilities" and 1,671 Palestinians who did take part in the hostilities (as well as 870 whose role in the hostilities is unclear) were killed by Israeli security forces during the Second Intifada. B'Tselem also reported that 577 Palestinians were killed by other Palestinians during the conflict, more than 100 of them because they were suspected collaborators with Israel ("Fatalities Before Operation 'Cast Lead,' Data by the date of event, 29 September 2000–26 December 2008," https://www.btselem.org/statistics/fatalities/before-cast-lead/by-date-of-event). As with so many aspects of this conflict, even the statistics are controversial. While most sources agree on the basic number of casualties, there is disagreement over the classification of those casualties (i.e., whether or not they were combatants). I've chosen to use these statistics because (a) B'Tselem is an internationally respected human rights organization, and (b) it is not affiliated with either the PA or the Israeli government. Full disclosure: I should note that B'Tselem is a grantee of the New Israel Fund.

Meanwhile, the outside world made attempts to stop the violence and resuscitate the peace process. In 2002, the Arab League announced a peace initiative, offering Israel peace and normalized relations with the countries of the Arab world in exchange for withdrawal from the occupied territories, a just resolution to the refugee question, and the establishment of a Palestinian state in the West Bank and Gaza, with East Jerusalem as its capital. Sharon rejected the deal out of hand because it mentioned UN Resolution 194 (which calls for the return of Palestinian refugees to Israel) and because it required Israel to withdraw to the 1967 borders.

Then, in 2003, the Bush administration, along with the European Union, Russia, and the United Nations (the so-called Quartet), presented their Road Map for Peace, a plan meant to lead to a two-state solution (on terms much friendlier to Israel than those of Camp David and Taba). The Road Map was short on details, but it called for a halt to all violence, a settlement freeze, security for Israel, and the establishment of a viable Palestinian state. Sharon accepted the idea in principle but with reservations; in particular, he rejected the settlement freeze. The new PA chairman, Mahmoud Abbas (a moderate who had been deeply involved in Oslo), accepted the plan. In the end, the attention of the Bush administration was focused on the war in Iraq, and the Road Map didn't lead the parties out of the mess they were in. The PA didn't stop the violence, and the Israelis refused to stop building settlements.

Despite the failure of the two peace initiatives, something was shifting for the Israeli prime minister. The relentless violence of the Second Intifada, the horror of the suicide bombing campaign, the need to send IDF soldiers back into big Palestinian cities—all this convinced him that something had to change. In 2003, Sharon addressed a group of Likud lawmakers, saying, "The idea that we can continue holding under occupation—and it is occupation; you might not like this word, but it's really an occupation—to hold 3.5 million

Palestinians under occupation is, in my opinion, a very bad thing for us and for them. It cannot continue forever. Do you want to stay forever in Jenin, in Nablus, in Ramallah, in Bethlehem? I don't think that's right." The word *occupation* is still controversial in some conservative Israeli and pro-Israel circles today—and here was the prime minister of Israel, the architect of the settlement enterprise, using it in 2003. What was going on?

Speaking to an Israeli journalist in 2003, Sharon provided the answer. "I have made up my mind to make a real effort to arrive at a real agreement. I'm seventy-five. I have no political ambitions beyond the position I now hold. And I see it as an aim and a goal to bring this people security and peace. Therefore, I shall make very great efforts. I think that this is something that I need to leave behind me: to try to reach an agreement." It would seem that once in power, Sharon, just like his predecessors Rabin, Peres, and Barak, had come to the same conclusion that Ben-Gurion had arrived at back in 1967: Israel could not remain a democracy and a Jewish state while holding on to all the territory (and the Palestinians who lived on it) captured in the Six-Day War. Even though Sharon's idea of what land to give up and how to do it differed greatly from that of his Labor Party predecessors, he had come to believe that Israel had to separate from the Palestinians; it had to get out of at least some of the territories.

In June 2004, Sharon announced a plan to withdraw unilaterally all Israeli settlers and troops from the Gaza Strip and from some isolated West Bank settlements. This would, essentially, remove (or at least reduce) one of the major points of conflict among Palestinians, settlers, and the IDF. To say this was a political earthquake would be an understatement. The godfather of the settlement enterprise had decided to dismantle a big part of it. Critics on the right, opposed to conceding *any* territory to the Palestinians, were horrified and felt betrayed. Critics on the left argued that unilateral disengagement wasn't a good idea; better that Israel coordinate with the PA in order to prevent a vacuum into which rejectionist Hamas, always a powerful force in Gaza, could step. (This is, of course, just what happened.) But Sharon didn't believe there was a reasonable PA partner with which to coordinate, and he wanted to do things on his terms.

In February 2005, Sharon and Abbas met in Egypt and pledged to end Israeli-Palestinian violence. With Arafat dead and Sharon's Gaza withdrawal plan in motion, the Second Intifada came to an end. Israeli troops withdrew from Area A, and a few months later, Sharon created a national unity government to carry out the disengagement from Gaza, bringing Labor into the ruling coalition to strengthen his hand. In September 2005, the Bulldozer sent bulldozers to Gaza. Israel dismantled its Gaza settlements and withdrew all Jewish settlers (between eight and nine thousand) and the IDF troops that protected them.

In November, facing a Netanyahu-led revolt in his Likud Party over the disengagement, which was deeply traumatic to the settler movement and its supporters on the political right, Sharon resigned

Soldiers evict settlers
from Gaza

as head of the party and formed a new centrist party called Kadima (meaning "Forward"). Polls showed it dominating the political landscape in advance of elections scheduled for March 2006. On January 4, 2006, Sharon suffered a stroke, went into a coma, and never recovered. (He died eight years later.) The last leader to emerge from Israel's founding generation was gone.

Sharon's endgame still isn't clear. He, no doubt, intended to withdraw from at least some parts of the West Bank in addition to Gaza (which seemed to most Israelis, with the exception of the settlers who lived there, a tar pit from which they desperately needed to extract themselves). And he had come to the conclusion that a Palestinian state was an unavoidable necessity. We don't know exactly what Sharon's next move would have been. What we do know is that his views had evolved to the point where he considered some separation with the Palestinians—and the relinquishing of territory that that would require, no matter how painful—necessary for Israel's survival. And his overwhelming popularity with the Israeli electorate at the time of his incapacitation suggested that Israelis would likely have followed where he led. It is yet another irony in a story full of them: The fierce Bulldozer evolved into a paternal, even beloved leader. The architect of the settlement enterprise began to deconstruct his own creation. Perhaps Sharon would've led Israel out of the conflict. We'll never know. Another Israeli warrior turned peacemaker had been struck down before getting to finish the job.

OLMERT AND THE SECOND LEBANON WAR

Sharon was replaced by his deputy, Ehud Olmert, finance minister and a former mayor of Jerusalem. Olmert had come up a staunch Likudnik, but like his boss, he had moved to the center, following Sharon to Kadima. Soon after becoming prime minister, Olmert unveiled his "Realignment Plan," in which Israel would withdraw—unilaterally, if necessary—from all of the West Bank except for the five largest settlement blocs there; these last it would then annex. But once again, events intervened. In July 2006, Iranian-backed Hezbollah fighters in Southern Lebanon fired rockets at Israeli towns and then killed and captured several IDF soldiers in a cross-border raid. Israel responded with air strikes, Hezbollah fired missiles into Israel, and then, announcing that it would hold the Lebanese government accountable for allowing Hezbollah's attacks, Israel launched a full-scale invasion of Southern Lebanon.

The Second Lebanon War was something of a debacle for Israel. The government was excoriated by the Israeli media for its handling of the war, as military supply lines into Lebanon bogged down and hundreds of thousands of Israelis fled the North of the country to avoid the Hezbollah missiles and rockets that rained down on small towns and big cities like Haifa. Internationally, Israel's image took another hit as up to a million Lebanese civilians fled the invading Israeli forces and as Israeli air strikes pummeled Hezbollah bases in Beirut, but also the international airport and other parts of Lebanon's civil infrastructure. Why, critics asked, had Olmert taken the bait of this deliberate provocation on Hezbollah's part? The radical Lebanese militant group had increased its power and prestige in Lebanon and beyond by successfully engaging much bigger and stronger Israel in a costly, no-win war.

After a month of this fighting, the UN Security Council passed a resolution demanding an end to the war, and a cease-fire went into effect. Hundreds of Lebanese civilians and hundreds of Hezbollah fighters were killed during the conflict. Forty-four Israeli civilians were killed by rocket and missile attacks, and 121 IDF soldiers were killed in the fighting. Hezbollah and its patron, Iran, had flexed their muscles, showing they could hit Israel almost anywhere from their bases in Southern Lebanon and proving that their fighters were dangerous foes on the ground. Israel had responded with overwhelming force, but Olmert had been badly damaged—at one point, his approval rating stood at 3 percent. An official government commission accused of him of mismanaging the war, and mass protests were held calling for his resignation.

Despite this, Olmert soldiered on, sharpening his belief that a two-state solution was necessary for Israel's continued survival as a democratic Jewish state. When the Arab League updated and reaffirmed its peace initiative from 2002, he responded positively, and in November 2007, President Bush hosted Olmert and PA president Abbas at a peace summit in Annapolis, Maryland. Once again, the parties got very close to a deal on terms close to those put forward seven years earlier, at Camp David and Taba. But by then, Olmert's political troubles had been compounded by legal troubles: he was facing indictment for corruption. And then Gaza interrupted.

Tensions between the two largest Palestinian factions, Fatah (which supported the Oslo Accords) and Hamas (which rejected them), had been rising in Gaza since Arafat's death in 2004 and had only increased after Israel's unilateral withdrawal from that territory in 2005. After Israel pulled out, it handed full control of Gaza to the PA, and in 2006, Hamas beat Fatah in Gaza in legislative elections. The United States, Israel, and other countries considered Hamas a terrorist organization and had supported Fatah in the election. Now they supported Fatah's attempts to retain control in Gaza. The two sides couldn't come to a political agreement, and fighting soon broke out between them. After several months of bloody conflict, in June 2007, Hamas prevailed, kicked Fatah out, and took control of Gaza.* There were now essentially two Palestinian polities: Hamas-

---

* Since 2007, numerous attempts at reconciliation have been made, none successful. Obviously, this further complicates the notion of any resumption of peace negotiations.

Gaza

controlled Gaza and PA/Fatah-controlled West Bank.

After the Hamas takeover, Israel imposed a total blockade (air, sea, and land) on Gaza, declaring that it would allow only humanitarian aid into the small, poor, crowded territory. (Egypt, which controlled the only other land border with Gaza, also heavily restricted who and what traveled in or out of the territory.) Some have taken to describing the Gaza Strip as the world's largest open-air prison. Indeed, in prison-break fashion, Hamas dug tunnels underneath the border fences into Israel and Egypt, through which it smuggled all manner of things, including arms, into Gaza.

With some regularity, Hamas and Islamic Jihad militants in Gaza fired rockets at nearby communities in Israel, and the IDF responded with artillery fire and air raids until, finally, a cease-fire brought a measure of calm to the region. But in December 2008, hostilities resumed—and soon escalated. In early January, Olmert ordered an Israeli ground invasion of Gaza to stop the attacks on nearby Israeli towns. By the time a cease-fire was declared after three weeks of fighting, some 1,400 Palestinians had been killed, about 900 of them unarmed civilians. Three Israeli civilians were killed by Hamas rocket fire into Israel, and 10 IDF soldiers were killed in the fighting.

Once again, Israel found itself facing strong international criticism, accused of using disproportionate force in Gaza that resulted in unconscionable civilian casualties. It asserted that it had every right to defend its civilians from unprovoked rocket attacks from Gaza. Hamas claimed that it was responding to Israeli provocations and the ongoing siege. Human rights organizations and the United Nations accused both sides of having committed war crimes.*

A couple of weeks later, badly damaged by the wars in Lebanon and Gaza, facing a criminal indictment for corruption, and deeply unpopular, Olmert announced that he was stepping down. His successor as Kadima Party leader, Foreign Minister Tzipi Livni, was given six weeks to put together a governing coalition, but she was unable to do so, triggering early elections in February 2009. Livni and Kadima won, but once again, Livni was unable to form a government. So, under Israel's electoral rules, the runner-up got a chance to do so. Because right-wing parties had won more seats overall than had centrist or left-wing parties, the second-place finisher succeeded in building a coalition. And with that, Likud's Bibi Netanyahu was back in business.

---

* The 2008–9 Gaza conflict, called "Operation Cast Lead" by Israelis and "the Gaza Massacre" by Palestinians, was just the first round in a series of short and bloody battles between Israel and Hamas. See the entry "Wars (and what to call them)" in the lexicon.

CHAPTER 14

THE DEMOCRACY RECESSION

NETANYAHU'S RETURN TO the top job marked a new phase of Israeli history—let's call it the Bibi Era. From 2009 to 2021, Bibi served as prime minister, clawing his way to victory in five more closely fought Israeli elections over ten years—there are no term limits in Israel—amid a growing set of personal and political scandals that resulted, in 2019, in three criminal indictments. (His trial began in 2020 and is ongoing at the time of this writing.) He led the country through several short, sharp, indecisive wars with Hamas in Gaza, increased the rate of settlement building, clashed with U.S. president Barack Obama over Iran, and moved closer to evangelical Christians and the Republican Party in America while growing further away from the liberal American Jewish community and the Democrats. He celebrated the rise of his friend Donald Trump, and Trump showered him with political gifts: U.S. withdrawal from the 2015 Iran nuclear deal, recognition of Israeli sovereignty on the Golan, relocation of

Netanyahu

the U.S. embassy to Jerusalem (see "Jerusalem (East and West)" in the "Lexicon of the Conflict," to see why that's important), a U.S. peace plan that would allow Israel to annex 30 percent of the West Bank, and U.S.-facilitated normalization of relations with two tiny, wealthy, not particularly democratic Persian Gulf states, the United Arab Emirates and Bahrain.

In March 2020, after yet another inconclusive election, Netanyahu once again managed to remain prime minister (and, he hoped, avoid criminal prosecution while in office) by forming a coalition government with his chief rival, the centrist Blue and White Party, ostensibly to combat the coronavirus pandemic. Bibi's political wizardry is unmatched in Israeli history. But all this has come at a price—and the price has been the quality and character of Israel's democracy.

For the last decade or so, the Economist Intelligence Unit's "Democracy Index" has consistently ranked Israel as a "flawed democracy," not a full one. Israel has begun to drift from its liberal-democratic founding principles. The succession of right-wing governments under Netanyahu over the last decade presided over a "democracy recession"* in Israel. New and proposed laws and policies strengthened the power of the ultra-Orthodox religious establishment, further marginalized Israel's Arab minority, placed new limits and restraints on freedom of expression and dissent, attempted to shut up and shut down human rights organizations that report on the occupation, and of course, dramatically strengthened the settlement project. (We'll discuss many of these issues in greater depth in part 2 of this book.)

This shrinking of democratic space is not unique to Israel; a tide of what some call "illiberal democracy" has washed across the globe, from Turkey and Russia to Hungary and Poland and Brazil, and on to Brexit Britain and Trump's America. But the rise of right-wing populism in Israel is, well, uniquely Israeli. And it is threatening to change Israel into a place that many of its supporters would no longer recognize. So, what happened to the plucky little Western-style democracy on the east coast of the Mediterranean?

At the heart of the change in Israel was the ascension to an uninterrupted decade of power of a right-wing coalition, under Bibi's leadership, made up of nationalist, religious, Russian, and settler parties. Israel had certainly had rightist coalitions before, but this was different. Not only was this new Israeli right less concerned than its predecessors with maintaining and protecting the values and institutions of liberal democracy, but also there was no serious political opposition. The once mighty Labor Party, the folks who had founded the country, had experienced a dizzying decline into near irrelevancy after the collapse of the peace process and the terror and violence of the Second Intifada. Labor's voters migrated to a series of large centrist parties or to small left-wing parties, weakening the opposition bloc. While the

---

* A term coined by political scientist Larry Diamond.

makeup of the new nationalist-settler-Russian-religious alignment changed a bit from election to election, and even sometimes included centrist parties, Netanyahu's six successive governments moved Israeli politics and policies significantly rightward. Without a powerful political opposition, the new ultranationalist ruling coalition—which represented only about half the Israeli electorate (sound familiar?)—pursued its shared agenda with fewer restraints than ever before. All this served to further divide an already divided society.

. . .

GAZA, THE GOLDSTONE REPORT, AND THE ATTACK ON HUMAN RIGHTS DEFENDERS

After the three-week war in Gaza in 2008–9, the United Nations launched a fact-finding mission to investigate allegations of violations of international human rights and humanitarian law by the combatants. The mission was led by the (Jewish) former South African Supreme Court justice Richard Goldstone. Israel refused to cooperate with the investigation, pointing to what it saw as a history of unfair treatment by the United Nations.* Nevertheless, the Goldstone Report, issued in September 2009,

---

* To be fair, Israel had a point. While the 1947 UN Resolution 181 set the stage for the establishment of Israel, in the years since then, the UN General Assembly in particular was often a stage for Israel's enemies and critics to single it out for a unique level of criticism and censure, including an infamous "Zionism equals racism" resolution in 1975 (which was repealed in 1991). That said, the Security Council, with the United States as one of the permanent members, has *not* evinced an anti-Israel bias, and its resolutions—including 242 and 338, passed after the Six-Day War, requiring Israel's withdrawal from the occupied territories and a peaceful resolution of the conflict based on the idea of land for peace—are considered binding on UN member states.

found that both Israel and Hamas had committed violations of human rights and war crimes during the fighting.

The Israeli government and its allies reacted with fury, focusing their anger on Israeli human rights organizations whose data and reportage the Goldstone team had used in preparing its report. Governmental officials and right-wing GONGOs ("government-organized nongovernmental organizations," created to further government policies and strategies) began a campaign of public, political, and legal intimidation aimed at delegitimizing and marginalizing human rights organizations just for doing their jobs. By documenting human rights violations in the Gaza fighting and in the regular course of enforcing the occupation in the West Bank, the human rights organizations, they alleged, were undermining the morale of soldiers, besmirching the good name of the IDF, and actively working against Israel. This was dangerous stuff in a country where the army is the most trusted and beloved institution (at least in the eyes of many Jewish Israelis).

Right-wing GONGOs first attacked the New Israel Fund (the organization I currently lead and a major funder of Israeli civil society organizations, including human rights groups), accusing it of being "behind" the Goldstone Report. (It was not.) And right-wing members of the Knesset threatened a parliamentary inquiry into the organization. This never happened, but more effective and dangerous attacks followed. Legislators passed a law, discussed later, designed to restrict the activities of human rights organizations. GONGOs launched an online video campaign featuring pictures of prominent human rights activists, describing them as terrorist-supporting traitors, and publishing their home addresses. Pro-settler organizations launched strategic lawsuits against anti-occupation and human rights activists in an attempt to intimidate them and tie them down with frivolous litigation. The assault by

Israel's right wing on Israel's human and civil rights sector can be seen as one of the first steps backward in the country's democracy recession. And it's still one of its hallmarks: ten years later, the attacks continue.

. . .

For over a decade, Netanyahu's ruling coalitions promoted rhetoric, policy, and, especially, a raft of legislation designed to strengthen the power of the Jewish majority at the expense of the Arab minority; constrain and diminish democratic institutions like the judiciary and civil society, which serve as a check and balance on the power of the ruling coalition; and protect, expand, and perhaps prepare the way for potential annexation of the settlements. This legislation (much of which we will take a closer look at in part 2) includes laws that:

- Made it a civil offense for Israelis to call for a boycott of Israel or its settlements and prohibited entry into Israel of foreigners who did the same. Yes, technically you can be denied entry into Israel if you've ever publicly called for people not to buy products made in Israel's West Bank settlements.

- Punished Arab municipalities and institutions for commemorating the 1948 war (known by Israelis as the War of Independence) as the Nakba, or "Catastrophe," by stripping them of state funding. This would be like the U.S. government telling Native Americans they can't mourn or protest on Columbus Day, or telling Black Americans they can't observe Martin Luther King Jr. Day, without losing federal aid.

- Allowed certain communities to ban "undesirables" (as in Arabs) from moving in.

- Restricted the activities of human and civil rights organizations that serve as society's monitors and watchdogs of government action. At one point, then Justice Minister Ayelet Shaked, a leader of the ultranationalist, pro-settlement "The Jewish Home" Party—the name really does say it all— actually demanded that the law require representatives of nongovernmental organizations that receive funding from foreign countries such as the United States or EU member states to wear badges identifying them as "foreign agents" when in the Knesset. As you can imagine, the idea of forcing people to wear special, identifying badges on their clothing didn't go over too well in Israel.

- Permanently prioritized Israel's Jewish character over its democratic character with 2018's controversial Nation-State Law, which asserts that only the Jewish people have the right to self-determination in the State of Israel.

And it wasn't just antidemocratic bills and laws. The Bibi Era also saw efforts to extend the power of the religious establishment over aspects of public life in Israel. For a number of years, ultra-Orthodox Jews, who oppose the intermingling of the sexes in public, had demanded that women be forced to sit at the back of public buses serving religious neighborhoods. They succeeded in having the front of these buses reserved for men only. By 2011, empowered by the new, illiberal zeitgeist, these ultra-Orthodox Jews had stepped up their campaign to remove images of women from billboards and advertisements on city streets and on public transportation. In supermarkets and on streets in religious neighborhoods, gender segregation was

increasingly enforced by private security. Meanwhile, the ruling coalition was silent. But the public was not. A coalition of civil society
organizations fought back, challenging these restrictions at the High
Court of Justice. They won, but Dorit Beinisch, the first woman to
serve as president (or chief justice) of the Court, warned that the cases
were harbingers of an ominous change in Israeli society. Gender segregation, she said, "began with buses, continued with supermarkets and
reached the streets. It's not going away, just the opposite."

During the first years of the Bibi Era, as Israel became more populist, more ethnonationalist, more illiberal, Netanyahu continued
his strong support for the settlement enterprise, but he maintained
his official (albeit tepid) support for a two-state solution with the
Palestinians, despite the increasingly prevalent position of some of his
coalition partners and, indeed, fellow Likudniks against the establishment of any Palestinian state, ever. But as right-wing, illiberal populism continued to rise around the world, the international atmosphere
became conducive to a more hard-line Israeli position on the question
of the settlements, the occupation, and the two-state solution. The
election of Donald Trump in the United States and the almost total
focus of the European Union, Israel's largest trading partner and a
critic of its settlement enterprise, on dealing with Brexit and a number
of other internal crises removed two of the last powerful checks on
Israel's policies in the West Bank.

Then, just days before Israel's April 9, 2019, elections—and with
what appeared to be tacit support from the Trump administration—
Netanyahu broke with fifty-one years of prime-ministerial precedent
and told an interviewer that, should he win, he would move to extend
Israeli sovereignty to all Jewish settlements in the West Bank. In other
words, he would annex at least some of the West Bank. The election
resulted in what was essentially a tie, and Netanyahu was unable to
form a government. As Israelis headed back to the polls in September

2019 for their second election in six months, Netanyahu renewed his pledge to annex the settlements if he won. He narrowly lost that election, but neither he nor his rival was able to put together a ruling coalition, plunging Israel into political uncertainty and, ultimately, a third election.

In the midst of this uncertainty, and having already broken with international consensus by recognizing Israel's annexation of the Golan, the Trump administration stated that "the establishment of Israeli civilian settlements in the West Bank is not, per se, inconsistent with international law," reversing decades of American foreign policy. The European Union immediately reiterated its position that Israeli settlements in the West Bank were indeed illegal.

A few months later, in January 2020, the Trump administration released its "Peace to Prosperity" plan for Israel and the Palestinians, which seemed to offer Israel a green light to annex territory on the West Bank. In March 2020, Israel held a third inconclusive election. Once again, Bibi pledged that, if elected, he would begin to annex. In April 2020, Netanyahu and opposition leader Benny Gantz announced their intention, in the face of the coronavirus pandemic sweeping the world, to form a unity government, with the two men rotating the prime ministership; they would be committed to working together on just two issues: fighting the virus and beginning to annex land in the West Bank.

In August, the United Arab Emirates, a tiny, oil-rich Gulf state, and Israel announced that they would normalize relations; this announcement was followed by the news that Bahrain, another small, oil-rich Gulf state, would follow suit. In exchange for the deal, Israel agreed to abandon its plans to annex territory in the West Bank—at least for the time being. In truth, the two Arab countries and Israel (which, it should be pointed out, had never actually been at war with each other) had quietly, but hardly secretly, fostered closer relations for years. Not only was their "normalization" of relations mutually advantageous economically, but also they had a common enemy: Iran. As America began to turn its attention away from the Middle East—first under Obama's plan to "pivot to Asia" and then under Trump's "America First" isolationism—Israel and a number of conservative, majority-Sunni Arab states began to build a de facto alliance of convenience against Iran, the Shia regional powerhouse that threatened them all. It was a modern-day example of the ancient Middle Eastern proverb "The enemy of my enemy is my friend."

By the fall of 2020, Israel's unwieldy unity government—struggling to contain the pandemic, riven by in-fighting, led by an indicted prime minister facing a criminal trial—was divided and paralyzed. Then, in November, Joe Biden defeated Donald Trump in the U.S. presidential election, signaling an end to the Trump-Netanyahu era of unconditional American support for the most hard-line of Israeli policies and a likely return to a more familiar U.S.-Israel relationship. By December, the unity government was in a state of collapse, and Israelis returned to the polls for an unprecedented fourth election in March 2021.

That election was as inconclusive as the three that preceded it; Netanyahu's Likud won the most seats but was once again unable to build a governing coalition. The mandate to do so then passed to Yair Lapid, the leader of the centrist Yesh Atid (There Is a Future) party, who set to work trying to assemble a collection of right-wing, centrist, left-wing, and Arab parties united only by their desire to get rid of Netanyahu. By early May, Lapid seemed, against all odds, to have done it. But as he prepared to present his "Change Coalition" to Israel's president, the Israeli-Palestinian conflict that Bibi (and Trump) had worked so hard to sideline exploded, once again, onto the scene.

This time, the spark was Palestinian fury over an attempt by

Israeli settlers to evict several Arab families from the homes in East Jerusalem in which they'd lived since losing their former homes in Israel and fleeing to Jordanian territory during the war of 1948–49. Having worked its way through the Israeli legal system, the case was slated to be heard by the High Court of Justice in May 2021, in the midst of Ramadan, and on the very day Israelis celebrate "Jerusalem Day," marking Israel's capture and annexation of East Jerusalem. Militant nationalist religious youth were planning a provocative "flag march" through the Muslim Quarter of the Old City. As the holiday approached, Israeli police prevented Palestinians from gathering in the plaza in front of the Damascus Gate to the Old City, the "town square" of East Jerusalem, stirring more rage. Soon, Palestinian and Jewish young people were demonstrating, clashing with police, and even attacking each other in the Holy City. Jerusalem boiled over. Realizing the situation had gotten out of hand, the police removed the Damascus Gate barriers, the attorney general petitioned the High Court to postpone the eviction hearing, and Netanyahu ordered the route of the "flag march" changed so that it avoided the Muslim Quarter. But it was too little, too late.

Hamas in Gaza watched the escalating tensions in Jerusalem. Autocratic, increasingly unpopular amongst the Gazans they ruled, and desperate for greater relevance, Hamas had found its bid for primacy in Palestinian politics stymied when, in April, Palestinian Authority president Mahmoud Abbas canceled what would have been the first PA elections in fifteen years. With Jerusalem in turmoil, and Israeli police and young Palestinians clashing at the Al-Aqsa Mosque compound, Hamas saw its chance to claim the mantle of defender of Jerusalem and champion of the Palestinian cause. It launched a barrage of missiles and rockets at Israeli communities west of Jerusalem, Israel responded with punishing air strikes, and all hell broke loose. After two weeks of air strikes and rocket attacks, with over 240 Palestinians and 12 people in Israel killed and with parts of Gaza reduced to rubble, Israel and Hamas agreed to an Egyptian-brokered cease-fire.

But something was different about this round of conflict. It was not contained to unrest in Jerusalem and fighting between the IDF and Hamas, as past flare-ups had been. Clashes between Palestinians, settlers, and soldiers took place throughout the occupied West Bank. Even more ominously, the fighting triggered the first serious intercommunal mob violence between Israeli Jews and Arabs in decades. Fury, violence, and destruction spilled into the streets of Israel's mixed cities.

And something else about this round of fighting was different, too: In Washington, the official line had long been that Israel had every right to defend itself in response to Hamas's attacks. But that message was tempered this time by other voices among the political class (especially within the Democratic Party), much louder than in the past, questioning Israel's policies in the West Bank and Jerusalem, criticizing the intensity of its response to Hamas and the number of innocent Gazans killed in the fighting, and calling for U.S. aid to Israel to be conditioned on Israeli policy and behavior vis à vis the Palestinians.

It seemed likely that the two-week war of May 2021 would upend the opposition's attempts to finally unseat Netanyahu. But it didn't. On June 13, after twelve years of divisive and consequential premiership, the longest in Israel's history, the Knesset swore in a new government and showed Bibi the door. The Netanyahu era, at least for the time being, was over.

That's as far as we are in this story at the time of this writing. The closer we are to these events, the harder it is to know how they will fit into the bigger narrative we are trying to understand. One thing's for certain: just like its past, Israel's future will continue to be written in shades of gray.

Part Two

WHY IS IT SO HARD TO TALK ABOUT ISRAEL?

In part 1, we looked at how we got here. We defined some key terms and familiarized ourselves with the story of Israel as well as the geography, history, and contours of the conflict. In part 2, we will take a deeper dive into some of the most important and, often, contentious and emotionally loaded issues that define Israel and the challenges it faces today. Can a country with a large non-Jewish minority successfully define itself as both Jewish and democratic? What does Israel's massive settlement enterprise mean for the future of Israelis, Palestinians, and any potential two-state solution? What is the state of the relationship between the two largest Jewish communities in the world, the one in Israel and the one in the United States? Why are there so many land mines when it comes to talking about, and criticizing, Israel and its policies? And what's the evangelical Christian obsession with Israel all about? Once we've unpacked these (and a few other) questions a bit, we may have a better sense of why they can drive so many otherwise sensible people a little bonkers.

CHAPTER 15

THE MAP IS NOT THE TERRITORY

IN THE LATE 1990s, I decided to photograph road and street signs in Israel (mostly in Jerusalem) that had been altered or vandalized, almost always to excise the Arabic place names from the bi- or trilingual signs. There were hundreds of examples. In the pictures, you can see the Arabic place names blacked out with paint or covered over by ultranationalist Hebrew-language bumper stickers. This attempt to cover up (literally) the Palestinian connection to and presence in the land, and to send the message to Arabs that they don't belong, was just one overt example of a dedicated effort at political and demographic wishful thinking.

Both Israelis and Palestinians have invested a great deal of energy and innovation in trying to strengthen their claim to the land by denying that of the other. Primary battlegrounds in this war over perception have been history, geography, cartography, and archaeology. In 2001, a top Islamic legal authority, the former mufti of

Jerusalem, claimed that "there isn't even a single stone of the Old City of Jerusalem that is Jewish. There is no proof at all that the Jews were ever in Jerusalem." And Palestinian leader Yasser Arafat alleged, completely falsely, that there was no evidence that a Jewish Temple had ever stood on the Temple Mount in Jerusalem, where the Dome of the Rock now stands. Meanwhile, as we saw in chapter 3, Palestinian Arabs trace their origins to the Muslim conquest of Palestine in the seventh century and earlier, but some pro-Israel advocates deny this connection, insisting that there is no such thing as a Palestinian people and that, even if there were, Palestinian Arabs all came to the region in the last couple of centuries.

Maps, in particular, are often weaponized by both sides to score propaganda points and shape perspectives, sometimes with almost comical symmetry. Official Israeli and Palestinian Authority maps of the territory often neglect to show the Green Line, or the fact of the other side's actual presence on the ground, instead portraying a fantasy of an undivided country—all Israel or all Palestine. But accuracy isn't the point of these official maps. They're meant to represent the wished-for world, not the world as it is. This makes them worse than useless; it makes them dangerous. Maps (e.g., Jerusalem's bus maps) can shape the way we perceive territory, even when they don't actually reflect reality. Generations of Palestinian and Israeli kids grow up with maps that tell them that they are the sole rightful owners of the land. And when those deeply rooted perceptions and assumptions don't match reality, look out. That's a key ingredient in the recipe for another generation of conflict and hatred. When it comes to this contested region, the map is not the territory.

Archaeology, too, is a conflict zone. Despite the fact that there is an abundance of actual historical and archaeological evidence clearly supporting the connections of both Jews and Palestinians to the land, a lot has been invested in not only establishing the best and most compelling historical claim, but also denying the connection of the "other." In the 1990s, Israel opened the Ir David (City of David) National Park archaeological site in the middle of the densely populated Palestinian East Jerusalem neighborhood of Silwan. Silwan and Ir David are located east of the Green Line, just outside the sixteenth-century Ottoman-built Old City walls, over the spot where a part of ancient Jewish Jerusalem once stood, spilling down the slope south of the Temple Mount.

The Ir David project was established by the Ir David Foundation, a right-wing national-religious organization dedicated to asserting an exclusive Jewish claim to Jerusalem. In particular, the site seeks to unearth evidence of King David's palace and the Temple built by his son Solomon, which was replaced by King Herod's Temple Mount complex (including the Western Wall), which was destroyed by the Romans and, ultimately, replaced with the Dome of the Rock.

While the Israel Antiquities Authority runs the actual dig, the Ir David Foundation uses the findings to support its narrative of the Jewish right to all of Jerusalem based on the biblical evidence. It also puts this narrative into practice, buying up Palestinian homes near the site and giving them to Jewish families—thus creating a new

Jewish settlement in the heart of a Palestinian neighborhood of East Jerusalem. As Dan Shapiro, the former U.S. ambassador to Israel, said, the Ir David Foundation's moves to alter the demography of East Jerusalem have "a clear political intent, which is to cement permanent Israeli control. And that isn't good for anyone who still has hope for a resolution." From the foundation's point of view, however, it is simply bringing Jews back to the Temple-adjacent neighborhood after a temporary absence of two-thousand-plus years. All this activity—the park, the archaeological site, the settlement—is supported by and coordinated with the government, which sends thousands of schoolchildren and soldiers to tour the foundation's state-of-the-art visitor center every year.

Aside from the geopolitical issues, there's just one problem: while archaeologists have uncovered some incredible findings that help us better understand ancient Jerusalem, no actual archaeological evidence has been uncovered to prove the existence of King David's palace or the Temple of Solomon. To be sure, there is an abundance of archaeological evidence demonstrating the ancient Jewish presence in Jerusalem and showing that Jerusalem was indeed the capital of the Jewish kingdom. No serious historian or archaeologist refutes this, and it is deeply offensive when some Palestinian leaders and their supporters claim otherwise. But it is just as offensive to Palestinians when Israel erects an enormous archaeological complex aimed at buttressing Israeli claims to all of Jerusalem in the midst of a neighborhood Palestinians claim as part of their future capital.

Still, today, tourists, Israeli schoolchildren, and IDF soldiers are taken through the complex, where guides make archaeologically dubious suggestions that, despite the lack of any actual evidence, the ruins they are seeing *might actually* have been David's palace. In fact, Israeli archaeologists, concerned about attempts to manipulate the rich archaeological record of Jerusalem to score political points,

Jerusalem

founded an NGO, Emek Shaveh, to correct some of the "alternate facts" and wishful thinking being proffered by Ir David.

Many modern Israeli communities are built on the ruins of Arab villages and towns that were abandoned, emptied, or razed during Israel's War of Independence. And those Arab communities were built over medieval and biblical-era Jewish settlements, so that both Jews and Arabs feel a deep sense of connection and ownership to the land—a sense that each side tries to argue is more justified than the other's. Indeed, partisans of each narrative often attempt to outright deny or negate the evidence of the other side's connection to and history in the land—like those altered street signs I mention at the beginning of this chapter.

This conflict also echoes in the changing names of places (a Hebrew place name replaces an Arabic one, which itself harks back to a Hebrew biblical name), but the attempts by each to erase the other's presence don't always work. In the 1950s, a major effort was undertaken to replace the remaining Arabic neighborhood names of West Jerusalem with Hebrew ones. This was seen both as an important Zionist project by some officials and as an affront to the actual history of the city by others. In the end, the neighborhoods received Hebrew names, but they didn't stick. I lived for a time in the Jerusalem neighborhood of Morasha, a Jewish district with a good Hebrew name that it received in the 1950s—except, nobody called it that. Everybody still referred to it by its old Arabic name, "Musrara," which is what the neighborhood's Arab Christian founders named it when it was built in the late nineteenth century, decades before their descendants would be forced to flee to neighborhoods east of the Green Line during the War of Independence/Nakba in 1948. But the battle over memory, history, and geography continues. In 2011, two right-wing Knesset members submitted a bill that would have forced the Jerusalem municipality to use the Hebraized neighborhood

names. The bill was defeated, but it seems unlikely that this is the end of the long war over place names in Jerusalem.

None of these attempts to erase the language, history, or reality of the "other side's" presence in or connection to the land have worked. Nor has any attempt to alter history or to assert historical primacy based on (often questionable) archaeology, map making, and place naming (and renaming). The connections to this place felt by Jews and Palestinians are just too deep to disappear. After all, Jews spent millennia in exile praying for a return to the land their ancestors lost, and Palestinians have spent most of the last century carrying, figuratively and sometimes literally, the keys to the homes from which their ancestors fled or were driven out.

At the end of the day, it doesn't much matter if King David really built his palace in Silwan, or if the Palestinians are descended from the Philistines. The fact is that history, myth, religious belief, and lived experience have created powerful bonds between Jews and Palestinians and the land they both claim. Trying to prove otherwise is a distraction and an exercise in futility. You might make yourself feel better, but you won't convince the other guy he doesn't feel the way he feels. Acknowledging the profound connection that both sides feel, then, is probably a good first step in trying to find a way out of the conflict—at least, as former ambassador Shapiro said, "for anyone who still has hope for a resolution."

CHAPTER 16

ISRAEL'S ARAB CITIZENS
Shared Society or Segregation?

WHAT DOES IT mean for a country that calls itself the Jewish state to have a non-Jewish minority that makes up a full fifth of its citizens? And how can a country that considers itself a democracy guaranteeing equality for all its citizens even *describe* itself as a state that belongs only to one particular class of those citizens? These questions are at the heart of the identity dilemma Israel has faced since its founding. They represent the balancing act Israel attempts as it tries to be all these things at the same time. And it is Israel's Arab citizens who bear the brunt and the burden of this aspect of the Israeli experiment— and who, perhaps, provide the best hope of resolving it.

The 156,000 or so Arabs who remained in what was now the State of Israel in 1948 received citizenship, but the state seemed unsure of what to do with them. They presented a problem that Israel's founders appeared not to have thought that carefully about. The challenge of the place of Israel's Arab citizens in Israeli society goes right to the heart of the unresolved nature of what Israel is meant to be.

On the one hand, it seems pretty clear. Israel's founding document, the Declaration of the Establishment of the State of Israel, set forth a vision that not only stated the aim of protecting the Jewish people, but also included explicit commitments to equality, liberty, justice, and fidelity to international law:

> The State of Israel will be open for Jewish immigration and for the Ingathering of the Exiles; it will foster the development of the country for the benefit of all its inhabitants; it will be based on freedom, justice and peace as envisaged by the prophets of Israel; it will ensure complete equality of social and political rights to all its inhabitants irrespective of religion, race or sex; it will guarantee freedom of religion, conscience, language, education and culture; it will safeguard the Holy Places of all religions; and it will be faithful to the principles of the Charter of the United Nations.

Israel is meant to be a refuge and homeland for the Jewish people, but also, just as important, a country developed for "the benefit of *all* its inhabitants" (emphasis mine).

On the other hand, in 1948, the new government of Israel found itself with a sizable minority population it did not trust and with whom it had just fought a war. After statehood, Israel enacted policies and laws meant to secure title to the land and resources of the country primarily for the benefit of its Jewish citizens. And while it granted citizenship to Arabs remaining in Israel after 1948, it also extended martial law to those areas containing the largest Arab populations: the Galilee in the North; the so-called Triangle of Arab towns bordering the central West Bank; and parts of the Negev in the South. While officially based on geography, in practice the curfews, travel restrictions, and deportation for those not properly registered with the authorities were applied only to Arab citizens, not Jewish ones. Arab Israelis lived under martial law until November 1966, at which point they were granted the same rights and privileges as all Israeli citizens. But because Israel assumed control of millions of Palestinian civilians after its victory in June 1967—and because West Bank Palestinians are not citizens, do not have the vote, and are still subject to Israeli military law to this day—some have noted that Israel was a true democracy for only about seven months.

The uncertainty of what it means to be an Arab citizen of a country that officially describes itself as a Jewish state is captured by the different names these citizens call themselves: "Palestinian Israelis," "Palestinian citizens of Israel," "Palestinians in Israel," "Palestinians with Israeli citizenship," "Arab citizens of Israel," "Arab Israelis," and "Israeli Arabs" (their Jewish fellow citizens tend to use the last two to describe them). Today, Arab citizens of Israel number about 1.9 million and make up just over 20 percent of the population of the country. That's a big proportion. By way of comparison, Black Americans make up about 13 percent of the U.S. population, and Jewish Americans less than 3 percent.

And the balancing act (or perhaps wrestling) between the poles of Israel's identity as a Jewish homeland and a democratic society ensuring equality for all its citizens continues to create tensions and challenges. On the one hand, Arab citizens of Israel officially have the same formal rights and privileges as Jewish citizens. They serve in the professions, as judges, and in the Knesset. On the other hand, it is very challenging to be a non-Jew in a country created for the safety and benefit of the Jewish people. Arab citizens speak Hebrew (although Arabic tends to be their first language) and live their lives, like all Israelis, according to the Jewish calendar. The overwhelming majority are loyal citizens, but very few would describe themselves as Zionists. And why should they? Their story isn't the Jewish story. Most Arab citizens simply want to be treated like equal citizens in their own country.

But while they are officially equal, in many ways they are not. Integration is not seen as a civic virtue by most Israelis, Arab or Jewish. Arab and Jewish Israelis live largely separate lives in separate social spheres, with separate school systems and often separate neighborhoods and communities. (Mixed cities like Haifa, Jaffa, and Akko are fascinating exceptions to this rule.) Most of the poorest municipalities in Israel are Arab. Because Arab Israelis by and large do not serve in the IDF (almost all non-ultra-Orthodox Jews do), they do not gain access to the networks and opportunities (especially in fields like high-tech) that military service provides.*

Worse, Arab citizens are subject to many kinds of discrimination, informal and official. In Israel's early years, the state exercised the power of eminent domain to take ownership of land that had belonged to Arabs in the pre-state years, and Arab villages were razed to make way for new Jewish communities. Officials didn't even try to hide their goal of "Judaizing" heavily Arab regions of the new country by building new Jewish towns in the Negev Desert in the South and Galilee in the North.

While some of this has changed for the better—due mainly to successful court cases brought by Israel's robust civil rights sector—in recent years, some aspects of this discrimination have gotten worse. In addition to the type of nastiness minorities face in many countries (landlords who refuse to rent to them, limited job and career advancement opportunities, etc.), Arab Israelis face some unique (or, at

---

* And this can also provide a pretext for discrimination: it is not uncommon for Help Wanted ads to read ARMY VETERANS ONLY.

least, rare) challenges for citizens of a democratic country. Whereas racial profiling is controversial and usually officially forbidden in most Western countries, in Israel it is simply a part of everyday life for the country's Arab citizens. Given the terrorist threats Israelis have faced since the country's inception, this is seen as necessary (if unfortunate) by many Jewish Israelis. But Arab citizens of Israel are routinely subjected to casual discrimination, humiliating treatment, and interrogation and detention at places like the airport despite decades of complaints over this kind of behavior.*

Arab Israelis

* This discrimination is commonplace for virtually all non-Jewish citizens of Israel. In 2019, the Israeli ambassador to Panama, a Druze citizen, stated that he, an official representative of the state, had been detained and harassed at the airport. Immediately after the incident, he posted this on his Facebook page: "I thought to myself while on the plane: Go to hell Ben-Gurion Airport. 30 years of humiliation and you are still not done. In the past, you would beat us at the terminal, today you've progressed to treating us as suspects at the checkpoint at the entrance [to the airport]." This sad story sums up an "only in Israel" circumstance: the often bewildering experience of Israel's non-Jewish citizens in a country where they are officially equal but always suspect. You can rise to a high position in government, but you're still going to get harassed at the airport because you're an Arab (or a Druze).

Even more troubling is the message Israel's Arab citizens hear coming from the highest leadership in the land. Attempting to mobilize his base on the eve of the 2015 elections, Prime Minister Netanyahu posted on Facebook (a primary vehicle for political communication in Israel) that "the right-wing government is in danger. Arabs are coming out to the polls in droves." This wasn't a racial dog whistle; it was plain old racism. That same year, then Foreign Minister Avigdor Lieberman, a proponent of instituting a "loyalty oath" for Arab citizens, said that "disloyal" Arabs should be beheaded. (Yes. You read that correctly.)

And in recent years, Israel's hard-right-wing ruling coalition has passed several laws that seem to have little purpose beyond making sure that Israel's Arab citizens know where they stand in the eyes of their own government. This includes the Budget Foundations Law of 2011, otherwise known as "the Nakba Law," which penalizes any institution (e.g., a school or a local municipality) that commemorates Independence Day or the establishment of the state as a day of mourning; any Arab community that wants to observe those events as "Nakba Day" will lose state funding. And 2011 also saw passage of the Admissions Committees Law, allowing small communities to create committees to determine whether potential new residents would fit into the community's "social cultural fabric." While the language of the law forbids discrimination against people because of their religion or ethnicity, civil rights activists argue that the law is intended to legalize discrimination, keeping Arabs (and other "undesirables," like LGBTQ+ people) out of communities that don't want them. An ultraright-wing Knesset member (who infamously stated that he wouldn't want his wife to give birth in the same maternity ward as Arab women) is now trying to extend the Admissions Committees Law to apply to larger communities.

But most concerning of all was the passage in 2018 of the

Nation-State Law. Israel does not have a written constitution. Instead, it has a set of Basic Laws, which have constitutional status and can be changed only by a parliamentary supermajority. Almost all fourteen current Basic Laws deal with either the establishment of Israel's institutions (e.g., the early Basic Laws establishing the government, judiciary, military, and economy) or the expansion and protection of the rights of Israel's citizens (e.g., Basic Law: Human Dignity and Liberty; and Basic Law: Freedom of Occupation).

The Nation-State Law, the newest Basic Law, is the exception to this rule. Officially, it is intended to secure Israel's status as a Jewish state. But if you've been to the country recently (say, at any time over the entire seventy-three years of its existence), you've seen that the Jewish character of Israel—the thriving Hebrew language; the living Jewish Calendar; the vibrant religious communities, folkways, food, arts, and culture—is under no threat and in no need of special protection. Rather, like Donald Trump's proposed "Muslim Ban," the Nation-State Law championed by Netanyahu and the Israeli right is a draconian solution to a problem that doesn't actually exist. The true intention of the law is to constitutionally enshrine a kind of Jewish supremacy that threatens to upend the decades-long, carefully calibrated balance between the Jewish and democratic aspects of Israel's identity, to weight the scales decidedly to the Jewish side. That, and poke a stick in the eye of Israel's Arab citizens, reminding them that they do not truly belong to or in Israel, at least not the way Jewish citizens do. The Nation-State Law is in line with the xenophobic ethnonationalism espoused by the right-wing ruling coalition that created and promoted the bill. (This nationalism is, of course, not unique to Israel; it's a virus currently sweeping the globe, attacking the health of liberal democracy in many countries, including our own.)

In the end, the law passed only narrowly and was opposed by

many in Israel and beyond, who saw it as antidemocratic and discriminatory toward Israel's Arab citizens. And not just those on the political left—Israel's president Reuven Rivlin, himself a man of the Likud but also a thoughtful champion of democracy, announced that if the law passed and came to his desk, he would sign it as required, but he would do so only in Arabic, to register his disapproval. Which is exactly what he did.*

What does the Nation-State Law actually do? First, it asserts that the right to exercise self-determination in Israel is "unique" to the Jewish people. This means that only Jews (not all Israel's citizens) have the right to determine and decide on the kind of society and country Israel will be. Non-Jewish (read: Arab) citizens do not share the same right. They may have the vote, but the Nation-State Law makes official that they are a different class of citizen. The law also reinforces this recalibration of how Israel views its Jewish and non-Jewish citizens by establishing Hebrew as the only official state language, thus downgrading Arabic, which had shared that honor, to a "special status" language. It also explicitly prioritizes Jewish settlement as a "national value." It never mentions the word *democracy*.

Still, despite the incendiary and divisive rhetoric from top governmental officials and the passage of antidemocratic laws, the last decade also saw major positive developments for Israel's Arab citizens and for the idea of a truly shared Arab-Jewish Israeli society and future. In 2015, the government passed Resolution 922. The anodyne name belied the decision's significance. Resolution 922 was a multi-year plan that aimed to close the economic gap between Arab and Jewish citizens by investing 15 billion shekels (about $4.3 billion) into housing, urban planning, education, employment, transportation,

---

* Israel's president is elected by the parliament and serves as Israel's official head of state, a largely ceremonial office but one with a powerful bully pulpit.

and other infrastructure in Israel's Arab community. It was achieved through a joint effort of Arab leaders, civil society organizations, and public officials and adopted by the most right-wing government in Israel's history. So, why would politicians who've never hesitated to engage in racist dog whistles pass such a law?

Well, insinuating that 20 percent of the population constitutes a threat to Israel, and warning that Israeli Arabs could be a disloyal fifth column, might be good politics for exciting your right-wing base. But allowing or creating circumstances in which one fifth of your population is so discriminated against, so economically disadvantaged, and so marginalized that it actually becomes a fifth column is probably not such a good idea. In fact, the very anti-Arab invective so often employed by Netanyahu and other coalition leaders may well have provided cover for them to address a huge societal problem without angering their voters, who likely paid more attention to rhetoric than finances. For Arab citizens of Israel, however, 922 and the unprecedented alliance that got it passed and implemented was a huge victory, an example of what successful coalition building can accomplish.

In politics, too, the ground is shifting. For decades, Arab citizens of Israel tended to support Arab parties that, with the significant exception of the Rabin era, were always relegated to the ranks of the opposition. Because Jewish-majority parties refused to include these parties in governing coalitions, Arab political power was limited, despite the size of the Arab population of the country. Frustrated by being permanently locked out of real power and demoralized by the ongoing conflict with Palestinians in the occupied territories and a right-wing legislative agenda that seemed designed to reinforce their marginal, second-class status in Israel, Arab Israelis voted at lower rates from 1967 onward. Some Arabs boycotted elections and called on others to disassociate from the Israeli political system in protest.

Others figured their vote didn't matter and gave up. And while this may have been just what the right-wing parties and politicians wanted, it wasn't good for Israeli Arabs.

In 2013, Prime Minister Netanyahu and then Foreign Minister Lieberman (the guy who suggested beheading "disloyal" Israeli Arabs) put forward, and the Knesset passed, a law raising the electoral threshold for the parliament—that is, the percentage of the national vote a party had to get to gain a seat in the Knesset—from 2 percent to 3.25 percent. Critics immediately saw this for what it was: an attempt to prevent small parties, especially Arab parties, from ever making it into the Knesset at all. Even the seemingly random new threshold number gave the game away. In the previous election, the Hadash ("New") Party (formerly Communist, now progressive, and the only truly mixed Arab-Jewish political party in Israel) had received 3 percent of the vote. Neither it nor any other majority-Arab parties would've cleared the 3.25 percent threshold now in place. It looked like Lieberman and Netanyahu had figured out a way to strip Arab citizens of what little electoral power they actually had.

But that's not what happened. In response to the new law, the small Arab parties came together to form a bigger one, "the Joint List," led by Ayman Odeh, an Arab-Israeli legislator from the mixed city of Haifa. In the election of 2015, Netanyahu scraped by to a narrow victory, but Arab citizens came out in force to vote. And the Joint List made history, emerging as the third-largest party in Israel.*

In 2019, elections ended in a virtual tie between Netanyahu and his chief rival, Blue and White Party leader Benny Gantz. Once again, Odeh made history, recommending to the president of Israel

---

* In what, I admit, I find a delicious irony, Lieberman's Yisrael Beiteinu (Israel Our Home) Party crashed and burned in the 2015 election, losing 7 seats and barely passing the electoral threshold. And until 2021, the Joint List was the third-largest party in the country.

Ayman Odeh

that Gantz be given the mandate to form a government—the first time since 1992 that an Arab party formally endorsed a Zionist candidate.

Odeh stands for something new in Israel, and this causes him no end of trouble. He is a proud Palestinian citizen of Israel who cherishes his Arab identity and fights tirelessly against institutionalized discrimination and for the rights of Arab citizens. He rejects separatism and extremism and condemns terrorism. He insists that Israel's future must be a shared future that includes both Arabs and Jews. He says he doesn't want to be a leader of Arab Israelis fighting for equality, but rather, a leader for *all* Israelis fighting for equality. He tells supporters that the job isn't to defend democracy in Israel, but to build it. "The day in which hundreds of thousands fill the streets," he says, "crying out in one voice and two languages, 'Democracy for all!'—this will be the first day of the joint future we build." This complex reimagining of what it means to be an Israeli and what Israel can be is threatening to many, Arabs and Jews alike. Odeh, a quiet and somewhat shy guy who comes across as anything but a revolutionary, makes a lot of people nervous precisely *because* his vision is so inclusive. For others, including me, his emergence as one of Israel's most important political voices is a major and much-needed shot of hope.

In discussing the situation of Arab citizens of Israel in relation to that of Jewish citizens, one often hears something along the lines of "Well, Arab Israelis have it *much* better than they would in most Arab countries." And while this may be true—Israel, for all its shortcomings, is a more democratic society and ensures the rights and liberties of its citizens better than neighbors like Syria, Egypt, and Saudi Arabia—it misses the point. Israel describes itself as and aspires to be a democracy; it must therefore be judged by how it lives up to *that* description, not by how it compares to its undemocratic neighbors.

CHAPTER 17

A LOVE STORY?
Israel and the American Jewish Community

THIS IS THE story of a long romance, a love affair between partners who don't really know or understand each other anymore, and perhaps never did. For generations, the American Jewish community contributed to the Zionist enterprise and the building of the State of Israel—and it used that relationship as a central organizing principle in postwar American Jewish identity. And for generations, Israeli leaders relied on that community to secure Israel's place at the top of America's foreign policy priorities, meaning that the two largest Jewish populations in the world viewed each other as "insurance policies." This symbiotic connection worked well for a long time, but it doesn't anymore. The historic relationship is changing as American Jews (overwhelmingly liberal and Democratic) and Israel (increasingly right-leaning and looking to Evangelical Christians and the Republican Party for support) grow further and further apart and as the leaders of America's Jewish organizations and institutions, long the relationship's primary custodians, seem incapable of checking these trends. This divide is tearing the American Jewish community apart. What will it mean for the future of Israel?

These days, the topic of Israel tends to dominate the American Jewish conversation and the priorities of many American Jewish communal organizations. But this wasn't always the case. At one time, many American Jews, and the institutions they built, weren't particularly enamored or even supportive of the Zionist project.

Most American Jews in the late nineteenth and early twentieth centuries felt no compulsion to support the return of Jews to the Promised Land. In fact, they felt they'd already arrived. Inside the domed sanctuary of Congregation Sherith Israel, founded in 1870 in San Francisco, a stained-glass window portrays Moses and the Children of Israel receiving the Ten Commandments. Only, instead of standing at Sinai, the Israelites are gathered before the unmistakable profiles of Yosemite National Park's Half Dome and El Capitan. That about sums it up: for those San Francisco Jews, the United States (specifically, California), not Israel, was the promised land.

Moses in CA

It made sense. Jews had been in what is now the United States since the early colonial period, first arriving in the early seventeenth century. And while American Jews sometimes experienced discrimination and antisemitism, it was not of the horrifically violent, government- and church-sponsored variety that afflicted the Jews of Europe. Racism was America's founding sin, not antisemitism. Here, for the most part, Jews were safe. Here, more than any other place in history, Jews were accepted; they not only survived, but also thrived.

This was the case from the earliest days of the republic. In August 1790, President George Washington responded to a letter of congratulations sent to him by members of the Jewish community of Newport, Rhode Island, with a powerful statement about the place of Jews in America. He wrote, in part:

> The Citizens of the United States of America have a right to applaud themselves for having given to mankind examples of an enlarged and liberal policy: a policy worthy of imitation. All possess alike liberty of conscience and immunities of citizenship. It is now no more that toleration is spoken of, as if it was by the indulgence of one class of people, that another enjoyed the exercise of their inherent natural rights. For happily the Government of the United States, which gives to bigotry no sanction, to persecution no assistance, requires only that they who live under its protection should demean themselves as good citizens, in giving it on all occasions their effectual support.

In other words, Jews were not equal and accepted in America because of the generosity of the majority; they were equal and accepted because they were human beings who subscribed to a shared vision of citizenship and, so, were just as American as anyone else. (It is, of course, a terrible irony that these enlightened and beautiful lines about what it means to be American were written by a slave owner.)

So, it should come as no surprise that the visionary desperation of late-nineteenth-century Zionism did not catch fire in the land of the free and the home of the brave. In fact, prominent American Jewish leaders were among the fiercest critics of early Zionism. It's easy to see why. American Jews saw themselves as a part of the great American melting pot: Jews by religion, Americans by nationality. They were wary of potential accusations of "dual loyalties," and they had little interest in a small, faraway plot of land in the middle of the desert that had no real relevance to their daily lives. They might say "next year in Jerusalem" at their Passover seders, but they certainly didn't mean it literally. The prevailing attitude of American Jews toward Jewish nationalism was summed up in this plank from the Pittsburgh Platform of 1885, the official statement of the principles of the Reform movement of Judaism (today, the largest denomination of Judaism in America): "We consider ourselves no longer a nation, but a religious community, and therefore expect neither a return to Palestine ... nor the restoration of any of the laws concerning the Jewish state."

These attitudes began to shift with the growth of the pioneering Jewish community in Palestine and the increasingly precarious situation of European Jewry with the rise of Hitler. The Reform movement's Columbus Platform of 1937 marked a radical change from the Pittsburgh Platform of half a century earlier: "In the rehabilitation of Palestine, the land hallowed by memories and hopes, we behold the promise of renewed life for many of our brethren. We affirm the obligation of all Jewry to aid in its upbuilding as a Jewish homeland by endeavoring to make it not only haven of refuge for the oppressed but also a center of Jewish culture and spiritual life."

After the war, the American Jewish community suddenly found itself the center of the Jewish world. The great and ancient

Jewish communities of Europe were gone. The Jewish community in Palestine was growing, but terribly vulnerable; it needed help, and now American Jews were ready to step up. The near destruction of the Jews of Europe and the unwillingness of the free countries of the world, including the United States, to provide refuge to them in their hour of need convinced most American Jews that a Jewish state was both morally just and desperately needed. And the Zionist idea of building a safe and strong haven for Jews in danger, wherever they might be, now seemed like a very good one, even to the secure and happy Jews of America.

The institutions of American Jewry, originally established to provide security, support, and resources for the American Jewish community, increasingly turned to the work of advocating for, funding, and supporting the Zionist project in Palestine. American Jewish leaders quickly became savvy at working the system on the Zionists' behalf. Eddie Jacobson, a traveling salesman, was a close friend, former army buddy, and past business partner of President Harry S. Truman.

Truman & Weizmann

American Jewish leaders implored Jacobson to intervene with his pal the president, who had grown irritated and exasperated by the Zionists' ceaseless lobbying. Truman couldn't say no to his old friend Eddie, who convinced him to meet with the leader of the movement, Dr. Chaim Weizmann, in 1948. Truman's conversations with Weizmann led to the United States becoming the first nation in the world to recognize the new State of Israel.* And Chaim Weizmann became its first president.

Once Israel was established, support for and defense of the new country became perhaps *the* central organizing principle for the American Jewish community. Jewish baby boomers remember the blue-and-white Jewish National Fund "pushke box" into which they would deposit their spare change to help plant trees in Israel. And American Jewish leaders advocated, Eddie Jacobson–like, on behalf of Israel in the halls of government. This was support Israel needed badly, and during the decades that followed the founding of the State of Israel, it became something of a secular religion for many American Jews.

In a way, this was a stroke of luck for the American Jewish communal establishment, too, as it faced the growing challenges of assimilation, acceptance, and intermarriage. Ironically, Israel's first decades of existence coincided with the removal of the last restrictions on Jews in America, such as the quotas that had limited Jewish attendance at elite colleges, the restrictive covenants that had kept them out of exclusive neighborhoods, and the discriminatory policies that had blocked them from membership in tony country clubs. With these formal barriers gone, communal leaders who for decades

---

* This story always reminds me of a quote attributed to Ben Hecht, a Hollywood screenwriter and fanatical Zionist activist of the era: "Do not tangle with the Jews. You will get a headache."

Pushke box

had advocated for security and equality for American Jews now turned to worrying about a different threat. Increasingly, they feared that American Jewish identity might be a victim of the success of American Jews themselves.* Young American Jews might be tempted to integrate completely: intermarrying; abandoning their Jewish heritage, practices, and community; and disappearing into the American melting pot. Israel was just what they needed: the great Jewish drama of modern times was also a compelling and powerful cause with which to identify, a way to keep a rising generation of American Jews connected to the community. And so a new, reciprocal relationship was established: Israel needed American Jews for its literal survival, and American Jews needed Israel for their survival as a community.

---

* American Jewish leaders *always* worry about the Jewish future. It's practically in their DNA. In 1948, the Polish-born American Jewish scholar Simon Rawidowicz published an essay called "The Ever-Dying People," in which he poked gentle fun at this trait, writing, "He who studies Jewish history will readily discover that there was hardly a generation in the diaspora that did not consider itself the final link in Israel's chain. Each always saw before it the abyss ready to swallow it up." And he wrote this three years after the Holocaust!

Israel soon became priority number one for many American Jewish organizations. Advocacy groups such as the Anti-Defamation League (ADL), the American Jewish Committee (AJC), and the Jewish Community Relations Councils (JCRCs) put Israel at the top of their agendas. In 1956, the Conference of Presidents of Major American Jewish Organizations was founded at the request of both the Eisenhower administration and the Israeli government, which wanted a "central address" in the American Jewish community to deal with. From day one, the most important project for this most important of organizations was support for Israel. In 1963, the American Israel Public Affairs Committee (AIPAC) was founded in order to (in its words) "strengthen, protect and promote the U.S.-Israel relationship in ways that enhance the security of the United States and Israel." Today, AIPAC is viewed by many as one of the most powerful lobbying organizations in the United States.

Together, these organizations composed what came to be known as "the Israel lobby," an informal network of entities working together to ensure support for Israel and whatever policies Israel chose to pursue—even when those policies, such as settlement building and annexation of the West Bank, were contrary to U.S. policy, violative of international law, or antithetical to the values and beliefs of most American Jews. Today, the lobby also includes Christian Zionist organizations, evangelicals who believe that a Jewish return to and conquest of the entire biblical Holy Land is necessary to bring about the return of Christ and the end-time, or Armageddon. (More on this in chapter 22.) To be sure, this match between evangelical Christian and Jewish organizations sometimes makes for strange bedfellows. (Just look at the differences between the two communities on, say, every single issue except Israel.) But if we've learned anything thus far, it's that, where Israel is concerned, normal rules don't always apply.

The Six-Day War of 1967 was a watershed moment for the American Jewish community, just as it was for the Israelis. American Jews watched with anxiety as Israel fought to prevent what they feared might be a second Holocaust and then rejoiced at Israel's astonishing victory. For American Jews, Israel's triumph provided not only relief but also a profound sense of pride. More than thirty thousand of them were inspired to move to Israel; tens of thousands more visited the country or chose to study there. The trials and tribulations that followed—the Munich Olympics massacre, the Yom Kippur War, the rescue by Israeli commandos of Jewish hostages at Entebbe in 1976—only served to strengthen this sense of pride and connection. Israel's political leaders—Moshe Dayan, Golda Meir, Yitzhak Rabin—acquired something like celebrity status. The IDF and Israeli soldiers were almost folk heroes. For many, if not most, American Jews, Israel could do no wrong. And they were beyond proud of the plucky David standing up to the mighty Arab Goliath, all while making the desert bloom.

Visiting Israel became a rite of passage for many American Jews, a trip to a welcoming and more appealing homeland than the eastern European countries from which most of their ancestors had fled. And then there was the Israel philanthropy industry. American Jews gave annual donations to the advocacy and lobbying organizations that worked on Israel's behalf in Washington and to charities that supported everything from soup kitchens to art museums in Israel itself. It became something of a joke in Israel that prominently displayed on the walls of every hospital, university, and museum in the country were the names of American Jewish donors. By 1975, American Jews were giving $1.5 billion in philanthropic contributions to Israel. (By 2007, it was $2.5 billion.)

Not everyone was satisfied with simply sending money. Others wanted a more meaningful and strategic way to connect and help. In

1979, a group of progressive young American Jews, concerned that Israel had yet to develop the robust civil society they believed necessary for a healthy democracy to flourish, partnered with a group of progressive young Israelis to build one. Israel needed its own ecosystem of organizations aimed at supporting marginalized and minority voices, defending civil and human rights, and promoting liberal values. To establish such a society, these progressive American Jews founded the New Israel Fund as an alternative way to support a liberal vision for Israel.

But for all the money and support they were sending, most American Jews paid little attention to Israel's expanding settlement enterprise in the West Bank and Gaza, or to its treatment of the millions of Palestinians who lived there. The first real bump in the road of the American Jewish community's love affair with Israel came after Israel launched the First Lebanon War in 1982. For the first time, American Jews watched Israel start what seemed to be a war of choice, rather than necessity, as it thrust itself into the midst of Lebanon's seemingly endless civil wars. For the first time, they watched as Israeli tanks besieged an Arab capital and shelled its inhabitants. And the massacres at the Sabra and Shatila refugee camps shocked American Jews to the core, just as they did the hundreds of thousands of Israelis who marched in protest of the atrocity and called for the resignation of the government.

The second bump—some would say the beginning of the rupture—came with the outbreak of the first Palestinian intifada, in 1987, and the Israeli crackdown on this largely unarmed uprising throughout the occupied West Bank and Gaza. The sight of armored vehicles carrying Israeli soldiers in full battle gear firing tear gas, rubber bullets, and sometimes live ammunition at young Palestinians throwing stones horrified the world and stunned American Jews. Israel, it seemed, might be a bit more complicated than many American Jews had thought.

For the first time, American Jews began to awaken to the situation of the millions of Palestinians living under Israeli occupation. Israel's various standard explanations for the longevity of the occupation—we are only here to protect Israel; we want to give it back, but there's no leadership to negotiate with; Palestinians are better off under Israeli rule than they were under Jordan; and so on—no longer seemed to answer all the questions raised by the images of armed soldiers beating teenagers. Watching live coverage of mass protests in rundown, chaotic Palestinian towns right next door to brand-new, heavily guarded, tidy, red-roofed Israeli settlements was jarring. But in 1987, it was no easy thing for American Jews to speak their minds where Israel was concerned.

Still, many didn't recognize the Israel they were seeing on the TV screens, and they were disturbed. I know I was; I was a sophomore in college when the intifada broke out, and I had insomnia for weeks. But the institutions of the Jewish community were unwilling or unable to voice virtually any criticism of Israel. Then as now, most of these institutions and leaders simply repeated, publicly at least, the official Israeli line coming out of Jerusalem.

Despite this unease with Israel's behavior during the First Intifada, and despite tensions caused by Israeli Orthodox political parties' hostility toward the liberal denominations of Judaism most American Jews belonged to, American Jewish support for Israel remained strong, and sympathies swung back in Israel's favor during the first Gulf War, when Saddam Hussein's Iraq fired dozens of missiles at Israel in an unsuccessful attempt to draw it into the fray.

The elections in 1992 of Bill Clinton in the United States and Yitzhak Rabin in Israel made the relationship even easier for a time. American Jews voted overwhelmingly for Clinton, and were much more comfortable with Rabin than they'd been with his predecessor, the hard-line right-wing Yitzhak Shamir. Clinton and Rabin established a genuine friendship, and each was popular in the other's country. Then, in 1993, came the Oslo peace process, which led to the famous handshake between Rabin and Arafat on the White House Lawn.

For many American Jews, it looked like the end of the hundred-year conflict between Arabs and Jews in the Promised Land. Peace seemed not only possible, but also inevitable, and American Jewish pride swelled for an Israel reaching out a hand to its neighbors. There was a sense of relief at not having to feel ambivalent about Israel anymore, to believe that it was doing everything it could to build a different, fairer future for everyone in the region.

This was certainly true in my case. During the mid-1990s, when I lived in Jerusalem, and when Israel and Jordan signed their peace treaty, my Israeli and Palestinian friends and I could sit in cafés and bars talking about our shared values and vision and dreaming about a new future.

The dream didn't last. The assassination of Rabin by an ultra-nationalist Jew in 1995, the waves of Palestinian terrorism, and the harsh Israeli responses to the Second Intifada (2000–2005) brought about the collapse of Oslo. And that marked the end of an era for the American Jewish community's relationship with Israel. Divisions and differences that had lurked underground began to appear out in the open. The two largest Jewish communities in the world, perhaps never as close as they thought they were, began to move further and further away from each other.

For their part, Israelis felt they had been badly burned by the risks they'd taken for peace. The horrific terrorism Israelis experienced in the first years of the new century eroded public faith in negotiations and peace treaties as a path to security and calm, and the Hamas rockets that rained down on Israel after its unilateral withdrawal from Gaza in 2005 only sealed the deal, confirming the worst fears of many

Israelis. More and more Israelis were convinced that there was no legitimate partner for peace, that further compromise would only bring more bloodshed. The new separation barrier went up, dividing Israel proper and many of the settlements in the occupied territories from Palestinian population centers in the West Bank. This, and the cooperation of Palestinian Authority police forces, who served almost as Israel's security contractors in the Palestinian territories, dramatically reduced terrorism in Israel. Meanwhile, Israel established a formidable matrix of control in the West Bank, a complex system of laws and rules and also infrastructure. Highways, tunnels, walls, military bases, and heavily armed and guarded checkpoints now crisscrossed the occupied territories, allowing Israel to expand the Jewish settlements there while integrating them into the economic, social, and political life of the country.

All this enabled many Israelis to ignore and remain inured to the harsh realities of the occupation going on in their name just a few kilometers away, on the other side of the Green Line. The fact that Israelis didn't have to see this reality facilitated a kind of cognitive dissonance: an unwillingness, or even inability, on the part of Israelis to connect Israel's actions to the roots of Palestinian misery and rage. For Israelis, things were relatively quiet, and the economy was good. As if in response, Israelis increasingly voted for right-wing governments who insisted that only they could ensure Israel's security and prosperity. Some Israeli Jews opposed this swing to the right; most just tried to get on with their lives, the hard-line rhetoric and policies emanating from Jerusalem an unfortunate but acceptable trade-off for the peace and quiet.

One thing's for sure: Israeli Jews didn't spend a lot of time worrying about what American Jews might think of all this. In fact, they didn't spend a lot of time thinking about American Jews at all. But whether or not Israelis cared, these changes served to alienate many

American Jews from Israel. The truth is, by the end of the twentieth century, the two largest Jewish communities in the world didn't know each other very well. For a long time, American Jews had imagined and related to the idea of an Israel that bore only partial resemblance to the actual country. And that actual country looked increasingly different from the American Jewish community.

American Jews were largely affluent, highly educated, and overwhelmingly liberal. For over a hundred years, a majority has voted for the Democratic candidate for president in all but one election.* Three quarters of American Jews voted for Barack Obama in 2008, proud to be a part of the coalition that elected the first Black president. And Obama, beloved in the liberal Jewish community, immediately clashed with the hawkish Prime Minister Netanyahu over the settlements, America's role in the Middle East, and what to do about Iran's nuclear ambitions. Despite the fact that the amount of security cooperation and aid to Israel was higher under the Obama administration than under any previous president, the ideological divide and sour personal relationship between the two leaders was apparent and toxic. Unlike previous U.S. presidents, Obama was unpopular in Israel. And unlike previous Israeli prime ministers, Netanyahu was unpopular among the American Jews who supported Obama. Among the 25 percent or so of the American Jewish community that voted Republican (which included a majority of American Orthodox Jews), Obama was seen as a threat to Israel, and Bibi was seen as a rock star.

The tensions and difficulties between the two leaders exposed preexisting fault lines between American Jews and Israel—and within

---

* The only exception was in 1920, when the Democrat got just 19 percent of the American Jewish vote. And that's because 39 percent of American Jews voted for Eugene V. Debs, the Socialist Party candidate. So, almost 60 percent voted against the Republican candidate.

Bibi & Barry

the American Jewish community itself. A full year before Obama's election, a new Israel advocacy organization, J Street, was founded as a more progressive alternative to AIPAC and the other traditional Israel lobbying organizations. J Street offered itself as home base for American Jews who cared about Israel, but who believed that a two-state solution was the only path that would ensure its survival. J Street grew exponentially and rocketed to the fore of the American Jewish Israel conversation. But despite the fact that J Street's position was shared by a vast majority of American Jews, embraced by a popular president, and welcomed by many high-profile Democratic members of Congress, establishment American Jewish Israel advocacy organizations (along with the right-wing Israeli government) treated it like a threat, even a pariah. The rise of J Street signified something important: the growing distance between American Jews and the organizations that claimed to speak in their name when it came to Israel.

In 2010, the journalist Peter Beinart wrote a piece for the *New York Review of Books* called "The Failure of the American Jewish Establishment," and almost immediately it went viral. Beinart, an observant Jew and the former wunderkind editor of the *New Republic*, argued that (a) American Jews were liberal; (b) the American Jewish establishment (that is, the organizations and institutions that serve and claim to represent the community) paid lip service to this liberalism on a host of issues; but (c) the American Jewish establishment demanded that American Jews abandon their liberal values when it came to Israel. This, he said, worked well enough for the generations of American Jews who witnessed the Holocaust and the founding of the State of Israel and the Six-Day War and were thus willing to forgive Israel almost anything, but it didn't work anymore. Given a choice between their liberal American Jewish values and Israel, younger American Jews (Gen Xers, millennials, Gen Zers) would choose the former. They would walk away from Israel, and they would also walk away from the Jewish community organizations that reflexively, unthinkingly, defended and justified every Israeli position or action. Beinart's piece set off a firestorm of debate, but he was right. Poll after poll, study after study, showed that American Jews, especially younger ones, were becoming less and less attached to Israel.

In 2015, the United States, the United Kingdom, France, Germany, Russia, and China came to an agreement with Iran in order to keep it from developing its nuclear program. Israel had considered attacking Iran to stop its development of nuclear weapons, and it fiercely opposed the Iran deal, which it felt let Iran off the hook without sufficient safeguards or sanctions. A plurality of American Jews, however, supported the Obama administration's efforts. Accordingly, organizations like AIPAC and the Conference of Presidents of Major American Jewish Organizations, taking their cue from Jerusalem, opposed the Iran deal, while J Street defended it. When the Republican Speaker of the House of Representatives invited Netanyahu to address Congress to make his case against the deal, it felt not just like a finger in the eye of the Obama administration, but also like a middle finger directed at the liberal American Jewish community. Worse, it put American Jews in the position of having to choose between the agenda of a Democratic American president on the one hand and that of AIPAC and Israel on the other. And while that was an uncomfortable place for some American Jews to be, it wasn't really a difficult choice in the end, just as Beinart predicted. While the establishment American organizations stood with Netanyahu, most American Jews sided with Obama.

The Iran deal pushed many American Jews further away from Israel and from the Jewish organizations that automatically defend it, but that vector of drift and disaffiliation was massively exacerbated and accelerated by the 2016 election of Donald Trump and his subsequent "bromance" with Netanyahu. The two were a sort of fun house mirror version of the Rabin-Clinton friendship of the 1990s. Instead of Clinton and Rabin's shared commitment to pragmatic liberalism, democracy, and peace, however, Trump and Netanyahu shared a right-wing ethnonationalist populism; a willingness to make use of previously unacceptable, racially charged imagery and language for political gain; and a palpable disregard and disdain for democratic institutions and norms. They were natural allies.

Not only were Trump and Bibi kindred neo-authoritarian spirits, but also Trump saw support for the hard right in Israel as a way of ensuring support from two important domestic constituencies: the late GOP megadonor and Israel uber-hawk Sheldon Adelson (who donated over $180 million to Trump and the GOP for the 2020 election) and the conservative evangelical Christian community, for whom Israel, and the role it plays in their apocalyptic worldview, was so important. Trump did everything Netanyahu could have hoped for. He appointed his bankruptcy lawyer, a longtime supporter of Israel's settlements in the occupied territories, as ambassador to Israel—though the man had no diplomatic experience. He dispatched his son-in-law, who had no conceivable credentials or experience at all, to lead his peace negotiations team. And he gave political gift after political gift to Netanyahu: he moved the American embassy from Tel Aviv to Jerusalem, he recognized Israeli sovereignty over the Golan Heights, he declared that the United States no longer considered the settlements illegal, and he released a so-called peace plan that served as a green light for unilateral Israeli annexation in the West Bank. These decisions upended decades of bipartisan American policy on Israel. They ended any pretense that the United States could serve as a fair arbiter of the conflict. And they were rejected out of hand by the Palestinians and by most of rest of the world. But they sure were popular in Israel.

If most Israeli Jews loved Donald Trump, the vast majority of American Jews couldn't stand him. They were appalled by his race-baiting, misogyny, and xenophobia. And they were frightened by his seeming willingness to tolerate, if not embrace, antisemites and white nationalists at home and abroad. After a neo-Nazi rally in Charlottesville, Virginia, in 2017 led to the murder of a counterprotester, Trump conceded only that there were "very fine people on both sides." White supremacists, like former KKK leader David Duke, applauded the president's comment. After a white nationalist who had spewed anti-immigrant invective massacred twelve Jews praying in a Pittsburgh synagogue in 2018, American Jews heard it all loud and clear. They did not feel safe in Donald Trump's America.

Netanyahu, the self-proclaimed leader of the Jewish world, refused to utter a word of criticism at Trump's winks and nods to antisemites and white nationalists. This was in line with Bibi's embrace of other right-wing ethnonationalists who flirted with antisemitism. Once, Israeli leaders had seen themselves as the protectors of Jews wherever they might live. (Remember that Bibi's own brother died upholding this very principle, in the raid on Entebbe, Uganda, in

1976.) But under Netanyahu, Israel made common cause with hard-line right-wingers like Hungarian prime minister Viktor Orbán, whose embrace of xenophobia and use of antisemitic imagery earned the rebuke of the Israeli ambassador. But did Netanyahu support his ambassador's move? On the contrary, he ordered him to withdraw his criticism of the Hungarian autocrat.* As long as they supported his hard-line agenda for Israel, Bibi welcomed the support of other hard-liners—even antisemites.

Liberal American Jews—already put off by Netanyahu's policies in the West Bank, his invectives against the Arab citizens of Israel, his demonization of the Israeli left, his dismissal of their concerns about religious pluralism, and his alliance with ultra-Orthodox rabbis who proclaimed themselves arbiters of "who is a Jew"—were dismayed by his embrace of autocrats like Orbán. Bibi's political courtship of American evangelical Christians and his love affair with Donald Trump, the most reviled American president in a lifetime, put them on notice: Israel was no longer interested in what they thought. It had found other, more ideologically attuned American allies. The traditional institutions of the American Jewish community seemed paralyzed by the dilemma: unwilling to criticize Israel and afraid to criticize Trump. Meanwhile, newer organizations less concerned with

---

* In July 2017, leaders of the Hungarian Jewish community approached the Israeli ambassador in Budapest to share their concerns about antisemitic imagery being used by the political party of Prime Minister Orbán, a staunch ally of Netanyahu's in smearing the Hungarian-born American Jewish financier George Soros. Soros, a very well-resourced, unabashed critic of hard-line policies in Hungary, Israel, the United States, and elsewhere, is a regular target of right-wing populist leaders (including Netanyahu). Alarmed, the Israeli ambassador issued a sharp statement: "The [Orbán] campaign not only evokes sad memories but also sows hatred and fear. It's our moral responsibility to raise a voice and call on the relevant authorities to exert their power and put an end to this cycle." This was the Israel that Jews around the world had come to expect, even rely on, to defend against antisemitism. But the very next day, Netanyahu ordered the statement retracted.

defending Israel and firmly opposed to the Trump agenda began to step into the vacuum. As these tectonic shifts began to alter the landscape of American Jewish life, it seemed to many American Jews that Israel was no longer particularly interested in them or their concerns; it had moved on. The question would be whether a new generation of American Jews would move on, and away from Israel, too.

CHAPTER 18

THE SETTLEMENTS

MORE THAN 440,000 Jewish Israeli civilians live in the settlements that were built over the Green Line in the West Bank after Israel captured and occupied the territory from Jordan in 1967. An additional 200,000-plus Israeli civilians live in neighborhoods built in East Jerusalem, also captured by Israel in the Six-Day War and also over the Green Line. Israel annexed East Jerusalem after 1967, applying Israeli sovereignty and declaring it a part of Israel (unlike the West Bank). However, this annexation is not recognized by the rest of the world, which regards East Jerusalem as a part of the Israeli-occupied Palestinian territories and the site of the capital of a future Palestinian state.

Most of the West Bank settlements are not "Wild West" outposts or temporary tent cities, but villages with tidy red-tile-roofed homes, parks, schools, cafés, shopping centers, libraries, and synagogues. They pretty much look, feel, and operate just like any village or city in Israel proper—except they aren't in Israel. They are in the occupied territories—Area C, to be exact.* And that's the point. They were built, and intended, to be permanent communities—facts on the ground that will make it difficult, if not impossible, for Israel to withdraw from the whole of the West Bank in any peace treaty. And, of course, the West Bank is what the Palestinians want, and the international community expects, to be the bulk of an eventual Palestinian state.

Israeli settlements

= settlements
= Palestinian population
= "Green Line"

---

* Remember, under the Oslo Accords, the West Bank occupied territories are divided into three administrative areas: A, B, and C. All the settlements—as well as between 180,000 and 300,000 Palestinians—are in Area C, which encompasses 60 percent of the West Bank ("Area C," B'Tselem, https://www.btselem.org/topic/area_c). See map on page 155.

254 CAN WE TALK ABOUT ISRAEL?

The majority of Israeli settlers live in large towns, or "blocs" of communities, built close to the border with Israel proper or in the post-1967 Jewish neighborhoods built in East Jerusalem. Despite the appearance of normalcy, living in the settlements, especially the more isolated ones deep in the West Bank, can be a dangerous business. Palestinian militants, aiming to push the Israelis out of territory they regard as their homeland and future state, have staged attacks on Israeli soldiers and civilians in the West Bank. In turn, Israeli security forces make enormous efforts to prevent attacks, running networks of agents and informants within the Palestinian population, erecting checkpoints within the West Bank and between the West Bank and Israel, and maintaining a significant IDF presence in army bases and around the settlements throughout the West Bank.

Almost every country aside from Israel considers the Israeli settlements illegal under international law, a violation of the Fourth Geneva Convention's prohibition on an occupying power transferring its civilians to territory it has occupied.* Israel disputes this, citing historical Jewish ties to the territory and arguing that given that there was no recognized sovereign power in the West Bank prior to 1967, Israel cannot be considered an occupying power. By that logic, the argument goes, the Geneva Convention doesn't apply. Since 1967, both Democratic and Republican administrations in the United States have rejected this argument and referred to the settlements as, variously, "illegal," "illegitimate," and "an obstacle to peace."

However, in 2019, the Trump administration broke with that

---

* The Fourth Geneva Convention is an international treaty put in place in 1949, after World War II, that provides protections for civilians in war zones, occupied territories, and other situations related to conflict. Israel is a signatory to the treaty, along with almost two hundred other countries, and in any case, the treaty is considered binding on *all* countries, whether they are signatories or not.

bipartisan policy by declaring that the United States had determined that the settlements did not violate international law—although the meaning and implications of that position were, as with so many other things related to the Trump administration, unclear.* In January 2020, in an even more radical break with American policy, the Trump administration's "deal of the century" peace plan appeared to offer American support for Israel's annexation of parts of the West Bank. The international community—including the European Union, Israel's biggest trading partner—strongly opposed any such move. But the apparent blessing of the world's only superpower provided Prime Minister Netanyahu with a unique opportunity to feel justified in making such a controversial and unpopular move, and he vowed to begin the process of annexation in July 2020 (he did not).

While Israel has not (yet) officially annexed the West Bank, the Israeli residents of the settlements there are citizens of the State of Israel and enjoy the same rights and benefits as all Israelis. They vote in Israeli elections, receive Israeli benefits, are subject to Israeli law, and are tried in Israeli courts. The Palestinians living in their cities, towns, and villages in the same territories are not Israeli citizens. They do not vote in Israeli elections and do not have the same rights and liberties as Israeli citizens. Yet they are subject to Israeli military law and are tried in Israeli military courts.

Almost one in ten Israeli Jews lives in a community built after 1967 over the Green Line. Some do so for ideological or religious reasons, and their communities tend to be made up of hard-line right-wingers. These settlers are fiercely dedicated to the project of

---

* As of February 2021, the new Biden administration had not yet indicated what, if anything, it planned to do about this change in American policy toward the settlements. It is unlikely, though, that the new president will share the former administration's warm embrace of and support for Israel's settlement enterprise.

keeping the biblical Jewish homeland in Jewish hands. Some are even more loyal to this vision than they are to the institutions and laws of the modern State of Israel. They protest, and even reject the authority of, any attempts by the state to reign in or limit the expansion of their communities. And they often express this rejection at the expense of their Palestinian neighbors. Some militant settlers have preached and practiced violence against local Palestinians, destroying olive groves and other property and, in some cases, attacking people.

The Palestinian city of Hebron, holy to both Jews and Muslims as the burial site of the biblical patriarchs and matriarchs Abraham ("Ibrahim" to Muslims) and Sarah, Isaac and Rebecca, and Jacob and Leah, is a case in point. It was home to an ancient Jewish community that was uprooted after the massacre by Palestinians following the riots that began in Jerusalem in 1929. After the city was conquered by Israel in 1967, religio-nationalist hard-liners, aiming to reestablish a Jewish community in Hebron, established a small, militant Jewish settlement of several hundred people right in the middle of the city's two hundred thousand Palestinian residents. To protect that small settlement, the IDF positioned hundreds of soldiers there, shut down the traditional local market (casbah), and closed off main city streets to Palestinians. This made life miserable for Arab residents, who were no longer permitted even to walk on some of the city center's sidewalks or drive on certain streets reserved for settlers. Just outside town, the militant settlement of Kiryat Arba boasts a park celebrating its most (in)famous resident: the American Israeli doctor who, in 1994, took his assault rifle and murdered twenty-nine Palestinians at prayer in the mosque in the Tomb of the Patriarchs.

Other Israelis live in the settlements for nonideological reasons. They live there because the communities in the West Bank are simply more affordable and attractive, with more fresh air and open space than similar places inside Israel. And they're close: a lot of settlers commute daily to jobs or schools in Israeli cities like Jerusalem or Tel Aviv, which are often just a few miles away.* Unlike their more militant brethren, these "settlers of convenience" don't, for the most part, think of themselves as religious visionaries fulfilling some mystical destiny, or as brave pioneers holding the line against a future Arab invasion. Encouraged by generous government subsidies, they're just trying to live the good life in Israel—except, of course, they're not actually in Israel. To enable the settlers to live in the midst of what is, essentially, hostile territory—among millions of Palestinians who do not want them there and who see their presence as the primary obstacle to the emergence of a Palestinian state in the West Bank—Israel has constructed its matrix of control. All this creates a nightmarish quality of life for millions of Palestinians, but it serves the Israelis' purpose: since 1995, the settler population in the West Bank has grown four times faster than that of the population of Israel proper.

While the international community condemns and mostly refuses to recognize Israel's expansionist moves, it hasn't stopped Israel from developing the territories as it pleases—with very few, if any, serious consequences. Even tentative steps by the European Union to label settlement goods sold in European supermarkets as coming "from the occupied territories" (as opposed to "from Israel") have faltered under withering criticism and claims of antisemitism from Israel and some of its supporters. And given the positive signals from the American right wing, why wouldn't Israel just officially annex the West Bank—or at least Area C, which amounts to about 60 percent

---

* Israel is about the size of New Jersey, and so the geographical intimacy of the conflict can be surprising. Distances between places in Israel and the West Bank are often a lot shorter than people think. The Palestinian city of Bethlehem is about five miles south of Jerusalem. Ramallah, the headquarters of the Palestinian Authority, is about six miles to the north. The whole area is one big Israeli-Palestinian conurbation. If it weren't for the checkpoints, you wouldn't even notice you'd left Jerusalem and entered these other cities.

of the territory and is where all the settlements are located? It's a good question, one with huge implications. The fact is, the ambiguity of the West Bank status quo over the last half century has worked to Israel's advantage. But it is unclear how much longer this will be the case. Let's look at why.

The official justification for Israel's continuing occupation of the West Bank has always been, first and foremost, security. Israel's early wars and the ongoing enmity of many of its neighbors underscored the country's lack of strategic depth. (Israel is just nine miles wide at its narrowest point, between Netanya, on the coast, and the West Bank.) Until those neighbors accept the State of Israel, the argument goes, Israel will be forced to maintain its occupation of the West Bank to ensure strategic control over the territory west of the Jordan River.* And as we learned earlier, after the Six-Day War, Israel stated that it was willing to trade land for peace. Indeed, in the case of Egypt's Sinai Peninsula, also occupied in 1967, it showed itself willing to do so. Remember, Israel gave the Sinai back to Egypt as a result of the Camp David peace accords that U.S. president Jimmy Carter negotiated between the two former enemies. Israel and Egypt have lived in peace, albeit a relatively cold one, ever since.

Sounds reasonable enough, right? Land for peace is a pretty good negotiating position. But it's not the whole story, because over the last half century, Israel has not simply maintained a military presence in the captured West Bank territories. Rather, as we've seen, it has established an entire infrastructure of new towns, cities, and roads for the hundreds of thousands of Israeli Jews whom it encouraged to settle there, essentially turning what it calls Judea and Samaria into new districts of the State of Israel. And while occupying territory captured in a war is not, in and of itself, a violation of the Geneva Conventions,

---

* Just in case anyone gets any stupid ideas.

moving civilians into occupied territory is. So, why did Israel do this? Certainly not simply for security reasons. The real reasons were ideological and religious. To understand why and how this happened, we need to understand the story of a once fringe radical movement that succeeded in mainstreaming its agenda and making its goals a top priority for successive Israeli governments.

After the Six-Day War in 1967, Israel set up army bases and built civilian settlements in all the territories it had captured. In the case of the Sinai, Gaza, and the Golan, this was largely a strategic move to enable Israel to create and hold on to a buffer between its territory and hostile neighbors. When Israel withdrew from the Sinai in 1982 and from Gaza in 2005, the settlements there were razed, and the settlers (4,300 in Sinai, 8,500 or so in Gaza) returned to Israel proper. Sure, the romance of those places had resonated with many Israelis, but not like that of the West Bank.

The West Bank (Judea and Samaria) was different. This was the birthplace of the Jewish story, the place where Abraham, Isaac, and Jacob had walked, and it was intoxicating for many Israelis finally to be able to trace their footsteps, to touch that newly accessible mystical landscape. And so, exhilarated by Israel's stunning victory in 1967, a fierce new movement blossomed in Israel, one that saw Jewish control of and return to the West Bank, the biblical heartland, as the divinely ordained, miraculous fulfillment of Jewish destiny. That movement, originally called Gush Emunim, "the Bloc of the Faithful," was inspired by the mystical and militant teachings of Rabbi Tzvi Yehuda Kook, son of Israel's first chief rabbi, who decreed that Israel was actually *forbidden* to relinquish any of the conquered territories. Gush Emunim became the heart of the national-religious pro-settlement movement in Israel, and it set out to build permanent Jewish communities in the occupied territories and to bind them forever to the State of Israel.

At first, leaders of the then ruling center-left Labor Party paid little attention to the Israelis setting up camp at the site of pre-state kibbutzim and villages that had been abandoned when the territory fell to Jordan in the war of 1948. After all, they weren't the only ones: an entire brigade of the IDF, the Nahal, made up largely of soldiers from kibbutzim and other collective communities, was tasked with setting up military bases in the territories. These were explicitly intended to one day become civilian settlements. Some Labor Party officials, such as Shimon Peres (a future prime minister and party leader), looked on approvingly, seeing in these new settlers the same pioneering spirit that had animated the early twentieth-century Zionist arrivals to Palestine. But while the early Zionists were largely secular, motivated by their dream of Jewish self-determination, the Bloc of the Faithful were religious, motivated by what they believed God wanted them to do. They had no intention of allowing any of the land on which they built their new settlements to be one day traded for peace. And so, through benign neglect and quiet support, the first settlements took root.

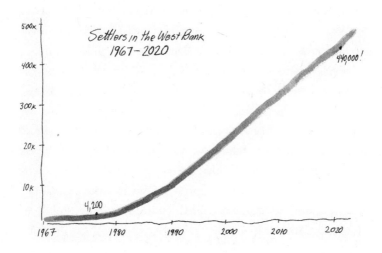

Everything changed with the rise to power of the right-wing Likud in 1977, which has dominated Israeli politics, with some exceptions, ever since. Under successive Likud governments, from Menachem Begin to Benjamin Netanyahu, the settlement movement found sympathetic cheerleaders and champions. And so, the settlements grew and grew. As they did, Israel provided military protection and created infrastructure to accommodate that growth. By 1977, ten years after the first West Bank settlements were built, the settler population comprised about 4,200 people. By 1988, it was 66,500. Ten years later, in 1998, it was 172,200. In 2008, it was 281,100. In 2018, it was north of 440,400.

This didn't happen by accident. The settler camp developed a powerful lobby to represent its interests and ideology in the halls of government and in the arena of public opinion. Like the Trumpist faction of the Republican Party in America, the settlement movement is a hard-line minority, and while its agenda is (still) unrepresentative of the views of the majority, it has become one of the prime drivers of Israeli policy and, indeed, of the national direction. That's because, like the conservative Christian right in America, it has built a formidable political machine aimed at changing not only Israeli law and policy, but also the hearts and minds of Israelis. And in this it is succeeding. Under Prime Minister Netanyahu, founders of the pro-settler Jewish Home Party served as the education and justice ministers of the State of Israel. If you want to change Israel's social fabric for the long term, there are no better places to start.

Supporters of the settlement project filled the ranks of the major parties of Israel's ruling coalitions throughout the second decade of the twenty-first century. And the movement's overarching goal was to secure the settlement enterprise—to ensure that the biblical heartland was never again severed from the rest of Israel. To this end, its leaders had long been proponents of Israeli annexation of the territories;

they wanted Israel to declare them a part of the state. But this was a marginal position, seen as fringe even by the mainstream Israeli right. Even though the right (and, at least in the early days, some on the left) enthusiastically supported—indeed, enabled—the astonishing growth of the settlements, few major figures seriously called for their formal annexation to Israel. All Israeli leaders, including the biggest supporters of the settlement enterprise, understood the crisis that annexation would precipitate, the international pariah status Israel would attain, and the rift it would create with the United States and with American Jewry. It just wasn't worth it.

What's more, there was no real *need* for annexation. In fact, in large part *because* Israel never annexed the territories, it was able to accomplish the de facto incorporation of the settlement enterprise into the fabric of Israel proper without incurring (too much) international opprobrium. And, crucially, it was able to do this without having to deal with the question of the political status of the millions of Palestinians who live in the West Bank.

And so, Israel's settler movement succeeded implicitly in practice, if not officially in law, in its primary objective of peopling the occupied territories with Jewish Israelis. In doing so, it also succeeded in changing the way Israelis think about the West Bank and the settlements. If you look at most Israeli maps of Israel, you'll notice that something is missing: namely, the Green Line that marks the border between Israel and the occupied territories. This cartographical absence is no oversight. It is a reflection of the settler movement's success in erasing the Green Line from the mental maps of many Israelis.

For many Israelis, the large settlements and settlement blocs are as much a part of the country as any towns or villages on the Israeli side of the Green Line. Today, there are many third-generation settlers, Israelis who think of themselves, and who are treated by the State, as Israelis living in Israel—despite the fact that they live in towns and cities that are not actually in Israel. Increasingly, this perspective is shared by their fellow Israelis living in Israel proper. When the government recently conferred university status on the public college in the large settlement of Ariel, many in Israeli academia and the left protested what they saw as "creeping annexation." But for other Israelis, this was yet another indication that Ariel was, essentially, just the same as Tel Aviv.

When it comes to all but the most isolated and extreme settlements (and, of course, the Palestinian population centers in Area A), the Green Line has essentially ceased to exist for citizens of Israel (at least for most of the Jewish ones). The separation barrier and the checkpoints prevent Palestinians from entering Israel or even traveling easily to and from areas A, B, and C in the West Bank. But Israeli

West Bank Barrier

citizens breeze through any checkpoints they encounter and, using tunnels and special roads, can move between Israel proper and most of the largest of the settlement blocs without even realizing they've crossed the border.

All this worked pretty well for Israel for a long time. Sure, there were ongoing security concerns and responses—including an increasingly frustrated and hopeless Palestinian population, the bloody Second Intifada, the construction of the separation barrier, regular bursts of violence and unrest, and the growth of a radical and violent movement of militant Jewish settler "hilltop youth," whose loyalty was to the settlement enterprise, not to the State of Israel—but these were deemed a reasonable price to pay for the benefits of retaining the status quo. And ironically, while the Oslo Accords are still ritually condemned by the Israeli right, they actually made Israel's control over the West Bank much easier: First, they created the Palestinian Authority, which oversees many aspects of governance in Area A and some in Area B, including policing, thus serving as Israel's security contractor, even as Israel retains ultimate control. Second, the Oslo Accords mitigated international pressure on Israel by serving to reassure the international community that, despite what the facts on the ground seemed to indicate, the status quo is only temporary and will one day lead to a two-state solution.

And so, even the leaders of Israel's right-wing governments knew better than to poke the hornet's nest that is the West Bank with talk of annexation. After all, why buy the cow when you get the milk for free? Other than regular protests by Israeli and international human rights organizations, the occasional light slap on the wrist from the international community, and the campaigns of the Boycott, Divestment, Sanctions movement (more on this later), Israel has faced astonishingly few serious consequences for its ever-expanding settlement enterprise.

And the cow, in this case, would come at a very high price—because if Israel annexes all or some of the West Bank, it creates a massive problem for itself: Namely, what does it do with the 2.3 million Palestinians who live there? (Remember Ben-Gurion's Triangle from chapter 8?) If it makes them all citizens with equal rights, it has just created millions of new Israeli voters who would likely vote to change Israel into the "State of Palestine." But if it annexes and doesn't grant citizenship and equal rights to those millions of Palestinians, or formalizes these little Bantustan-like* islands of "autonomous" Palestinian enclaves surrounded by Israeli-annexed territory, Israel will no longer be a democracy. It will be something else entirely. There is a word for this type of political arrangement, but it isn't in English or Hebrew; it's in Afrikaans: *apartheid*.

Faced with these options, most Israeli leaders have chosen the status quo: continuing to expand the settlements and quietly integrating them into the fabric of Israeli society, while avoiding the issue of what the ultimate political status of the occupied territories should be. But can an occupation that's lasted over half a century, during which time Israel has built towns and cities in the occupied territory and moved a sizable portion of its civilian population to live in them, really be called temporary? And as those settlements continue to grow, how long can a status quo like this remain sustainable?

For a long time, Israelis and their supporters were able to get by without really addressing these questions. But now this may be changing. Powerful voices are now challenging the status quo.

On the Israeli right, the traditional calls for annexation are

---

* Bantustans (or "homelands") were territories within apartheid-era South Africa created by the white government and aimed at concentrating Black Africans in manageable territories, nominally self-governing but, in reality, totally controlled by South Africa, thereby denying them participation, including voting rights, in South African political and civic life.

now gaining traction and resonating in a new way. This is reflected in shrinking Israeli support for a two-state solution (in late 2018, it stood at about 43 percent) and in growing numbers of Israelis (about half, according to recent polls) who say they support annexation of either Area C or the whole West Bank, with no political rights for Palestinians. Reasons for this shift include the success of the settler movement and its allies in government in changing the mental maps of Israelis to include the settlements as an integral part of the country, the lack of any progress* in the peace process, the dysfunction of the PA, and very real fears of terrorism born of the experience of the Second Intifada and rockets from Gaza. But it is also the result of a steady diet of fear, ethnonationalism, and even Jewish supremacy from Israel's leaders over the last ten years—hallmarks of the global trend of tribalism, democratic recession, and rising neo-authoritarianism affecting not only Israel, but also Europe, Brexit United Kingdom, Russia, India, Brazil, and the United States. This trend has hardened us-versus-them attitudes and eroded faith in compromise and support for peace.

For all these reasons, support for a two-state solution—which, remember, is still the official position of the Israeli government—has lessened, and support for annexation has moved into the mainstream. For example, Naftali Bennett, Israel's former minister of education and the leader of a hard-right settler party, a man who opposes the two-state solution, calls for annexing Area C. He says that he would support granting citizenship to the Palestinians living there if certain

---

* And, I would argue, any real desire for progress on the part of too many decision makers. In 2019, Prime Minster Netanyahu stated, quite clearly, "A Palestinian state will not be created, not like the one people are talking about. It won't happen" (Tovah Lazaroff, "Netanyahu: A Palestinian State Won't Be Created," *Jerusalem Post*, Apr. 8, 2019, https://www.jpost.com/arab-israeli-conflict/netanyahu-a-palestinian-state-wont-be-created-586017).

conditions, such as mandatory loyalty oaths, were met. As for the millions of Palestinians living in areas A and B, well, under his plan, they would enjoy a permanent "autonomy on steroids": citizens of no state surrounded on all sides by Israel, which would maintain security control. To critics, this sounds like Bantustans with a Hebrew accent. Keep in mind that Bennett is not a marginal figure; indeed, in June 2021 he became prime minister of Israel. And lest we forget: just days before Israel's general election of April 2019, Prime Minister Netanyahu crossed a rhetorical redline, declaring that, if he were reelected, Israel would begin annexing West Bank settlements. Upon forming a government in April 2020, Netanyahu reiterated that pledge, this time with what seemed like a thumbs-up from the Trump administration. The peace deals with the UAE and Bahrain in the autumn of 2020 required Israel to back-burner annexation, and the new Biden administration will almost certainly reinstate the traditional American position opposing the settlements and annexation. Still, the annexation genie is out of the bottle, and what ultimately happens to the status quo of the last fifty-four years, or to any remaining chance for a two-state solution, is anyone's guess.

Recent polls put the level of Palestinian support for a two-state solution at about 43 percent,* but the preferred alternatives are unclear. What is clear is that decades of Israeli occupation, ever-increasing settlement activity, a moribund peace process, and a corrupt Palestinian leadership have eroded horizons and hopes for change for millions of Palestinians who do not believe Israel will ever agree to a Palestinian state. Palestinians face a daily reality of checkpoints, walls, tunnels, roads, and military bases that reinforce

---

* It is much higher among supporters of the Fatah Party, which rules the West Bank, and those who don't identify with a particular political movement, and lower among those who support Hamas, which rules in Gaza.

Israel's control over them. Recognizing that both diplomacy and violence have failed to achieve their national goals, some Palestinians are turning to a new position, one that, if it continues to grow, may represent the greatest challenge that Israeli rule in the West Bank has yet faced. These Palestinians no longer call for a two-state solution because they do not believe one will ever come to pass. Rather, their demand is simple: one person, one vote.

Ahed
Tamimi

How would Israel, liberal American Jews, the United States, and the international community respond to an organized movement making this demand? How long would the status quo of occupation and disenfranchisement last if this were the official Palestinian position? Would the two-state solution suddenly become much more appealing to Israelis? Would it be too late?

In early 2019, I sat in the home of Bassem Tamimi, in the village of Nabi Salih, in Area B. Tamimi, a lifelong anti-occupation activist, told me his family had been resisting foreign domination since the Ottoman era. Bassem is a well-known figure in the ranks of Palestinian advocates of nonviolent resistance, but today he is perhaps best known as the father of Ahed Tamimi, who became something of a celebrity in activist circles in 2017 when, at seventeen years old, she was sentenced to eight months in a military prison for slapping an Israeli soldier moments after her fifteen-year-old cousin was shot in the head with a rubber bullet during a protest in her village. Bassem Tamimi told me he no longer supports a two-state solution. Not for "ideological reasons," he said, but because he knew it would never happen: Israel would never allow it; it would never stop building settlements. I asked him what he wanted, if he felt the two-state solution was off the table. Tamimi set his tea glass down on the table between us. "I want to take my children to the beach," he said simply. "It is only seventy kilometers away, but the Israelis will not let me. I want to take my children to the beach." And then he looked me in the eye and said, "And I want the vote."

CHAPTER 19

WHAT WE TALK ABOUT WHEN WE TALK ABOUT BDS

A GREAT DEAL of energy, angst, and ink has been expended on the debate around the Boycott, Divestment, Sanctions (BDS) campaign against Israel. Initiated by Palestinian activists, BDS aims to compel local and international governments and people around the world to treat Israel like apartheid-era South Africa in order to pressure it to change. The issue has become a kind of Middle Eastern Rorschach test, driving many people on all sides of the debate to distraction, confusion, and, I would argue (given the relatively modest impact of BDS to date), complete disarray.

But what are we actually talking about when we talk about BDS?

In June 2005, a number of Palestinian civil society groups issued a call for boycott, divestment, and sanctions against the State of Israel, a call since endorsed by various organizations around the world. This is the global BDS movement, and it calls on Israel to be thrown out of all international organizations and for all countries to cut ties with, boycott, divest from, and sanction Israel until it fully complies with international law by, in the BDS movement's own words:

> Ending its occupation and colonization of all Arab lands and dismantling the Wall [see "West Bank barrier" in the "Lexicon of the Conflict"];

> Recognizing the fundamental rights of the Arab-Palestinian citizens of Israel to full equality; and

> Respecting, protecting, and promoting the rights of Palestinian refugees to return to their homes and properties as stipulated in UN Resolution 194.

It is important to keep in mind that the BDS movement is nonviolent and that it was created, after the end of the Second Intifada, by Palestinians with real, legitimate grievances who wished to peacefully oppose what they saw as the ongoing theft of their homeland. So, why is a movement that rejects violence and terror labeled as unacceptable, anti-Israel, and even antisemitic by, among others, Israel, the U.S. government, and many in the American Jewish community? After all, these are nonviolent tactics designed to harness moral, economic, and political pressure to persuade a more powerful opponent to change its behavior.

In fact, boycott and divestment have been used successfully in the United States and elsewhere to confront injustice for many years. The Montgomery Bus Boycott that began in December 1955 helped end segregation in the United States. In the 1980s and '90s, the state of Arizona lost the Super Bowl, many rock and pop concerts, and hundreds of millions of divested business dollars until it recognized

Martin Luther King Jr. Day as a paid holiday. More recently, Indiana passed a law seen as discriminatory to LGBTQ+ people and lost tens of millions of dollars as businesses (including Apple and Salesforce), sports leagues (including the National Basketball Association and the National Collegiate Athletic Association), and even other American states boycotted. Thanks to such campaigns, Indiana amended the law. MLK Day was recognized. Segregation was ended. And as for sanctions, the United States and other Western countries have leveled them against numerous countries to protest violations of international law and to punish behavior such as invasions by neighbors, arms dealing, and human rights violations. In other words, the tactics of BDS are not only peaceful and nonviolent, but they can also effect massive change, and they're often used in support of perfectly legitimate and reasonable goals.

But Israel has reacted as if the BDS movement, and its tactics themselves, were an existential danger. In 2015, Prime Minister Netanyahu declared BDS a "strategic threat" to Israel, adding it to a list that includes Hamas, Hezbollah, and Iran. He claimed that the goal of boycotting Israel had nothing to do with changing Israel's actions, but rather, aimed to call the state's very existence into question. Netanyahu even appointed a cabinet minister, and invested a lot of money, to combat BDS.

So, what's all the fuss about?

Well, for one thing, the aim of the BDS movement isn't clear. While many of those who support BDS simply want an end to the occupation of the West Bank, the language of the actual BDS movement does not limit itself to that goal. Rather, it calls for the return of Palestinian refugees to their homes in what is now Israel. And this leads many critics of the BDS movement to believe that its ultimate aim is not just to end Israel's occupation of the Palestinian territories, but rather, to change Israel into a country that is no longer a homeland for the Jewish people. This is because if all the millions of descendants of the Palestinian refugees of 1948 were to return to their old homes in what is now Israel, the Jewish population would soon be in the minority—and the new Arab majority would likely vote to change Israel into a very different kind of country, one that was no longer a Jewish state.*

Certainly, this is true for many BDS supporters, some of whom want to see a single democratic state between the river and the sea. And while that may seem like a just and reasonable goal, many supporters of Israel feel it tends to ignore the fragility of Jewish life in a world without a sovereign Jewish state; without that state, Jews are at risk of persecution, oppression, and, ultimately, genocide.

And the idea of a single state to replace the State of Israel is probably not very realistic at the current time. Most Israelis don't want to live in a single democratic country with the Palestinians. And large numbers of Palestinians still favor the establishment of an independent Palestinian state next to Israel. So, if it's not what either of the parties to the conflict actually wants, it doesn't seem like this version of a "one-state solution" is likely to succeed at the moment.

Still, there are more than a few people who support applying boycotts, divestment, or sanctions to Israel who aren't part of the official BDS movement, don't want to see Israel disappear, and aren't really concerned with future theoretical regional political arrangements. They just want to see an end to the occupation, a modicum of justice for 2.7 million Palestinians, and a two-state solution. Pressuring Israel

---

* There are approximately six million Palestinians living in the Palestinian diaspora around the world. It is probably no more likely that most of those people would choose to return to their ancestral homes in what is now Israel than it is that Jews in America would pick up and move to Israel—which they've had the opportunity to do for more than seventy years now. But that doesn't allay the fears of many Israelis.

through nonviolent means like boycotts, divestment, and sanctions seems like a reasonable way of working toward this goal. In fact, the U.S. government applied just this kind of pressure on Israel in the not-so-distant past, when President George H. W. Bush threatened to withhold loan guarantees if Israel didn't stop building settlements. People can disagree about whether this is an effective or appropriate strategy. But the motivation of these supporters of the tactics of boycott, divestment, and sanctions isn't necessarily based on hatred for Israel or opposition to the very idea of its existence; it's based on a desire for fairness, justice, and conflict resolution.

Critics of BDS object to the way the movement singles out Israel for special opprobrium as if it alone among the nations of the world were deserving of this kind of punishment. Where, they ask, are the BDS movements against China, Saudi Arabia, Iran, or any number of worse state actors than Israel? And, some argue, the movement is counterproductive. As recent elections show, the Israeli electorate is divided, and moderate, pro-two-state-solution candidates have come very close to winning. The international BDS campaign is, therefore, too blunt a tool to use in a situation like this and would put Israelis on the defensive and make them less likely to take a chance on peace. And anyway, why punish Israel in this way when it agreed to the UN partition plan back in 1947 and then got invaded by its neighbors; offered Palestinians a two-state solution at Camp David in 2000 and then got the Second Intifada; and withdrew from Gaza in 2005 and then got rocket and missile fire in return?

Supporters of BDS respond that those other bad-actor countries aren't the recipients of more U.S. military aid than all other countries combined; that honor is held by Israel. And, they argue, the occupation and settlement enterprises are now over half a century old, and Israel shows no interest in ending either—quite the contrary, given its recent pledges to annex territory in the West Bank. A permanent occupation is a monumental injustice that can be solved only by the international community, these supporters say, and if there is no political will in the international community to pressure Israel, then it's up to regular people everywhere to create that pressure.

These are all fair points. That's why BDS is such a difficult issue to get one's head around.

CONFLATING CALLS TO BOYCOTT THE SETTLEMENTS WITH CALLS TO BOYCOTT ISRAEL

Muddying the waters further is the fact that the Israeli government and its allies love to purposefully conflate criticism of Israel's West Bank settlements, especially any calls by Israelis or anyone else to hold Israel accountable for the settlement enterprise, with the BDS movement proper. Remember the anti-boycott law we read about in chapter 14, which made it a civil offense for any Israeli to call for boycotts against Israel, including the settlements? This is all part and parcel of the Israeli government's campaign to erase the Green Line from the mental maps of all Israelis and from the consciousness of the world. If you want Israelis to think of the settlements as a part of Israel, declare that boycotting the settlements is tantamount to boycotting Israel, and therefore anti-Israel and antisemitic. See how the logic works?

In 2010, a group of Israeli artists, writers, and performers published an open letter saying that because they opposed the settlement enterprise and believed it to be morally and strategically wrong and lethal to Israel's democracy, they would refuse to perform at a state-funded theater in the large settlement of Ariel, and they called on fellow artists to join them. This open letter was not a call for anyone to boycott Israel, and it had nothing to do with the BDS movement. These were patriotic Israeli artists protesting their government's policy in the West Bank by refusing to patronize it. But the government of Israel and its allies immediately accused them of participating in the BDS movement. In fact, the artists' open letter was one of the rationales put forward by the drafters of the Anti-Boycott Law of 2011.

Another case in point is the European Union. Israel is an "associated state" of the European Union, which means it gets "most favored nation" trade status with EU countries. But the European Union opposes Israel's occupation and settlement enterprise (because it harms the potential for a two-state solution, which the European Union supports), so it wants to label products from settlements as MADE IN ISRAELI SETTLEMENTS, not MADE IN ISRAEL. Mind you, they're not moving to *ban* such products or even boycott them: they're just saying that Israel cannot label them as made in Israel if they're going to be sold in EU markets. This makes sense because . . . well, they're *not* made in Israel—they're made in Israeli settlements that exist in occupied territory. The European Union says its member countries and consumers have a right to know this, and it has adopted a policy called "meaningful differentiation." Here's what it has to say about the rationale for it:

> Differentiation [between Israel and its settlements] disincentivizes Israel's illegal acquisition of territory and re-affirms the territorial basis of a two-state solution. It also feeds an Israeli debate over national priorities by framing the negative consequences that Israel will face in its bilateral relations if it continues its annexation of Palestinian territory.

In other words, the EU policy of prohibiting settlement-made products from being labeled MADE IN ISRAEL is an effort to leverage its trade relations with Israel to support the two-state solution and to signal to the Israeli public that it may have to choose between the settlements and annexation on the one hand and its warm and bene-ficial economic relationship with the European Union on the other. Reasonable people can disagree about whether this is too tough or not tough enough, fair or unfair. But it is certainly not support for the global BDS movement, let alone antisemitism.

Yet, this is exactly what many Israeli officials and their supporters abroad claimed, including Michael Oren, a Knesset member and the former Israeli ambassador to the United States, who said, "The EU decision to label Israeli products is antisemitic." This was, of course, absurd. Israel hasn't annexed the West Bank settlements (at least not yet), so even *Israel* doesn't view the territory in which these goods were made as Israel. Oren's description of goods made there as "Israeli products" is dubious at best. But whether or not you think those settlement products are Israeli, it is ridiculous to claim that the EU requirement that they not be labeled as MADE IN ISRAEL is antisemitic. EU opposition to Israel's settlements has nothing to do with whether or not the settlers are Jews; it has to do with the fact that the European Union (and most of the rest of the world) holds that Israel's West Bank settlement project is a violation of the Fourth Geneva Convention's prohibition on an occupying power moving its civilian population into occupied territory.

The official Israeli attempt to equate any opposition to Israel's occupation and settlement enterprise with Jew hatred is dishonest, inflammatory, and dangerous, suggesting as it does that any criticism of Israeli policies in the West Bank is, essentially, an attack on Israel and the Jewish people. To be clear: it's not. But it is a useful fear to exploit if you want to delegitimize critics of the occupation. And it's useful to characterize any opposition to Israel's settlement enterprise as opposition to Israel itself, if what you're trying to do is convince people that there is no difference between Israel and the settlements. So, who actually believes that there is no difference between the two?

BDS'S STRANGE BEDFELLOWS

Herein lies the most striking irony of the whole BDS conversation: the main parties who maintain that there is absolutely no difference between a West Bank settlement like Ariel and an Israeli city like Haifa are the government of Israel and its right-wing allies on the one hand and some of the most zealous supporters of the BDS movement on the other. Although they view each other as polar opposites, when it comes to the issue that matters the most to them both, they're actually on the same page. Israel argues that boycotting the settlements is the same as boycotting Israel; if you're against one, you must be against the other. The BDS movement agrees—only, in reverse: the settlements are an extension of Israel into land it has occupied, so Israel should be the target of any boycott opposing them.

Virtually the entire world accepts that Israel is legitimate within the Green Line. But the settlement enterprise—and in particular, the idea of annexing the West Bank to integrate those settlements permanently into Israel while denying millions of Palestinians basic rights or equality—undermines this legitimacy. Blaming that problem on BDS is a form of gaslighting: creating a problem, then blaming others for trying to fix it, and in doing so, denying reality. In other words, Israel doesn't have a BDS problem; it has an occupation and settlement problem. It doesn't have a PR problem; it has a policy problem. Or, in Clintonian terms: It's the occupation, stupid.

BDS IN THE UNITED STATES

In the United States, BDS activity, especially on college campuses, among church movements, and in some corners of the political left, has become an issue of great concern to some in the Jewish community establishment. To listen to certain Jewish communal leaders, and to look at the websites and literature of the traditional organizations they lead, you would think that the BDS movement poses a greater threat to the American Jewish community than did the rise of violent white nationalists during the Trump era. Once the Israeli government declared BDS an antisemitic existential threat, many of Israel's supporters took those new marching orders seriously and began to organize accordingly.

In 2015, the casino magnate billionaire Sheldon Adelson* gathered other megadonors and a number of Jewish communal leaders for a "secret" conference in Las Vegas, at which they pledged millions to fight BDS on college campuses. And in 2018, a shadowy new organization, the "Canary Mission," began harassing and blacklisting American university students and professors whom it deemed insufficiently pro-Israel by accusing them, among other things, of supporting BDS. When its McCarthyite tactics—these included, I kid you not, ominous figures dressed in giant bird costumes menacing people critical of Israel at campus events—were exposed, several major philanthropists were embarrassed into ending their support.

But it's not just the right-wing fringe; even the mainstream Jewish community in the United States tends to treat BDS as a red-alert threat. Around the country, Jewish Community Relations Councils, organizations founded to serve as an "official" Jewish community voice, send out fund-raising emails informing supporters that detractors of Israel are (in the words of one I received from my local JCRC) "spending millions each year in [our] area alone," and warning that the BDS movement is a threat to our local community's "vital interests." Among certain sectors of the American Jewish community,

---

* Adelson also funded an Israeli newspaper so devoted to supporting Netanyahu and the Israeli hard right that it is nicknamed *Bibitone*, a mashup of Netanyahu's ubiquitous nickname and the Hebrew word for newspaper, *etone*. It is now the largest-circulation newspaper in Israel. Guess why? It's free!

BDS has become almost a byword for "enemy of the Jews and Israel."

The BDS debate is even affecting U.S.-Israel relations—and not in a good way. In the summer of 2019, the government of Israel took an unprecedented and extraordinary step against two Democratic American congresswomen, Ilhan Omar and Rashida Tlaib. The congresswomen are both people of color, the first two Muslim women ever to serve in the U.S. House of Representatives; Tlaib is a Palestinian American with family living in the West Bank.

While the congresswomen had both been very critical of the occupation and had even expressed some support for the campaign to boycott Israel in protest of its policies in the West Bank, it has always been almost a sacrament for successive Israeli governments to maintain strong bonds with the U.S. government and America's two major political parties. After all, it was only a matter of time before the party out of the White House was back in.

But that was before Donald Trump decided to weaponize the issue of Israel in an attempt to burnish his end-time bona fides with evangelical Christian voters for whom support for Israel is sacrosanct and to try to divide Jewish voters from the Democratic Party by casting it as anti-Israel. And so, after a series of tweets and statements by Trump attacking the congresswomen as antisemitic and urging Israel to ban them, Netanyahu obliged the will of his patron in the White House and declared that Omar and Tlaib would be banned from entering Israel because of their political views. The refusal to admit them was an unprecedented and extraordinary step. No U.S. official had ever before been denied entry to Israel.

In doing so, Netanyahu furthered the divide that he had done so much to exacerbate between American Jewish Democrats and Israel. Concerned commentators across the political spectrum, including some mainstream American Jewish organizations that are usually loath to criticize anything Israel does, condemned the move. With good reason: they worried what it would mean for Israel's future standing with the Democratic Party.

But the rationale for refusing the congresswomen entry to Israel was even bigger than Netanyahu's allegiance to Trump. Omar and Tlaib were denied future entry based on a 2017 amendment to Israel's Entry into Israel Law, which bans supporters of BDS from the country.* This law was part of a campaign to cast the BDS movement as an antisemitic challenge to Israel's very existence.

And so, Donald Trump's desire to paint the Democrats as radically anti-Israel, Bibi's reluctance to break with his American patron and his calculated decision to adopt a divide-and-conquer strategy in American partisan politics, and the frenzy over BDS in Israel combined to produce an act of diplomatic foolishness. And a counterproductive one, if the goal is to build up, not tear down, support for Israel: Israel insulted the Democratic Party (supported by an overwhelming majority of American Jews) and made support for Israel an even more partisan issue than it already was.

And the battle over BDS is being felt in the United States at the legislative level, too. Over the past several years, Congress and more than thirty states have passed or considered laws that would ban American citizens from calling for boycotts of Israel or the settlements. These bills and laws essentially copy the language of Israel's own Anti-Boycott Law. Their supporters claim the laws are aimed at showing support for Israel and combating antisemitism. Critics argue that they are misguided attempts to achieve these goals,

---

* Amendment 27 to the Entry into Israel Law states that Israel will deny entry to any noncitizen "who knowingly issues a public call for boycotting Israel that, given the content of the call and the circumstances in which it was issued, has a reasonable possibility of leading to the imposition of a boycott—if the issuer was aware of this possibility." The amendment stipulates that this refers not only to boycotts of Israel, but also to boycotts of any Israeli institutions or "any area under its control."

instead amounting to unconstitutional gag orders that run contrary to long-established American policy distinguishing between Israel and the settlement enterprise. While some American Jewish organizations have supported the laws, others have fiercely opposed them, as has the American Civil Liberties Union, which filed a lawsuit challenging them.

Passing constitutionally dubious laws that compromise the free speech of American citizens in order to defend an Israeli settlement enterprise that the United States traditionally opposes? Responding to a set of nonviolent pressure tactics as if they constituted an existential threat to Israel? Banning U.S. congresswomen from entering Israel because of their criticism of that settlement enterprise? Running around in giant canary costumes to intimidate college students with whom you don't agree? None of this is very rational. But when it comes to the debate about BDS, *rational* isn't usually the first word that comes to mind.

CHAPTER 20

THE A-WORD

OF ALL THINGS about this conflict that make people unglued, the question of whether Israel is an apartheid state is one of the most explosive of them all. Many supporters of Israel are horrified and truly shocked by the comparison to apartheid-era South Africa, arguing that Israel, as imperfect as it may be, is a democracy and not remotely in the same awful league.

As you've probably guessed by now, the answer is complicated, and it requires more than the typical kinds of soundbites that both sides tend to employ in this debate. Here's what I say when the question of the *A*-word comes up (and believe me, it comes up):

If you give me a group of intellectually honest and open-minded BDS sympathizers and let me take them for two weeks up and down the length and breadth of the State of Israel *on the Israeli side of the Green Line*; if they speak to all kinds of Israelis—Jewish and Arab, Ashkenazi and Mizrachi, and Ethiopian and Russian and Druze—if they meet with politicians and police officers and civil society leaders and academics; if they visit the big cities and the tiny towns; if they really see Israel, they will have to acknowledge that what they've seen is an often fragile, seriously flawed democratic society—a work in progress, imperfect and stumbling along its way.

They will see inequalities between not only Arabs and Jews, but also between different kinds of Jews, between secular and religious, haves and have-nots, people at the center of the country and those on the periphery. They will see discrimination and populism, but also a vibrant civil society pushing back against those things. They will see laws aimed at excluding Arab citizens from full acceptance and equality, and they will see Arab Israelis on the Supreme Court and in charge of the third-largest political party in the country. They will see government corruption and also a fiercely free press that reports on it. They will see a conservative, hidebound, state-sponsored religious establishment attempting to assert its fundamentalist mores on society, and feminist and LGBTQ+ movements that have fought long, hard, and successfully against those mores to achieve a measure of equality and inclusion. They will see a country still trying to figure out how to be a liberal democracy, one that offers equality to all its citizens while at the same time serving as a homeland for the Jewish people. At the end of the day, if those BDS sympathizers were truly intellectually honest, they would have to admit that what they saw in Israel in no way resembled apartheid South Africa.

Now, if you give me a group of intellectually honest and open-minded right-wing supporters of Israel and let me take them for two weeks up and down the length and breadth of the Israeli-occupied West Bank *on the other side of the Green Line*, if they speak to all kinds of people (Palestinians, Jewish settlers, and IDF soldiers); and if they meet with human rights activists and journalists, with Palestinian Authority leaders and top brass in Israel's Civil Administration of the West Bank; if they visit the settlements with their neat red roofs, lush lawns, and tidy streets, and then visit the streets of Hebron, the largest Palestinian city, where, to protect a few hundred zealous settlers who live amid hundreds of thousands of Arabs, the IDF has shuttered the historic markets at the heart of the city, denying Palestinians who live in the neighborhood the use of streets and sidewalks, which are reserved for the settlers; if they see the inequitable distribution of land and water, the ever-expanding and strategically placed settlement enterprise, with soldiers and the checkpoints that protect them and impede the daily lives of Palestinians, checkpoints that separate not only the West Bank from Israel proper, but also Palestinian towns and cities within the West Bank from one another; if they see the massive security presence and the matrix of Israeli control, the Israeli-only roads and tunnels ensuring the freedom of movement for settlers while denying it to Palestinians, the two systems of justice (Israeli law for the 440,000-plus Israeli settlers, military law for the 2.7 million Palestinians treated so differently because of an immutable characteristic of birth)—at the end of the day, if those right-wing supporters were truly intellectually honest, they would have to admit that what they saw in the Israeli-occupied West Bank *did* resemble some of the more pernicious aspects of apartheid-era South Africa.

That's not an easy answer, and it's not a sound bite. Israel proper does not resemble an apartheid state; the Israeli-occupied West Bank does. If Israel moves to annex the occupied territory, the answer to the question may become clearer; the problem also looks different when the word *apartheid* is used in its narrower, more legal sense.* But for now, the truth is that while a debate about "the

---

* In 2020, the Israeli human rights organization Yesh Din published a legal opinion concluding that, under international law, "the crime against humanity of apartheid is being committed in the West Bank. The perpetrators are Israelis, and the victims are Palestinians" (https://www.yesh-din.org/en/the-occupation-of-the-west-bank-and-the-crime-of-apartheid-legal-opinion/). In January 2021, B'Tselem released a report entitled "A Regime of Jewish Supremacy from the Jordan River to the Mediterranean Sea: This is Apartheid" (https://www.btselem.org/publications/fulltext/202101_this_is_apartheid). And in April 2021, the

A-word" may get the blood boiling, the value of such comparisons is limited; they tend to distract from the real issues at hand.

Meanwhile, the occupation, more than half a century old, continues to make life miserable for millions of Palestinians while eroding the fabric of Israel's democracy. In the end, I defer to a friend of mine, Talia Sasson, an expert on the settlements and a former high-ranking official in the Office of the State Attorney of Israel as well as a legal adviser to former prime minister Ariel Sharon. When I asked her about the use of the word *apartheid* to describe the occupation, she told me, "It's bad enough what it is without using complicated and imperfect analogies." And that's about right: it's bad enough what it is.

---

international human rights organization Human Rights Watch (HRW) released a lengthy report entitled "A Threshold Crossed: Israeli Authorities and the Crimes of Apartheid and Persecution," which, like Yesh Din's, concluded that Israeli officials had committed the crimes against humanity, under international law, of "apartheid" and "persecution" in the occupied West Bank. HRW was careful to state that they were not using the term "apartheid" as a comparison to South Africa or labeling Israel an "apartheid state." Rather, they argued, they referred to the term as a legal definition (as defined by the Apartheid Convention of 1973 and the Rome Statute of the International Criminal Court of 1998), and found that the elements of the crime of apartheid as defined in the Rome Statute ("inhumane acts . . . committed in the context of an institutionalized regime of systematic oppression and domination by one racial group over any other racial group or groups and committed with the intention of maintaining that regime") had been met in the West Bank (https://www.hrw.org/report/2021/04/27/threshold-crossed-israeli-authorities-and-crimes-apartheid-and-persecution).

CHAPTER 21

THE *OTHER* A-WORD

IS CRITICISM OF Israel antisemitic? No (except when it is). Does being an anti-Zionist make you an antisemite? No (except when it does).

Sometimes, legitimate, reasonable criticism of Israel, including harsh criticism, is labeled as antisemitic by certain zealous (or just misinformed) defenders of Israel in an attempt to delegitimize and chill *any* criticism of Israel at all. Obviously, criticizing Israel or disagreeing with Israeli policy is not antisemitic, just as criticizing America or disagreeing with U.S. policy isn't anti-American.

But unfortunately, antisemitism (and all kinds of other hatreds) is alive and well in this era of rising white nationalism and political polarization. And sometimes criticism of Israel *can* amount to, or be a subterfuge for, antisemitism. The human rights activist Rabbi Jill Jacobs has come up with some useful ways of identifying when criticism of Israel crosses that line. I'll paraphrase some of them here, adding my gloss.

Does the criticism cast Jews as "insidious influencers behind the scenes of world events"? This is a popular trope in the antisemitic fringes on both the extreme right and left. Whether it's right-wing talk about a global conspiracy of cosmopolitan elites funded by George Soros or left-wing talk about an all-powerful Zionist conspiracy responsible for the world's ills, if someone is alleging that the Jews (or "cosmopolitan global elites" or "Zionist Elders") control the world, they're engaging in antisemitism.

Does the criticism deny Jewish history ("the Holocaust never happened" or "the Holocaust is exaggerated") or Jewish connection to and history in Israel ("today's Jews aren't connected to Jews who lived in Israel thousands of years ago" or "there's no evidence that there was ever a Jewish Temple in Jerusalem")? These allegations are totally baseless. Denying Jewish history and experience is intended to undermine the Jewish need for and connection to Israel. You can disagree with everything Israel does and stands for without having to rely on antisemitic lies erasing centuries of pain and trauma to make your point.

Does the criticism assume that the government of Israel speaks for all Jews or that all Jews support the government of Israel? If you're lumping Jews and Israelis together and holding all Jews accountable for Israel's actions; if you're conflating Jews with Israel and assuming that Jews must be supporters of right-wing Israeli policies and the occupation, guess what? You're being antisemitic.

Of course, there is a flip side to all this. Right-wing Israelis and some of Israel's defenders abroad occasionlly deploy a rhetorical move that goes like this: opposition to Israeli policy equals anti-Zionism, and anti-Zionism equals antisemitism. And in recent years, this line of thought has grown teeth.

In 2016, the International Holocaust Remembrance Alliance (IHRA), an intergovernmental organization focused on Holocaust-related issues, issued a "working definition" of antisemitism.* The definition itself seemed reasonable, if unwieldy. But IHRA also provided examples to illustrate its definition, among which were these two:

> "Denying the Jewish people their right to self-determination, e.g., by claiming that the existence of the State of Israel is a racist endeavor"; and

> "Applying double standards by requiring of it [Israel] a behavior not expected or demanded of any other democratic nation."

Now, reasonable people can disagree over whether claiming the State of Israel is a racist endeavor is, by definition, antisemitic; civil libertarians and a number of prominent Jewish leaders felt this was overreach. (I tend to agree with them.) And the question of whether it is antisemitic to criticize Israel but not other countries for similar bad behavior is certainly worth debating. (In my opinion, as I suggest in the opening lines of this chapter, it depends.)

---

* The IHRA working definition reads, "Antisemitism is a certain perception of Jews, which may be expressed as hatred toward Jews. Rhetorical and physical manifestations of antisemitism are directed toward Jewish or non-Jewish individuals and/or their property, toward Jewish community institutions and religious facilities."

290 CAN WE TALK ABOUT ISRAEL?

Whatever your opinion, nobody at the IHRA *ever* intended for the working definition to be turned into binding law or into hate speech codes. In fact, the IHRA specifically stated its intention that it *not* be. Its primary author attests to the fact that it was devised mainly to help data collectors studying antisemitism determine what to count and what not to count. It never meant for it to be used to intimidate critics of Israeli policy or to chill freedom of expression.

However, over the last few years, several countries, including the United States, have done exactly that, taking steps toward adopting the definition as policy and even codifying it into law. In December 2019, then president Trump issued an "Executive Order on Combating Antisemitism," which states that Civil Rights Act violations can be proved by citing the IHRA working definition and examples of antisemitism as evidence to establish "discriminatory intent." And in late 2020, the U.S. State Department cited the IHRA definition when it announced that it planned to label leading international human rights organizations (including Amnesty International and Human Rights Watch) as "antisemitic" based on their critical reporting on Israel's policies in the West Bank and Gaza.

These moves open the door for the IHRA definition to be abused and wielded as a cudgel to classify legitimate criticism of Israel and of its actions and policies (including rejecting the legitimacy of its settlement project in the West Bank) as antisemitic. This poses a very real threat to academic freedom and protected political speech. As a group of 122 Palestinian and Arab academics wrote in response to these developments, "To level the charge of antisemitism against anyone who regards the existing state of Israel as racist, notwithstanding the actual institutional and constitutional discrimination upon which it is based, amounts to granting Israel absolute impunity. Israel can thus deport its Palestinian citizens, or revoke their citizenship or deny them the right to vote, and still be immune from the accusation of racism."

These are, of course, upsetting things for many supporters of Israel to hear, let alone agree with. But one cannot ignore Israel's complicated past, the rhetoric of some of its leaders, and some Israeli politicians' enthusiasm for annexing the West Bank while denying equality and citizenship to most of the Palestinians living there. It is understandable why some scholars might criticize Israel as "racist"— and why they believe strongly that such criticism is not antisemitic. Surely, protesting a government's policy that you feel is racist by calling it racist isn't antisemitic just because the country in question happens to be Israel.

CHAPTER 22

RED COWS IN THE HEARTLAND
Israel and Armageddon

IN 2014, A red heifer was born at an undisclosed location in the United States. This was big news for some evangelical Christians because, according to them (and to some fundamentalist Jews), an unblemished red cow is required for sacrifice at the Third Jewish Temple in Jerusalem.

What's that? you say. There is no Third Temple? The Second Temple was destroyed by Rome in 70 C.E., and that's where the Dome of the Rock, the third-holiest site in Islam, stands today. Well, you're right. But not for long, if a new alliance of evangelical, dispensationalist Christians and fundamentalist Jews have their way.

While the radical fundamentalist Jews who dream of erecting the Third Temple—going so far as to re-create Temple garments and rehearse sacrificial rites described in the Bible in preparation for the

Red

Holy cow!

real thing—remain a small, fringe group in Israel, the same cannot be said of the evangelical Christians who support them in America.

About a quarter of Americans identify as evangelical Christians, and 80 percent of those who do say they believe that the Jewish return to Israel and the establishment of the state is the "fulfillment of Bible prophesy that shows we are getting closer to the return of Jesus Christ."* Christian Zionists are a powerful and growing advocacy constituency and a major influence within today's Republican Party. And while plenty of evangelical Christians support Israel for the same cultural, geopolitical, and historical reasons that many other Americans do, for a large number of evangelicals, support for Israel

---

* Eighty percent of evangelical Christians also say they believe that God's covenant with Abraham, promising the Land of Israel to the Jews, was for "all time." Only 23 percent support a two-state solution, in stark contrast to the almost 80 percent of American Jews who do. Interestingly, one place where conservative Christian Zionists and liberal American Jews seem to have something in common when it comes to Israel is when it comes to their kids. Just like young American Jews, young evangelical Christians are more ambivalent about Israel than their seniors.

is a critically important religious imperative. The Jewish people and Israel are central elements of their theology, and they believe that the United States has a divinely appointed role to play in their version of Israel's story. As the conservative evangelical icon Rev. Jerry Falwell said in 1981, "We believe that history and scripture prove that God deals with nations in relation to how they deal with Israel." Evangelical Christians were a major force within the Trump administration. Former vice president Mike Pence recently told a gathering of fellow Christian Zionists that "my passion for Israel springs from my Christian faith." And when Trump's secretary of state Mike Pompeo, also an evangelical Christian, was asked whether Donald Trump had been appointed by God to "save the Jewish people," he responded, "As a Christian, I certainly believe that's possible."

The largest pro-Israel organization in America today—bigger than AIPAC, bigger than J Street, bigger than the Zionist Organization of America—is Christians United for Israel (CUFI). Its leader, Pastor John Hagee, wielded significant influence within the Trump administration and reportedly played a role in convincing Trump to move the U.S. embassy from Tel Aviv to Jerusalem. Hagee, a guy who preached that the 2014 Ebola outbreak was God's punishment for Obama's Israel policy, was tapped by Trump to offer a benediction at the ceremony marking the new embassy's opening. CUFI, which claims to have more than nine million followers, describes its mission as "educating and empowering millions of Americans to speak and act with one voice in defense of Israel and the Jewish people."

Prime Minister Netanyahu has praised them, saying, "I consider CUFI a vital part of Israel's national security." Indeed, over the course of the past ten years, Netanyahu seems to have arrived at the strategic decision that Israel does not need the support of liberal American Jews who are ambivalent about his policies. Instead, he is forging a new primary partnership with these evangelical Christians, whose views on a host of issues are antithetical to those of American Jews, but who are passionate supporters of a territorially maximalist vision of Israel.

So, who are these Christian Zionists who have the ear of both the Israeli prime minister and the former American president, and who, during the Trump administration, had such a major influence on U.S. policy toward Israel? And what kind of Israel do they support? To understand, we need to understand dispensationalism, the religious perspective that animates their powerful commitment to Israel.

Dispensationalism has its roots in the teachings of a nineteenth-century English Bible enthusiast, John Nelson Darby. In Darby's understanding of the Bible, history is divided into eras, or "dispensations." The current era would end with the Rapture, when true Christians would be removed to heaven. Next would be the rise of the Antichrist and the era of Tribulations, the Battle of Gog and Magog, and then, at the end of the Tribulations, the Battle of Armageddon, when Jesus returns to earth to defeat the armies of the Antichrist on the plains of northern Israel.* This inaugurates the Messianic age. After the good guys win, then comes the Judgment, followed by the Millennium, a thousand-year period when Christ reigns on earth; then the Last Battle and the end of the story. In order for all this to happen, Darby believed, the Jews had to return to Jerusalem and the rest of the Holy Land, both of which were promised to them by God. That's what starts the end-time clock ticking, leading the way to the Rapture and all that follows.

Darby's dispensationalism is at the heart of the modern Christian

---

* The word *Armageddon* comes from the Hebrew *Har Megiddo*. *Har* means "hill" or "mountain" in Hebrew, and *Megiddo* was an ancient city in northern Israel. A *tel*, or "archaeological mound," stands at the site, near a modern-day kibbutz that bears the name. In the Book of Revelation in the New Testament, this is the location of the epic, end-of-the-world battle between the forces of God and Satan.

Zionist movement. After Israel's stunning victory in the Six-Day War, the Armageddon prediction industry really took off. It seemed that biblical prophecy was being fulfilled by the Jewish soldiers, tanks, and fighter jets of the IDF as they captured East Jerusalem, the West Bank, and wide swaths of the Holy Land. Today, dispensationalist Christian Zionists see the history of modern Israel as the fulfillment of those prophesies. That's why so many evangelical Christians are so supportive of Israel, no matter what, including its settlement enterprise. In fact, they oppose territorial compromise and a two-state solution. After all, God promised the Jews *all* of the Holy Land, not just that within the pre-1967 borders.

The belief that Israel plays a major role in fulfilling end-times prophesy also explains why Christian Zionists are so aligned with the fringe Jewish fundamentalists who want to rebuild the Temple in Jerusalem. Both these groups believe that building the Third Temple on the Temple Mount will hasten the Messianic age—thus the red heifer, sacrificial rite rehearsals, and the Bible-approved priestly robes. Sure, the dispensationalist Christians know that in the end-time, after the Jews' role in the story is over, up to one third of them will convert to Christianity and be saved, while the rest will be damned for all eternity. But that doesn't bother the Jewish Third Temple crowd, who are equally certain of a very different outcome in the world to come. And it sure doesn't bother an Israeli government that increasingly relies on the ironclad support of the Christian Zionist "Armageddon Lobby" in Washington and beyond.

Israel also helps explain why so many evangelical Christians were so devoted to Donald Trump, despite his less-than-Christian behavior. For them, Trump was a modern-day Cyrus, the ancient Persian king who conquered Babylon in the sixth century and allowed the exiled Jews to return to Jerusalem and rebuild their Temple. Just like Cyrus, according to the dispensationalists, Trump was an irreligious and personally flawed leader who nonetheless had been chosen to serve as an instrument of God. His support for Israel's hard-line government and its desire to annex territory in the West Bank were proof of this. Indeed, the very character flaws that would seem to damn him in the eyes of religious Christians were in fact further proof of his Cyrus-like stature. The more Trump misbehaved while delivering on Israel, the more it just went to show that he was their man. And they weren't the only ones making the comparison: after Trump moved the U.S. embassy to Jerusalem in 2018, Prime Minister Netanyahu proclaimed that Israel would remember Trump as the Jewish people remember Cyrus.

Many conservative Israelis and their American supporters smile and shrug at the end-time theology of their dispensationalist Christian Zionist allies. In the here and now, they say, these folks have proved themselves to be some of Israel's most reliable American friends and, in the Trump era, some of the most powerful. That's true, but aside from whether it's geopolitically wise to support the expansionist impulses of Israel's current hard-line leadership, there is this very real question: What happens when U.S. policy toward Israel is shaped and guided by devout Christian Zionists who believe, quite literally, that the end is nigh, that their policies are helping to bring it closer, and that Israel and the Jews have a major, violent role to play in that story? At a rally in 2015, three years before he would become secretary of state, then congressman Mike Pompeo told a crowd at a church in Kansas that "there is a never-ending struggle until the rapture . . . Be a part of it. Be in the fight." Joe Biden's election means that Christian Zionist end-time true believers will likely have little role in shaping U.S. policy toward Israel and the Middle East for at least the next four years. But among the early leading contenders for the Republican presidential nomination in 2024 are Mike Pompeo and Mike Pence.

CHAPTER 23

THE CASE FOR HOPE

So, I HOPE you now feel better prepared for that Israel conversation you've been avoiding. As we've seen, when it comes to Israel, people disagree about what to call the places and people involved, they disagree about the history of what happened, and they disagree about how to understand the issues roiling the region today. No wonder Israel makes so many people come unhinged. At times, the sheer weight of the history there, the intensity of the conflict, and the adamancy of the attitudes can make a person pessimistic about the potential for a just and peaceful future for Israel and Palestine.

But lest you feel like throwing this book across the room in desperation, I will conclude with a few stories of ordinary people living in Israel today who are doing extraordinary things to build bridges, heal wounds, and create a better future for everyone in this tortured land between the river and sea. Listen to their voices. Their stories remind us that the most precious export that the great faith traditions forged in Israel thousands of years ago is the one we need most now: hope.

MAISAM JALJULI, 47—Palestinian Citizen of Israel, Feminist, and Social and Political Activist

I was eleven years old when I first heard the term *transfer.**

The year was 1984, and Meir Kahane, an ultranationalist rabbi, tried to enter my hometown, the Arab Israeli city of Umm al-Fahm, in order to convince its residents, citizens of the State of Israel, to transfer themselves to other Arab countries.

I could not understand why someone would think I'd want to move away from my home and my country. It was shocking to me.

And then something extraordinary happened. Tens of thousands of Arabs and Jews blocked the city's entrance with their bodies. We stood there so that Kahane the person could not enter; but more important, we stood there so that Kahane the *idea* could not enter. And on that day in Umm al-Fahm, Kahane and his people did not enter the city.

We didn't let him divide us, we didn't let him infect us with hatred for one another. We were a human dam against the fascism.

Unfortunately, the optimistic lesson from that day—that Jews and Arabs could be partners in promoting shared values and goals— was shattered in my twenties, when I was a young mother working with at-risk youth in the city of Tira.

In October 2000, in a tragic event that preceded the Second Intifada, the Israeli police force shot to death thirteen young demonstrators, Arab-Palestinian Israeli citizens. This time, there was no one there with us. Jewish Israelis simply did not seem to care. We were alone.

---

* *Transfer* is, in the Israeli political lexicon, the term for the idea of expelling Arab citizens of Israel from the country. In other words, ethnic cleansing.

My heart was aching. But rather than let my spirit break, I became an activist to create a more just society.

Five years later, the municipality where I worked was trying to cut the jobs of women who were earning a minimum wage and supporting their families. I had two options: to quit my job or stay and fight. For me, the choice was clear.

It almost cost me my life—twice, my house was shot at—but in the end, we kept those jobs for those hardworking women, and I can guarantee you that if *that* didn't stop my battle for women's equality, which is really the fight for equal rights for every citizen, nothing will. I didn't quit then, and I haven't stopped since.

In 2018, Yaara Ayub and Silvana Tzagai, two teenage girls, one Arab, one Jewish, were both murdered a few hours apart on the exact same day by men they knew. They were female homicide victims number twenty-three and twenty-four in Israel that year. In fact, twenty-six women were murdered in 2018, the highest number of femicides in a decade.

Yaara was sixteen years old, and Silvana was thirteen. Imagine.

Women from all over the country—Jewish, Arab, secular, religious, asylum seekers—all understood it was time to cry out and do something dramatic. The shock of girls', and women's, lives being so devalued rocked the country, and actions were taken overnight. It was the biggest women's protest ever to take place in Israel.

As for me, someone used to having society overlook murders within the Arab community, I found myself fighting shoulder to shoulder with thousands of women (and men, Jews and Arabs) in Rabin Square, in Tel Aviv, shouting together, in both Arabic and Hebrew: "Stop the murder of women!"

Just like back in Umm al-Fahm, when Kahane tried to bring his hatred to town, we proved that our voices are stronger when we come together. We showed that when women set their minds on change, we can make it happen. We are not afraid to fight—we have a desire for life. We are powerful, and we can change the world order.

For the past four years, my friends and I have continued to build a strong and meaningful partnership as part of "Standing Together," a grassroots Israeli movement that organizes Arabs and Jews in Israel around campaigns for peace, equality, and social justice to help transform Israeli society and build a shared future for Jews and Arabs in Israel. We stand together in the struggles against the occupation, against racism, against the Nation-State Law and home demolitions in Arab villages. We stand together for the rights of all citizens.

Choosing to be courageous is often a hard choice, for all of us. It's much easier to ignore aggressive actions taken by the government, to find excuses and explanations for killing protesters in Gaza, to agree with the saying "There is no partner on the other side," and to allow for the continued exclusion of Arab citizens and their leaders.

More than ever, we deserve—and we demand!—brave leaders who will look honestly at reality and create the change we all need.

When we understand that Israel is the home for all of us, and that there is a place for everyone, we can create partnership, with respect for one another and with hope for a new path forward.

I may be stating the obvious, but everyone deserves to live, to study, and to feel free to speak their native language in their homeland. My own son does not feel that freedom—he chose to leave the country to study abroad. That, among other things, is what drives me to continue my political, social, feminist activities. I want my children to experience Israel the way I did, back in Umm al-Fahm. Only together can Arabs and Jews turn Israel into a better place for all of us to live in.

As Mahmoud Darwish, the national Palestinian poet, said, I have passion for life, and everything on this land is worth living for.

We each have a chance to write our own history. In mine, I hope to tell of the changes I helped bring about in my country.*

MUTASIM ALI, 34—Sudanese Political Asylum Seeker to Israel, Immigrant Rights Activist, Lawyer, and Refugee

I was raised by a loving father and mother in Darfur, a region of Sudan.

From the time I was five years old, my parents told me about the importance of education and community work. Our society is broken, they said, and it has to be fixed.

When I turned six, my parents began sending me away to stay with relatives and family members and sometimes even with strangers. I thought this was because my parents didn't love me. I could not have been more wrong.

In 2003, while I was studying for my undergraduate degree in Khartoum, our village in North Darfur was attacked by Janjaweed, a militia recruited by the Sudanese regime to wipe out African ethnic groups, take our land, and obliterate our identity. I was not at home at the time, because my parents had sent me away. This was when I truly understood the depth of their love for me. On that day, dozens of people were murdered, our houses were burned down, water sources were poisoned, trees were cut down, and the village was reduced to ashes. My parents fled to live in a displaced persons' camp in North Darfur. I could never return home.

I have not seen my parents since that day.

While I was a student activist in Khartoum, I was put several times in solitary confinement. And after I graduated, I had two

---

* Maisam Jaljuli, relayed via email message to the author, Dec. 20, 2020.

choices: remain silent and close my eyes to what was happening in Darfur, or pick up a weapon and go back home and fight. But neither of these choices was who I am. Instead, I sought asylum so that I could become a voice for my people.

Many people ask: Why Israel?

It is true that in our schools, we never learned anything positive about Israel; we heard only about hatred and war. And it is also true that most of us are Muslims who speak Arabic. But when the genocide in Darfur began in 2003, hardly anyone was there to advocate for us. One voice that we heard clearly was from Jews from America and around the world. Synagogues and Jewish youth movements took part in intensive campaigns such as Save Darfur to stop the systematic murder of innocent civilians. The people of Darfur heard that voice, and it was so moving to all of us. Jews have experienced mass murder and unspeakable human tragedy. From this rises the commitment to prevent and combat any genocide from happening ever again.

All this made me believe that the Jewish state would be a safer place for me.

I arrived in Israel in 2009. I was [housed in a] prison for four and a half months. I was released with a bus ticket to Tel Aviv. I didn't have family or even friends—I knew nobody.

I was given a three-month visa by the Ministry of Interior, but they would not allow me to file an asylum request. After years of attempts and advocacy, I finally managed to submit an application for refugee status in 2012.

Remembering my parents' lessons, I got involved in organizing the community. *Our society is broken*, I thought, *and it has to be repaired.* The challenges were great, the community's need for support was high, and change seemed impossible. But we reached out to the Israeli people and the decision makers. We protested for our rights. We became more visible.

Still, no word came on my claim for asylum nor the claims of many, many others.

In 2014, I was sent to the Holot detention facility for political asylum seekers and refugees. I remained there for fourteen months. Holot is located in the Negev Desert, in the South of Israel. It is a place designed to break our spirits, to serve as a deterrent to prevent other African asylum seekers from coming to Israel in search of refuge. At that time, thousands of people were held arbitrarily in detention for no other reason than that they were seeking safety from genocide, murder, and torture.*

It is difficult to arrive to a country with so much hope, only to be labeled as a "demographic threat." Asylum seekers, like so many, came to Israel to seek safety from terrible atrocities we had no choice but to escape. Some argue that we will damage Israel's social fabric and security. But we came to contribute to Israeli society. We are an asset, not a threat.

In the summer of 2016, after years of protest, detention, and advocacy, I am proud to say that I was finally granted refugee status. I then completed a degree in public international law (the first African migrant to graduate from an Israeli law school) and went on to receive a master's in international and comparative law at George Washington University.

I took every risk possible just to make it to the place where I am today.

Asylum seekers, more than anyone else, appreciate the opportunities that people have in Israel. The fact that I can speak out loudly and freely without fear of arrest is something I praise and value. I use

---

* The Holot detention center was shut down in 2018 as part of the Israeli government's plan, thus far unsuccessful, to expel tens of thousands of mostly sub-Saharan African political asylum seekers.

these precious opportunities to do my part to make Israeli society better, because I am part of Israeli society.

The founding fathers of Medinat Yisrael [the State of Israel] proclaimed in the Declaration of Independence that "the State of Israel . . . will be based on freedom, justice and peace as envisaged by the prophets of Israel; it will ensure complete equality of social and political rights to all its inhabitants irrespective of religion, race or sex." These are values we all cherish. When I left Sudan, I made a commitment to do whatever I could to advocate for my people in Darfur. But now, my contribution expands beyond those borders, to Israel and Israeli society. As a lawyer and as the first officially recognized Sudanese refugee, I continue to advocate for and to revive those values and to build a society of which we can all be proud.*

GADI GVARYAHU, 64—Jewish Israeli, Religiously Observant Human Rights Activist

I am the founder of Tag Meir, a coalition that encompasses fifty organizations and movements across the social and political spectrum in Israel. We started Tag Meir in response to the "price tag" campaign, a loosely organized movement of extremist Israeli settlers and their supporters who attack Palestinian people and property (and also peace activists and even sometimes Israeli army outposts) in response to any move by the Israeli government to dismantle or evacuate illegal settlement outposts. The idea behind this terror campaign is to make innocent Arabs pay a "price" for anything that pushes back against the goals of the extremist Israeli settlers. The Hebrew for "price tag" is *tag machir*;

---

* Mutasim Ali, relayed via email message to the author, Dec. 19, 2020.

that's why we named our movement Tag Meir, which means "light tag." Not only does its name rhyme with "price tag" in Hebrew, but we founded it during Chanukah, the Festival of Lights. Together, we—Jews, Arab citizens of Israel, and Palestinians—advocate for peace, tolerance, and compassion among the different nations and ethnic groups that live in Israel and the West Bank.

I was inspired to start Tag Meir after a mosque in Yasuf, a village south of Nablus, which is divided between Areas B and C in the West Bank, was torched by Jewish arsonists. I went there with a rabbi and his wife to show solidarity and support for the victims. We tried to get an entry permit from the IDF but didn't succeed, so, instead, we met with village notables at a junction in the road. The rabbi brought copies of the Koran. We sang and danced together. It was a profound and powerful experience, there at that crossroads. I learned then what still guides me today: you have to embrace, and you have to talk.

Tag Meir hosts solidarity meetings and events that bring Jews and Arabs together: marches, candle lighting during Chanukah, and joint iftars.* We operate student chapters at several universities. The students engage in Tag Meir activities, like giving out dates to break the Ramadan fast, helping out families of foreign workers, and assisting elderly people during the coronavirus pandemic. During the first COVID-19 lockdown, we handed out tens of thousands of masks in Bnei Brak.**

Our representatives visit sites of hate crimes as promptly as possible to stand in solidarity with the victims and to offer emotional, financial, and moral support. For example, in Sakhnin, in northern Israel, two large Christmas trees outside one of the largest churches

---

* Iftar is the meal eaten by Muslims after sundown during the holy month of Ramadan.

** Bnei Brak, a city near Tel Aviv, is a center of the ultra-Orthodox Jewish community and one of the poorest places in Israel.

in the city were set on fire. Sakhnin has a population of thirty-two thousand people—75 percent Muslim and 25 percent Christian. The incident caused quite a stir in the Arab community. We went there as a joint delegation, together with the Women Wage Peace* movement, to express our sympathies about the incident. As always, we brought an olive tree sapling, which we planted near a new church slated to be built in the city.

Recently, we went to express our condolences to the Horgan family in the Tel Menashe settlement, in the West Bank. Esther, a mother of six, had gone out for a morning run in the forest, and a Palestinian terrorist ambushed her and killed her in cold blood. Esther's father, Binyamin, gave us a warm welcome. He told us he really likes the name "Tag Meir" and asked everyone to let the security forces—and them alone, not Jewish vigilantes—handle the response and the security. When we asked him if Arab members of Tag Meir could come to the pay their respects, he replied, "Of course." The Horgan family received phone calls of support from people in Wadi Ara.** Ziad Sabatin, a Palestinian Tag Meir member from the town of Husan, near Gush Etzion,*** came to pay his respects to the Horgan family together with Israeli friends. The family welcomed them and were moved by the visits.

The camaraderie in times of both sorrow and happiness that takes place during Tag Meir's solidarity visits can lead to real acceptance, by both sides, that we are all human beings born in the image of God and that the time has come for peace.

---

* Women Wage Peace is, as it sounds, a grassroots movement of Israeli and Palestinian women demanding that their leaders pursue peace.

** Wadi Ara is a heavily Arab region in northern Israel.

*** Husan is a Palestinian town in the West Bank, located near the city of Bethlehem and Gush Etzion, a large bloc of Israeli settlements.

Between the Jordan River and the Mediterranean Sea, there are two nations, a Jewish people and a Palestinian people. We are not going to throw the Palestinians out into the desert, and they aren't going to throw us into the sea. The faster we accept the fact that we have no choice but to live together, the better it will be for both sides. This is true for secular and religious folks, for both those who have lived in this land for generations and for those among us who arrived in Israel more recently from the former Soviet Union and Ethiopia. Instead of investing our energies in hate, we all have to invest our energies in learning one another's languages, histories, pain, and cultures. We have to invest our energies in connection.

Tag Meir believes in the message from Psalms: "Depart from evil, and do good. Seek peace, and pursue it."*

. . .

Maisam, Mutasim, and Gadi—three very different people, one common commitment to work for a different, better, shared future for Israel. Each of them taking small but powerful steps to try to heal and build a bridge. Next time you read or see or hear something depressing or discouraging about the potential for peace and reconciliation in this over-promised, too-holy land (and you will); the next time you lose hope and start to give in to despair that things will never be better, think of them and take courage.

There is room on the raft for everyone living between the river and the sea. They haven't given up. Neither should we.

---

* Gadi Gvaryahu, relayed via email message to the author, Dec. 28, 2020.

A LEXICON OF THE CONFLICT

LANGUAGE IS POLITICAL, important, and confusing. How people refer to the geography of, wars fought during, or parties to the conflict often says a lot about where they're coming from, both literally and figuratively. Here we define some key terms.

Declaration of the Establishment of the State of Israel. Israel does not have a formal written constitution, so its Declaration of Independence of May 14, 1948, while not binding law, serves as its founding document, laying out a vision for the country. The heart of the Declaration, the part that describes the founders' idea of what Israel should be, is the thirteenth paragraph:

> The State of Israel will be open for Jewish immigration and for the Ingathering of the Exiles; it will foster the development of the country for the benefit of all its inhabitants; it will be based on freedom, justice and peace as envisaged by the prophets of Israel; it will ensure complete equality of social and political rights to all its inhabitants irrespective of religion, race or sex; it will guarantee freedom of religion, conscience, language, education and culture; it will safeguard the Holy Places of all religions; and it will be faithful to the principles of the Charter of the United Nations.

Diaspora. Refers to the exile and dispersion of Jews from the **Land of Israel** and to the Jewish community outside Israel today. It also refers to the dispersion of any group from its homeland and its community outside that homeland. So, there is, for example, both a Jewish and a Palestinian diaspora.

Druze. An Arabic-speaking ethnoreligious community in Israel, Lebanon, Syria, and Jordan. Druze do not consider themselves Muslim and are seen as a distinct subgroup within the Arab-Israeli community. The largest Druze communities are in the North of the country, and unlike most other Arabic-speaking citizens of Israel, a majority of male Druze Israelis serve in the **IDF**. Druze, a minority group wherever they find themselves, are traditionally loyal to the country in which they live.

Fatah. An acronym in Arabic for Palestine National Liberation Movement, a secular, nationalist Palestinian political party. Fatah joined the **PLO** in 1967, and it is the dominant force there. It is also the dominant party in the **Palestinian Authority**.

Gaza (or Gaza Strip). A narrow coastal strip of territory running between Israel and Egypt and the Mediterranean Sea that is almost completely cut off from the Palestinians in the **West Bank** and, indeed, from the rest of the world. Gaza is one of the most crowded places on earth, with 1.8 million Palestinians crammed into 140 square miles. In the misery Olympics, Gaza is a perennial contender for a medal. It was a part of British Mandate–era Palestine that came under Egyptian control as a result of the 1947–48 war. Israel captured Gaza during the 1967 war and built **settlements** there. Tellingly, Anwar Sadat, who was willing to break with the Arab world to get back the Sinai, was not keen on seeing Gaza returned to Egypt. He was perfectly happy to let the Israelis deal with the territory.

Palestinians claim Gaza as part of a future Palestinian state, and as a result of the **Oslo** peace process in 1994, the Palestinian Authority took control of civil matters in Gaza. Israel unilaterally withdrew from the territory in 2005. Since 2007, Gaza has been controlled by the authoritarian militant Islamist group **Hamas**, which displaced the Palestinian Authority after several days of fighting. Israel maintains an air, sea, and land blockade of Gaza, and Israel and Egypt tightly limit the entry and exit of goods and civilians through their border crossings. Since 2008, Gaza and Israel have engaged in repeated clashes, resulting in thousands of Palestinian and dozens of Israeli civilian deaths.

Golan Heights (or Golan). A high plateau in southwestern Syria overlooking the Galilee region in northern Israel. Syrian forces on the Golan and Israeli forces below clashed frequently in the decades following the 1948 Arab-Israeli War. Israel captured the western two thirds of the Golan from Syria during the Six-Day War in 1967. It began building **settlements** there in the 1970s, and in 1981, it extended Israeli law to the occupied territory, essentially annexing it. With the exception of the United States under Donald Trump, who recognized Israeli annexation in 2019, the rest of the world considers the Golan Israeli-occupied territory. Today, about twenty thousand **Druze** (still formally citizens of Syria) live in the Golan (tens of thousands of others fled or were forced out during the fighting in 1967); they are considered permanent residents of Israel under Israeli law. Around twenty-two thousand Israeli settlers live in communities built in the Golan since 1967. Most Israeli settlers who live in the Golan today see themselves as pragmatists, as opposed to ideologues or religio-nationalists, playing an important role in protecting Israel from the threat of Syrian aggression and, since Syria's descent into civil war, chaos.

Greater Land of Israel. More politically loaded than the **Land of Israel** (see below), the name is usually used by right-wing and/or (see above) **religio-nationalist** Israelis and their supporters to describe the territory they would like the State of Israel to one day control. Maps of "the Greater Land of Israel," which have been used by right-wing Zionist and Israeli groups since the early twentieth century, often show an aspirational Israel that includes Israel, the **West Bank**, **Gaza**, Jordan, and parts of Syria, Egypt, Saudi Arabia, and other nearby counties.

Green Line. Also called "the pre-1967 border," "the 1967 border," or "the 1948 armistice lines." Named for the color of the ink used to draw it, the Green Line refers to the armistice lines drawn between Israel and its neighbors in 1949 after the War of Israeli Independence/Palestinian **Nakba.** The territory Israel controlled at the end of the war "within the Green Line" (about 78 percent of historic Palestine) was ultimately recognized by the nations of the world as part of the new State of Israel.

Beyond the Green Line lay the **West Bank**, controlled by Jordan. The Green Line also went right through the city of **Jerusalem**, dividing it into Israeli West Jerusalem and Jordanian East Jerusalem. Israel captured the territories to the east of the Green Line in the Six-Day War of 1967, and since that time the international community has viewed the Green Line as the border between Israel and the Israeli-occupied Palestinian territories.

Hamas. An Arabic acronym for "Islamic Resistance Movement"; refers to a militant Islamist Palestinian political movement. It contains both a social service wing and a military wing. It is the main political rival of **Fatah** and has controlled **Gaza** since 2007. During this time, it has been involved in several localized wars with Israel in which thousands of Palestinians in Gaza have been killed. Israel, the United States, the European Union, and many other countries consider Hamas (or, at least, its military wing) a terrorist organization.

Hebrew. I know you know what Hebrew is. I've included it here to provide some guidance on how to pronounce its trickiest sound. When transliterating a Hebrew word in English, I use the letters *ch* for the Hebrew letter *chet*. It's pronounced *not* like the *ch* in the word *choice*, but rather, with a stronger *h* sound; more like the *ch* in the Scots-Gaelic word *loch* (as in "Loch Ness Monster") or the German word *achtung* (as in the U2 album *Achtung Baby*). So, the Hebrew letter *chet* isn't pronounced like the name "Chet" (as in the Prince of Cool, Chet Baker), but rather, like . . . well you get the point.

IDF, Israel Defense Forces. The Israeli military.

Intifada. Literally, "shaking off" in Arabic. Refers to the two distinct Palestinian uprisings against Israeli occupation and military rule in the **West Bank** and **Gaza.** The First Intifada, which lasted from 1987 to 1991 (some say 1993), was a series of protests, demonstrations, strikes, and riots, occasionally violent—stones and Molotov cocktails were thrown at **IDF** security forces; IDF forces responded with overwhelming force. The Second Intifada, which lasted from 2000 to 2005, was far more violent, with militants carrying out multiple terrorist attacks on Israeli civilians and fighting with IDF troops and IDF responding with massive force and reoccupying parts of the occupied territories from which it had withdrawn troops during the **Oslo Accords.**

Israel. The State of Israel, established in 1948, is a parliamentary democracy with just over 9.1 million citizens, about 74 percent of whom are Jewish and 20 percent Arab. Israel's internationally accepted borders were established by the 1949 Armistice Lines at the end of the first Arab-Israeli War. What the borders of Israel *should* be remains a source of disagreement and contention.

Jerusalem (East and West). The capital of Israel, a holy city to Jews, Christians, and Muslims. It was the focus of yearning for Jews for thousands of years during their **diaspora**; Jews end the Passover seder celebration with the words "next year in Jerusalem." West Jerusalem is mostly Jewish. East Jerusalem is traditionally mostly Arab, and it includes the Old City, the ancient historic core of the Holy City.

At the end of the 1948 War of Israeli Independence/Palestinian **Nakba**, the armistice line (the **Green Line**) ran right through the middle of the city: Israel held the (mostly Jewish) western half of the city, Jordan the (mostly Arab) east—including the Old City, whose Jewish residents were forced out by Jordanian troops. Nineteen years later, during the Six-Day War, Israel captured the eastern half of the city (including the Old City). Israel then annexed East Jerusalem, but this annexation was not recognized by the international community. Israel also unilaterally expanded the municipal boundaries of the city to include large swaths of land in the West Bank, and it built enormous new Jewish neighborhoods that ring

the city on this territory. While Israel considers Jerusalem its capital, most countries in the world keep their embassies in Tel Aviv, because of the unresolved status of the eastern part of the city, which Palestinians call Al Quds ("the Holy," in Arabic) and claim as the capital of a future Palestinian state. These countries indicate that they will move their embassies to Jerusalem when that status is resolved in a final peace agreement. In 2017, President Donald Trump broke with that long-standing consensus and moved the U.S. embassy to Jerusalem.

Knesset. The parliament of Israel. It has 120 seats, and in order to govern, the political party that wins the most seats in an election must assemble a coalition of parties that includes at least 61 seats. No party in Israeli history has ever gained 61 seats on its own, and so every Israeli government has, by definition, been a coalition government. This has resulted in Israeli governments in which the larger parties are often reliant on, and beholden to, smaller, more extreme "special interest" parties to form governing coalitions.

Land of Israel. The traditional Jewish name for a geographically undefined area that includes Israel and the **West Bank** as well as additional territories mentioned in the Hebrew Bible. Usually used in a religious or cultural context, it's somewhat akin to the name "the Holy Land" (which is how many Christians, as well as others, refer to the same basic territory) or "the Promised Land." Also used by Israeli settlers as a designation of the land that they regard as sacred and part of God's plan.

Nakba. Arabic for "Catastrophe"; how Palestinians refer to the 1947–48 war that Israelis refer to as their "War of Independence." "The Catastrophe" refers to the defeat, forced displacement, and dispossession of the Palestinian Arabs, hundreds of thousands of whom either found themselves as stateless refugees or living under Israeli military rule.

Old City of Jerusalem. The Old City is made up of four traditional "quarters": Armenian, Christian, Jewish, and Muslim. It also contains the holiest site in Judaism and the third-holiest in Islam, which the Jews call the **Temple Mount** (Har ha-Bayit) and Muslims, "the Noble Sanctuary" (Haram al-Sharif).

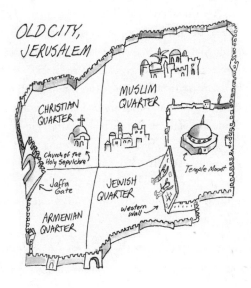

Oslo Accords (aka "Oslo," aka "the peace process"). The agreements between Israel and the **Palestinian Liberation Organization**, signed and sealed by the famous handshake on the White House Lawn by Israeli prime minister Yitzhak Rabin, PLO chairman Yasser Arafat, and U.S. president Bill Clinton in 1993, which initiated the official Israeli-Palestinian peace process. Called "the Oslo Accords" because the preliminary secret negotiations took place in the Norwegian capital, the agreements resulted in PLO recognition of Israel's right to exist, Israel's recognition of the PLO as the sole representative of the Palestinian people, the creation of the **Palestinian Authority**, and ultimately and at least officially, a commitment on the part of both parties to a two-state solution. The process was meant to resolve outstanding issues between Israel and the Palestinians (including borders; the status of **Jerusalem**, which both parties claim as their capital; the future of Israeli **settlements** in the occupied territories; and the question of the rights of Palestinian refugees and their descendants). These issues were never resolved: the Oslo peace process ran aground after the assassination of Rabin in 1995, the failure of a 2000 summit at Camp David, and the outbreak that year of the Second **Intifada**.

Palestinians. The Arab inhabitants of what was, until Israel's establishment in 1948, Palestine. Today the name is usually applied to Arab residents of the **West Bank** and **Gaza**, though many Arab citizens of Israel identify as Palestinian and refer to themselves as "Palestinian Israelis" or "Palestinian citizens of Israel." A majority of Palestinians are Sunni Muslim; a minority are Christian. Some Palestinian Arabs are Bedouin, nomadic people who live mostly in the deserts of the region. To make matters more complicated, prior to 1948, Jewish residents of Palestine, including the Zionists, were referred to as—you guessed it—Palestinians. And as if *that* weren't enough, some supporters of Israel insist that there is no such thing as a Palestinian people. This is contrary to history and common sense, but this conflict tends to do that to people.

Palestinian Authority (PA) (or Palestinian National Authority). An interim Palestinian self-governing body established in 1994 as a result of the

Oslo Accords between Israel and the **Palestine Liberation Organization**. It is controlled by the Palestinian political party **Fatah**, the dominant force in the PLO. The PA was created to handle civil affairs in the areas under its control. It was supposed to be in existence for just five years, until a final resolution of the status of the territory could be achieved, but because of the breakdown in the peace process following the Second **Intifada** of 2000, it still operates today. It is headquartered in Ramallah, in the **West Bank**.

Palestine Liberation Organization (PLO). Founded in 1964, the PLO began as the national liberation movement of the Palestinian people, an organization dedicated to the liberation of Palestine from Israel through armed struggle. In its early decades, under the leadership of the charismatic Yasser Arafat, it engaged in terrorism and armed attacks against the **IDF** from its bases in neighboring Arab countries. In 1988, its leadership declared its support for the two-state solution. In 1993, the PLO formally recognized Israel's right to exist and called off its armed struggle. In return, Israel recognized the PLO as the sole representative of the Palestinian people, meaning it is the official body with which Israel and the rest of the world negotiates. In 1996, the PLO removed from its official charter language about armed struggle and the destruction of Israel. The relationship between the PA and the PLO is not always totally clear, but the PA is meant to be responsible for local governance in the Palestinian territories, the PLO for international relations. Like his predecessor, Arafat, the PLO's current chairman, Mahmoud Abbas, is also the president of the **Palestinian Authority**.

Road Map for Peace (aka "Road Map"). A George W. Bush–initiated 2002 attempt by "the Quartet" (the United States, the United Nations, the European Union, and Russia) to revive the peace process after Oslo's collapse two years earlier and to resolve the Israeli-Palestinian conflict through the establishment of a two-state solution. Both sides signed on to the idea in principle, but after years of fruitless negotiations, the Road Map collapsed in the wake of the massive Israeli attack on **Gaza** in response to **Hamas** rocket and missile fire into Israel in 2008.

Settlements. Jewish communities built in the territory conquered by Israel during the Six-Day War of 1967. During the Six-Day War, Israel captured the West Bank and East **Jerusalem** (both from Jordan), the **Gaza Strip** and the Sinai Peninsula (both from Egypt), and the **Golan Heights** (from Syria). Israel set up military bases and civilian settlements in all the captured territories. The international community considers the settlements illegal under the Fourth Geneva Convention.

After it signed a peace treaty with Egypt in 1979, Israel returned the Sinai Peninsula and uprooted its settlements there. Similarly, after it unilaterally withdrew from the Gaza Strip in 2005, it razed its settlements there and brought the nine thousand or so Jewish settlers back to Israel proper.

For the purposes of this book, "settlements" (as well as "settlers," "settlement enterprise," and "settlement project") refers to the Israeli civilian centers established in the West Bank and East Jerusalem after 1967. Around 650,000 Israeli Jews live in these communities east of the Green Line. Some argue that because Israel unilaterally annexed East Jerusalem after the war, a distinction should be made between the settlements established in the West Bank (which was not annexed) and the new Jewish neighborhoods built post-1967 in East Jerusalem. But while it is true that Israel governs these two territories differently (since it considers East Jerusalem to be a part of a unified Israeli city), it is important to keep two things in mind here: First, after the Six-Day War, Israel not only annexed East Jerusalem, but also expanded the boundaries of the city to include territory deep in the occupied West Bank. Second, Israel's expansion and annexation of East Jerusalem is not recognized by the international community (including the United Nations, the United States, the European Union, and Russia).

"State of Palestine." Is there one? In 1988, after it declared that it supported a two-state solution with Israel, the PLO announced the establishment of the "State of Palestine," made up of the **West Bank**, **Gaza**, and East **Jerusalem**. This was more a PR stunt than an actual declaration of independence; after all, the PLO controlled zero percent of Palestine in

1988. In 1994, the **Palestinian Authority** was established to handle civil affairs in the territories it controlled as a result of the **Oslo** peace process. In 2012, the UN General Assembly voted to upgrade the status of Palestine to "non-member observer state." In 2013, the PA began referring to the "State of Palestine" in its official documents.

However, Israel does not recognize the existence of a "State of Palestine"; nor do the United States, Canada, Mexico, Australia, Japan, and most of the EU countries, all of whom support a two-state solution and say they will withhold recognition of a Palestinian state until that is achieved. Still, 138 of the 193 members states of the United Nations (and the Holy See, the Vatican) recognize the existence of a "State of Palestine," represented by the PA on the ground and the PLO abroad.

Temple Mount. Known as "Har ha-Bayit" in Hebrew and "Haram al-Sharif" ("Noble Sanctuary") in Arabic, a hill in the southeast of the **Old City of Jerusalem**. It is topped by a thirty-seven-acre man-made plaza (built during the time of Herod the Great, in the first century B.C.E.), on which the Second Jewish Temple, destroyed by the Romans, once stood—Jewish tradition has it that the First Temple, built by King Solomon, also stood there—and on which now stand the Muslim holy sites of the Dome of the Rock and Al-Aqsa Mosque. The hill is fortified by retaining walls, one of which, on the western side, is the Western Wall.

Wars (and what to call them). Since its inception, Israel has been involved in many clashes with its neighbors and in five or six major wars. And while it is true that, in general, the name the victors use for a war tends to stick, when it comes to the wars between Israel and its neighbors, things are sometimes more complicated. As is often true with Israel, what you call these wars can say a lot about who you are and what "side" you might be on. Here's a quick look at how some of the major wars are described by the parties and their partisans—and by everyone else.

1947–48: Israel's "War of Independence" is the Palestinians' "Catastrophe" ("Nakba" in Arabic). Each is true for the respective party. This war is also called "the 1947–48 Arab-Israeli War" and "the First Arab-Israeli War."

1956: The Israeli invasion of Egypt's Sinai Peninsula (supported by France and the United Kingdom, which then entered the fray) is usually referred to as "the Suez Crisis" or "the Second Arab-Israeli War." Israelis call this "the Sinai War." In the Arab world, it is sometimes known as "the tripartite aggression."

1967: Israel launches a preemptive strike when, after weeks of bellicose rhetoric coming out of Cairo and Damascus, Egypt closes the Straits of Tiran to Israeli shipping and demands that UN peacekeepers leave their posts keeping the sides apart (which they do). Israelis and many others call this "the Six-Day War." (You can guess why.) In the Arab world, it is described variously as "the Setback" ("An-Naksah" in Arabic) or "the June War." It is also called "the 1967 Arab-Israeli War" and "the Third Arab-Israeli War."

1968–70: Known as "the War of Attrition," a prolonged and inconclusive series of clashes and battles initiated by Egyptian president Nasser in an attempt to retake the Sinai Peninsula back from Israel. See "Second" and "Third" Arab-Israeli wars.

1973: Egypt and Syria shock Israel with a surprise attack that Israel ultimately repulses. Israelis call this "the Yom Kippur War." (Again, you can guess why.) Arabs call it "the Ramadan War" (same) or "the October War" (ditto). It is also referred to as "the 1973 Arab-Israeli War" and "the Fourth Arab-Israeli War."

1982: Israel invades Lebanon. Initially called "Operation Peace for Galilee," and then "the Lebanon War," or "the First Lebanon War," by the Israelis. Called "the Invasion" by the Lebanese. Everyone else calls it "the 1982 Lebanon War."

2006: Israel invades Lebanon again. Israel calls this "the Second Lebanon War," and Lebanon, "the July War." Also known as "the 2006 Lebanon War" and "the 2006 Israel-Hezbollah War."

2006–present: Gaza-Israel conflict. Starting with Israeli disengagement from and **Hamas** takeover of **Gaza** in 2005, there have been several intense rounds of fighting between Israel and Gaza. Israelis call the 2008–9 clash "Operation Cast Lead"; in the Arab world, it is known as "the Gaza Massacre." There was another major round of fighting in 2012; the **IDF** called that "Operation Pillar of Defense," and Hamas called it "Operation Stones of Shale." The IDF called the 2014 round of fighting "Operation Protective Edge," while others referred to it as "the 2014 Gaza War." The year 2018 saw massive Palestinian protests near the border fence between Gaza and Israel. May 2021 saw the worst round of fighting since 2014; the IDF called it "Operation Guardian of the Walls," and Hamas called it the "Sword of Jerusalem Battle." An estimated 3,650 Gazans have been killed in these clashes, many of them civilians. Almost two hundred Israelis, most of them soldiers, have also been killed.

West Bank (aka "occupied territories," aka "disputed territories," aka "administered territories," aka "occupied Palestinian territories," aka "Palestine," aka "Judea and Samaria," aka "areas A, B, and C"). All these names refer to the land between the Jordan River and the **Green Line**, captured by Israel from Jordan during the 1967 Six-Day War. Among 2.8 million Palestinians, about six hundred and fifty thousand Jewish Israeli civilians live in Israeli **settlements** in the West Bank and **Jerusalem**—behind the Green Line. The name you use to describe this territory can say a lot about what you think. For the purposes of this book, I refer to the territory in question (for the most part) as "the West Bank." This is the most neutral, least political, and most internationally used of the names I've just listed. It is, in fact, wonderfully literal: it simply refers to the land between the western bank of the Jordan River and the Green Line in Israel. I also use the slightly more charged "occupied territories," which has the benefit of being simple and accurate and which also reflects the general international consensus. Although some Israelis and supporters of Israel reject the designation "occupied," they are largely alone in this; the rest of the world recognizes the territories as occupied Palestinian territory.

Under the **Oslo Accords**, the West Bank was divided into three administrative areas: A, B, and C. Area A includes the major Palestinian cities, the bulk of the Palestinian population, but only 18 percent of the territory. It is administered by the **Palestinian Authority (PA)**, which is responsible for maintaining security and providing everyday services (e.g., trash collection, policing, and mail delivery). But the cities and towns of Area A are not contiguous. They are isolated from one another and surrounded by Israeli-controlled territory. The Israeli shekel is the local currency, and despite the PA's having responsibility for internal security and policing, Israeli security forces retain the right to operate throughout Area A. But there are no Israeli settlements there (with the exception of the Jewish neighborhood/settlement built in the heart of the city of Hebron), and for the most part, Israel forbids its citizens from entering the territory.

Area B is under PA civil authority and joint Palestinian-Israeli security control. It comprises just over 20 percent of the territory of the West Bank and includes no Israeli settlements. There are more than four hundred Palestinian villages in Area B. The vast majority of the 2.8 million Palestinians living in the West Bank are crammed into areas A and B.

Area C is under full Israeli civil and security control and comprises about 61 percent of the territory of the West Bank. It also contains most of the open space and natural resources in the West Bank. All Israeli settlements (about 135, with another 100 unofficial settler "outposts") are located here, as are Israeli army bases, nature reserves, and roads intended only for the settlers. In the early 1970s, a few thousand settlers lived in Area C. Today, over 400,000 do, alongside between 150,000 and 300,000 Palestinians. Israeli policy makes it extremely difficult for Palestinians to obtain building permits in Area C, and the vast majority of the territory and its resources is reserved for Israeli use only.

As you can see on the map, areas A, B, and C are all mixed together, turning the map of the West Bank into something resembling a slice of Swiss cheese. Israel controls travel between the three areas of the West Bank through its military presence and checkpoints. Israel also controls who crosses from the West Bank into Israel proper. And Israel, not the Palestinian Authority, controls the single crossing point between the West Bank into neighboring Jordan.

Many Israelis, including Israeli officialdom and some of Israel's more hard-line and religious supporters abroad, refer to the territories by their biblical names, "Judea" and "Samaria," the south and north of the West Bank, respectively. The normalization of these names in Israeli discourse is a linguistic victory of sorts by Israel's right wing. By harkening back to the origins of the Jewish story, these names suggest that the territories are an integral part of both the biblical **Land of Israel** (which they are) and also the modern State of Israel (which officially, even according to Israel, they are not) and seek to legitimize Israel's claim to the land and settlement presence there. This rankles many Palestinians and critics of Israel's settlement policy, who see it as an act of linguistic appropriation or imperialism. The international community* does not employ these names to refer to the West Bank.

Some Israelis simply refer to the West Bank as "the Territories."

Many Palestinians and their supporters refer to the West Bank (plus **Gaza** and, indeed, sometimes the State of Israel) as "Palestine." This was the name of the Roman province that included what is now Israel and the West Bank. Despite the fact that Israel maintains de facto control over the West Bank, more than 130 countries have officially recognized the **"State of Palestine."** The United States and the European Union have not yet done so, and the matter is currently being debated at the United Nations, which has granted "non-member observer status" to what it now refers to as the "State of Palestine." (It used to refer to "the Palestinian Territories,

---

* "International community" refers to the broad group of countries and governments, international organizations and associations, and individuals that share a basic common view of things such as civil and human rights and the authority of the United Nations and other international bodies.

occupied"; I know this is confusing.) Use of the name "Palestine" rankles many on the pro-Israel side, who see it as, at best, premature and, at worst, an act of linguistic appropriation or imperialism. The rankling is exacerbated when the name is used in reference to the territory that makes up the entire State of Israel, not just the West Bank and Gaza.

Yishuv ("the Settlement"). The Hebrew name for the Jewish community in Palestine prior to the establishment of the State of Israel in May 1948. Sometimes the name "Old Yishuv" is used to describe the Palestinian Jewish community that predated the arrival of the Zionists in the late nineteenth century, while "New Yishuv" refers to the community established by the waves of Zionist immigration.

West Bank barrier (aka "separation barrier," "security fence," "separation wall," and "apartheid wall"). Refers to the barrier (in some places, a high concrete wall; in others, fencing) that Israel is constructing to separate Israel proper (and Israeli **settlements** in the West Bank closer to the border of Israel proper) from Palestinian population centers. The barrier

The Wall

runs on or near the **Green Line** in some areas and winds deep into the West Bank in others. Israelis began building the West Bank barrier during the Second **Intifada** in 2002 and claims that the goal of the barrier is to keep suicide bombers out of Israel. Palestinians and others claim that its true intention is to separate and segregate Israelis and Palestinians while making a de facto land grab of Palestinian territory in the West Bank that lies on the "Israeli" side of the barrier. As with so many aspects of this conflict, there is probably some truth to both these positions.

Zionism. The belief that the Jewish people should be able establish a national homeland in the ancestral territory of "Zion"—what is now Israel—and the movement dedicated to realizing that belief.

ACKNOWLEDGMENTS

My profound thanks:

To Nancy Miller (who understood this book even before I'd written it), Ben Hyman, Morgan Jones, Barbara Darko, Emily Fisher, Lauren Ollerhead, Marie Coolman, Nicole Jarvis, and the entire team at Bloomsbury, along with Jenna Dolan, Elizabeth Van Itallie, Tanya Heinrich, and Harvey Lee Gable, for their enthusiasm and faith and for making this process painless, exciting, and fun.

To Charlotte Sheedy, the best advocate, ally, and agent I could've asked for. And to Ally Sheedy for her early read and thoughtful feedback.

To Serra Falk Goldman, George Goldman, and Pietro Bonanno for their love and friendship, and for providing me with the perfect place to write the end to this book.

To Sam Counter and Alex Kurtzman for believing in this project from before the beginning, and for providing me with the perfect place to start it.

To Anne Germanacos and Robert Mailer Anderson for their generosity and hospitality.

To the Moore Institute at the National University of Ireland, Galway.

To the many Israelis and Palestinians who have been my teachers and guides—especially Mutasim Ali, Amal al-Jafawi, Elah Alkalay, Jaber Asakla, Sharon Avraham Weiss, Hillel Ben Sasson, Vadim Blumin, David Broza, Avrum Burg, Naomi Chazan, Yossi Dahan, Robi Damelin, Itsik Danziger, David Ehrlich, Hagai El-Ad, Amal Elsana Alh'jooj, Nabila Espaniloa, Yitzhak Frankenthal, Ron Gerlitz, Avner Gvaryahu, Gadi Gvaryahu, Nasreen Hadad Haj-Yahya, Ronit Heyd, Rami Hod, Anat Hoffman, Hassan Jabereen, Maisam Jaljuli, Fida Jiryis, Rachel Liel, Menachem Lorberbaum, Mikhael Manekin, Fathi Marshood, Merav

Michaeli, Yonatan Mizrahi, Jessica Montell, Shula Mula, Achinoam Nini, Yuli Novak, Ayman Odeh, Yudith Oppenheimer, Debra Pell, May Pundak, Talia Sasson, Michael Sfard, Alice Shalvi, Yehuda Shaul, Yael Sternhell, Bassam Tamimi, Nathan Thrall, Reem Younis, Sawsan Zaher.

To David, Joanie, Yiftach, Amir, Maayan, Roee, and Keren Yogev (and their ever-growing clan), my home team—and my home—in Israel.

To my colleagues and friends who offered wisdom, comments, critiques, advice, and assistance whenever I asked (and sometimes when I didn't, but should have)—especially Sultan Abu Obaid, Peter Beinart, Jeremy Ben-Ami, Shira Ben Sasson, Ben Brandzel, Becky Buckwald, Paul Egerman, Hannah Ellenson, Mickey Gitzen, Andrew Goldblatt, Sharon Goldtzvik, Jill Jacobs, David Katznelson, Libby Lenkinski, Daniel Levy, Merav Mizrachi, Max Reinhardt, Harry Reiss, Steve Rothman, Seth Rubin (for artistic inspiration), Susan Sawicki, Esther Sivan, Jennifer Spitzer, Gideon Stein, Mary Ann Stein, and Yuval Yavneh.

To the board, staff, and grantees of the New Israel Fund, who inspire me with their commitment to work, every day, to build a better, fairer Israel.

To Peter Dreier, Brian Lurie, Aaron David Miller, Taylor Norman, and Niall Ó Dochartaigh for the time they spent helping me wrestle with some of the thornier parts of this book. I am incredibly grateful.

To David Myers, for his friendship, guidance, and close, critical, and careful read of this book.

To Daniel Handler, for his cheerleading, coaching, cooking, and companionship during our numerous writing retreats, and for insisting that the idea for this book become a reality.

To Christopher Noxon, for his partnership and passion, and for making this book more beautiful than I ever imagined it could be.

And in memory of Stephen Reinhardt and Ramona Ripston, whose epic passion for justice continues to inspire my own.

To my mom, Ann, and my brother, Andrew, who read various versions of this manuscript and offered love, support, and plenty of constructive criticism (both during the writing process and over the course of my life).

And in memory of my father, Sy, who shared my fascination with Israel, and who would have been so proud and pleased to see this book. I am incredibly lucky to come from our family.

To my daughters, Noa and Zoe, the bright and shining lights of my life.

And to Dana Reinhardt, the real author in the family, my love and partner, and the best person I know. Thank you for making me do this, and for making our lives so beautiful.

BIBLIOGRAPHY

Ajami, Fouad. *The Arab Predicament: Arab Political Thought and Practice Since 1967*. Cambridge, UK: Cambridge University Press, 1992.

———. *The Dream Palace of the Arabs: A Generation's Odyssey*. New York: Pantheon, 1998.

Avishai, Bernard. *The Hebrew Republic*. San Diego, CA: Harcourt, 2008.

Beinart, Peter. "The Failure of the American Jewish Establishment." *New York Review of Books*, June 10, 2010. https://www.nybooks.com/articles/2010/06/10/failure-american-jewish-establishment/.

Benvenisti, Meron. *Sacred Landscape: The Buried History of the Holy Land Since 1948*. Translated by Maxine Kaufman-Lacusta. Berkeley: University of California Press, 2000.

Bollens, Scott A. *On Narrow Ground: Urban Policy and Ethnic Conflict in Jerusalem and Belfast*. Albany, NY: SUNY Press, 2000.

Brenner, Michael. *In Search of Israel: The History of an Idea*. Princeton, NJ: Princeton University Press, 2018.

Carroll, James. *Constantine's Sword: The Church and the Jews*. Boston: Houghton Mifflin Company, 2001.

Chabon, Michael, and Ayelet Waldman, eds. *Kingdom of Olives and Ash: Writers Confront the Occupation*. New York: Harper Perennial, 2017.

Cleveland, William L. *A History of the Modern Middle East*. Boulder, CO: Westview Press, 1994.

Darwish, Mahmoud. *Why Did You Leave the Horse Alone?* Brooklyn, NY: Archipelago Books, 2006.

Djerejian, Edward, Marwan Muasher, Nathan J. Brown et al. "Two States or One? Reappraising the Israeli-Palestinian Impasse." Carnegie Endowment for International Peace, 2018. https://carnegieendowment.org/files/CarnegieBaker_Palestine_Finalı.pdf.

Dowty, Alan. *Israel/Palestine.* 3rd ed. Cambridge, UK: Polity, 2012.

Ephron, Dan. *Killing a King: The Assassination of Yitzhak Rabin and the Remaking of Israel.* New York: W. W. Norton, 2015.

Ezrachi, Yaron. *Rubber Bullets: Power and Conscience in Modern Israel.* Berkeley: University of California Press, 1997.

Friedman, Thomas. *From Beirut to Jerusalem.* New York: Anchor Books, 1989.

Gilbert, Martin. *Jerusalem History Atlas.* New York: Macmillan, 1977.

Goldberg, J. J. *Jewish Power: Inside the American Jewish Establishment.* New York: Basic Books, 1997.

Goldberg, Jeffrey. "Arafat's Gift." *New Yorker*, Jan. 22, 2001. https://www.newyorker.com/magazine/2001/01/29/arafats-gift.

Gorenberg, Gershom. *The Accidental Empire: Israel and the Birth of the Settlements, 1967–1977.* New York: Times Books, 2006.

———. *The End of Days: Fundamentalism and the Struggle for the Temple Mount.* New York: Free Press, 2000.

———. *The Unmaking of Israel.* New York: Harper Perennial, 2012.

Grossman, David. *Death as a Way of Life.* London: Picador, 2003.

———. *Sleeping on a Wire: Conversations with Palestinians in Israel.* New York: Farrar, Straus and Giroux, 1993.

———. *The Yellow Wind.* London: Picador, 1987.

Harkabi, Yehoshafat. *Israel's Fateful Hour.* New York: Harper and Row, 1988.

Heller, Mark A., and Sari Nusseibeh. *No Trumpets, No Drums: A Two-State Settlement of the Israeli-Palestinian Conflict.* New York: Hill and Wang, 1991.

Hertzberg, Arthur, "Israel: The Tragedy of Victory." *New York Review of Books*, May 28, 1987.

———. *The Zionist Idea.* 16th ed. Philadelphia, PA: JPS, 1986.

Jabotinsky, Ze'ev. *The Iron Wall.* Original in Russian, *Razsviet*, Apr. 11, 1923. http://en.jabotinsky.org/media/9747/the-iron-wall.pdf.

Katz, Elihu, Shlomit Levy, and Jerome M. Segal. "The Status of Jerusalem in the Eyes of Israeli Jews." Center for International and Security Studies, University of Maryland, Baltimore, 1997.

Knell, Yolande. "Israel's First Settlement University Stirs Controversy." *BBC News*, July 17, 2012. https://www.bbc.com/news/world-middle-east-18879786.

Laqueur, Walter. *A History of Zionism.* New York: Schocken Books, 1989.

Lustick, Ian S. *Paradigm Lost: From Two-State Solution to One-State Reality.* Philadelphia: University of Pennsylvania Press, 2019.

Mendes-Flohr, Paul R., and Jehuda Reinharz, eds. *The Jew in the Modern World: A Documentary History.* New York: Oxford University Press, 1980.

Montefiore, Simon Sebag. *Jerusalem: The Biography*. New York: Vintage Books, 2011.

Morris, Benny. *The Birth of the Palestinian Refugee Problem*. Cambridge, UK: Cambridge University Press, 1987.

———. *Righteous Victims: A History of the Zionist-Arab Conflict, 1881–2001*. New York: Vintage Books, 2001.

Nusseibeh, Sari. *Once Upon a Country: A Palestinian Life*. London: Picador, 2008.

"On 1948." Interview with Benny Morris. YouTube, Mar. 1, 2018. https://www.youtube.com/watch?v=YzN3hHEvGdc.

Oren, Michael. *Six Days of War: June 1967 and the Making of the Modern Middle East*. Oxford: Oxford University Press, 2002.

Oz, Amos. *How to Cure a Fanatic*. Princeton, NJ: Princeton University Press, 2002.

———. *In the Land of Israel*. Translated by Maurie Goldberg-Bartura. San Diego, CA: Harvest, 1983.

———. *Israel, Palestine and Peace*. New York: Vintage Books, 1994.

Pawel, Ernst. *The Labyrinth of Exile: A Life of Theodor Herzl*. London: Vintage Publishing, 1990.

Pfeffer, Anshel. *Bibi: The Turbulent Life and Times of Benjamin Netanyahu*. Toronto: McClelland and Stewart, 2018.

Pressman, Jeremy. "Visions in Collision: What Happened at Camp David and Taba." *International Security* 28, no. 2 (Fall 2003): 5–43.

Rabin, Yitzhak. *The Rabin Memoirs*. Translated by Dov Goldstein. Berkeley: University of California Press, 1996.

Rabinovich, Abraham. *The Yom Kippur War: The Epic Encounter that Transformed the Middle East*. New York: Schocken Books, 2004.

Rabinovich, Itamar. *Yitzhak Rabin: Soldier, Leader, Statesman*. New Haven, CT: Yale University Press, 2017.

Reinharz, Jehuda. *Chaim Weizmann: The Making of a Zionist Leader*. Oxford: Oxford University Press, 1985.

Remnick, David. "Seeds of Peace: Ayman Odeh's Unlikely Crusade." *New Yorker*, Jan. 25, 2016. https://www.newyorker.com/magazine/2016/01/25/seeds-of-peace.

Ross, Dennis. *The Missing Peace: The Inside Story of the Fight for Middle East Peace*. New York: Farrar, Straus and Giroux, 2004.

Sachar, Howard M. *A History of Israel*. 2nd ed. New York: Alfred A. Knopf, 1996.

Sadat, Camelia. *My Father and I*. New York: Macmillan, 1985.

Said, Edward. *Orientalism*. New York: Vintage Books, 1979.

———. *The Politics of Dispossession: The Struggle for Palestinian Self-Determination, 1969–1993*. New York: Pantheon, 1994.

Savir, Uri. *The Process: 1,000 Days that Changed the Middle East*. New York: Vintage, 1998.

Scheindlin, Dahlia. "The Logic Behind Israel's Democratic Erosion." The Century Foundation, May 29, 2019. https://tcf.org/content/report/logic-behind-israels-democratic-erosion/.

Segev, Tom. *A State at Any Cost: The Life of David Ben-Gurion*. Translated by Haim Watzman. London: Apollo, 2019.

Sfard, Michael. *The Gate and the Wall: Israel, Palestine, and the Legal Battle for Human Rights*. New York: Metropolitan Books, 2018.

Shapira, Anita. *Ben Gurion: Father of Modern Israel*. Translated by Anthony Berris. New Haven, CT: Yale University Press, 2014.

———. *Land and Power: The Zionist Resort to Force, 1881–1948*. Redwood City, CA: Stanford University Press, 1999.

Shavit, Ari. "The General." *New Yorker*, Jan. 15, 2006. https://www .newyorker.com/magazine/2006/01/23/the-general-5.

———. *My Promised Land*. New York: Spiegel and Grau, 2013.

Shikaki, Khalil, and Dahlia Scheindlin. "The Role of Public Opinion in the Resilience/Resolution of the Palestinian-Israeli Conflict." Palestinian Center for Policy and Survey Research, Jan. 2019. Pcpsr .org/en/node/742.

Simon, Leon ed. *Selected Essays of Ahad Ha-'am*. New York: Atheneum, 1981.

Smith, Charles D. *Palestine and the Arab-Israeli Conflict*. 3rd ed. New York: St. Martin's Press, 1996.

Tessler, Mark. *A History of the Israeli-Palestinian Conflict*. Bloomington: University of Indiana Press, 1994.

Thrall, Nathan. *The Only Language They Understand: Forcing Compromise in Israel and Palestine*. New York: Metropolitan Books, 2017.

Van Creveld, Martin. *The Sword and the Olive: A Critical History of the Israeli Defense Force*. New York: PublicAffairs, 1998.

Wright, Lawrence. *Thirteen Days in September: Carter, Begin, and Sadat at Camp David*. New York: Alfred A. Knopf, 2014.

Yehuda, Limor et al. *One Rule, Two Legal Systems: Israel's Regime of Laws in the West Bank*. Tel Aviv: Association for Civil Rights in Israel, Oct. 2014. https://law.acri.org.il/en/wp-content/uploads/2015/02/Two -Systems-of-Law-English-FINAL.pdf.

NOTES

INTRODUCTION

5 what the historian Benny Morris has called "righteous victims": Benny
Morris, *Righteous Victims: A History of the Zionist-Arab Conflict,
1881–2001* (New York: Vintage Books, 2001).

8 looked up to see a massive commercial jetliner fly low from the
east: Bruce Riedel, "25 Years On, Remembering the Path to Peace
for Jordan and Israel," Brookings.edu, Oct. 23, 2019, https://www
.brookings.edu/blog/order-from-chaos/2019/10/23/25-years-on
-remembering-the-path-to-peace-for-jordan-and-israel/.

CHAPTER 1: JEWS AND ISRAEL: WHERE DO WE START?

19 Whether Sephardic or Ashkenazi, Jews were the ultimate outsiders:
James Carroll, *Constantine's Sword: The Church and the Jews* (Boston:
Houghton Mifflin Company, 2001), 243.

21 new form of hatred became known in 1879 as antisemitism: Carroll,
Constantine's Sword, 447.

CHAPTER 2: THE ZIONIST IDEA: ORGANIZING,
IMMIGRATING, BUILDING (1860S–1917)

23 About twenty-five thousand Jews, overwhelmingly Sephardic and
traditionally religious: Howard M. Sachar, *A History of Israel*, 2nd ed.
(New York: Alfred A. Knopf, 1996), 24.

25 It was his time in Vienna and what he saw in Paris: Walter Laqueur, *A
History of Zionism* (New York: Schocken Books, 1989), 90.

25 including Argentina and East Africa (in what is now Kenya): Laqueur, *A History of Zionism*, 126–28.

28 argued in his essay "The Iron Wall (We and the Arabs)": Ze'ev Jabotinsky, *The Iron Wall* (Original in Russian, *Razsviet*, Apr. 11, 1923), http://en.jabotinsky.org/media/9747/the-iron-wall.pdf.

29 "In every Cabinet where the prime minister is a Jew": Michael Brenner, *In Search of Israel: The History of an Idea* (Princeton, NJ: Princeton University Press, 2018), 115.

30 their bicultural vision remains the Zionist road not taken: Laqueur, *A History of Zionism*, 161–71.

34 In his masterpiece *In the Land of Israel:* Amos Oz, *In the Land of Israel*, trans. Maurie Goldberg-Bartura (San Diego: Harvest, 1983), 148.

CHAPTER 3: WAIT, THERE WERE PEOPLE HERE: WHAT ABOUT THE PALESTINIANS?

35 "a land without a people for a people without a land": Anita Shapira, *Land and Power: The Zionist Resort to Force, 1881–1948* (Redwood City, CA: Stanford University Press, 1999), 42.

35 One school of thought has today's Palestinians descending directly: Mark Tessler, *A History of the Israeli-Palestinian Conflict* (Bloomington: University of Indiana Press, 1994), 69–70.

36 More recent and serious scholarship suggests: Alan Dowty, *Israel/Palestine*, 3rd ed. (Cambridge, UK: Polity, 2012), 221.

39 Palestinian Arab nationalism began to take shape in part as a result of: Charles D. Smith, *Palestine and the Arab-Israeli Conflict*, 3rd ed. (New York: St. Martin's Press, 1996), 36.

CHAPTER 4: THE BRITISH ARE COMING: WORLD WAR I,
THE BALFOUR DECLARATION, AND THE ESTABLISHMENT
OF THE BRITISH MANDATE (1917–39)

45   it adhered, at least in theory: Sachar, *A History of Israel*, 214.

46   The IDF inherited the concept of "purity of arms": "Protecting Our
Home: Maintaining Purity of Arms," Israel Defense Forces, Mar. 30,
2016. https://www.idf.il/en/minisites/press-releases/protecting-our
-home-maintaining-purity-of-arms/.

49   there were already almost half a million Jews: Smith, *Palestine and the
Arab-Israeli Conflict*, 107.

50   "aid the English in their war as if there were no White Paper [i.e.,
no British restrictions on immigration], and we must stand against
the White Paper as if there were no war.": Tom Segev, *A State at Any
Cost: The Life of David Ben-Gurion*, trans. Haim Watzman (London:
Apollo, 2019), 288.

53   But Ben-Gurion: Sachar, *A History of Israel*, 267.

53   By 1947, the population of Palestine was about 1.8 million people:
Smith, *Palestine and the Arab-Israeli Conflict*, 136.

CHAPTER 5: ISRAEL AND THE NAKBA: INDEPENDENCE
AND CATASTROPHE (1947–49)

56   There, they massacred between 100 and 250 people: Tessler, *A History
of the Israeli-Palestinian Conflict*, 291.

56   Prominent Jews in the United States, among them Nobel Laureate
Albert Einstein: Ruth Schuster, "1948: N.Y. Times Publishes Letter
by Einstein, Other Jews Accusing Menachem Begin of Fascism,"
Haaretz, Apr. 12, 2014, https://www.haaretz.com/jewish/.premium
-1948-n-y-times-letter-by-einstein-slams-begin-1.5340057.

57 As Begin later bragged, there is little doubt that the massacre: "On 1948," interview with Benny Morris, YouTube, Mar. 1, 2018, video, 14:10, https://www.youtube.com/watch?v=YzN3hHEvGdc.

57 some defenders of Israel's image deny that it even occurred: Eliezer Tauber, "*Deir Yassin*: There Was No Massacre," *Times of Israel*, May 28, 2018, https://blogs.timesofisrael.com/deir-yassin-the-end-of-a-myth/.

58 "The declaration of the new state by David Ben-Gurion": Gene Currivan, "Zionists Proclaim New State of Israel," *New York Times*, May 15, 1948, https://archive.nytimes.com/www.nytimes.com/library/world/480515israel-state-50.html.

59 "We hereby declare the establishment of a Jewish state": Anita Shapira, *Ben Gurion: Father of Modern Israel*, trans. Anthony Berris (New Haven, CT: Yale University Press, 2014), 162.

CHAPTER 6: THE DISPOSSESSED

65 In his memoir, former prime minister Yitzhak Rabin writes: Yitzhak Rabin, *The Rabin Memoirs*, trans. Dov Goldstein (Berkeley: University of California Press, 1996), 383–84.

68 The historical evidence suggests a more complicated story: "On 1948," 6:40–7:40.

68 and indeed, no serious evidence has been found that such broadcasts were made: "On 1948," 8:00–9:06.

68 in the mixed Arab-Jewish city of Haifa, the Jewish mayor: Tessler, *A History of the Israeli-Palestinian Conflict*, 302.

68 Golda Meir, a high-ranking official and future prime minister: David Margolick, "Endless War," review of *1948: A History of the First Arab-Israeli War*, by Benny Morris, *New York Times*, May 4, 2008, https://www.nytimes.com/2008/05/04/books/review/Margolick-t.html.

68 But historians are divided over whether there was a master plan: "On 1948," 5:17; Segev, *A State at Any Cost*, 416–21.

68 Some Israeli historians argue that without the forced population transfers: Ari Shavit, "Survival of the Fittest," *Haaretz*, July 1, 2004, https://www.haaretz.com/1.5262454.

75 "Sure, God promised it to us, but what does that matter to them?": Nahum Goldmann, *The Jewish Paradox*, trans. Steve Cox (New York: Grosset & Dunlap, 1978), 99.

CHAPTER 7: THE FIFTIES: STATE BUILDING AND SUEZ

76 His vehicle for accomplishing this was his concept of *mamlachtiut*: Shapira, *Ben-Gurion: Father of Modern Israel*, 174.

78 "Israel in the early 60s was afraid that from the west would come a bad wind of sex, alcohol and rock'n'roll": Toni O'Loughlin, "Truth After 42 Years: Beatles Banned for Fear of Influence on Youth," *The Guardian*, Sept. 21, 2008, https://www.theguardian.com /world/2008/sep/22/israelandthepalestinians.thebeatles.

78 He was also intent on overcoming the ideological tensions, rivalries, and factionalism that had led to clashes among Zionist groups: Shapira, *Ben-Gurion: Father of Modern Israel*, 174.

78 radio broadcast programs listing the names of survivors: Greer Fay Cashman, "Radio Program Aids Search for Holocaust Survivors," *Jerusalem Post*, Nov. 5, 2007, https://www.jpost.com/israel/radio -program-aids-search-for-holocaust-survivors.

80 hundreds of thousands of Mizrachi immigrants were sent to transit camps: Sachar, *A History of Israel*, 403–5.

80 The 1950s saw civil unrest in Haifa and elsewhere: Sachar, *A History of Israel*, 422.

81 Some claim that the reason hummus and falafel are considered the national dishes: Reem Kassis, "Here's Why Palestinians Object to the Term 'Israeli food': It Erases Us from History," *Washington Post*, February 14, 2020, https://www.washingtonpost.com/lifestyle/food /heres-why-palestinians-object-to-the-term-israeli-food-it-erases-us -from-history/2020/02/14/96974a74-4d25-11ea-bf44-f5043eb3918a story.html.

81 An authoritarian and a fierce advocate of pan-Arab nationalism: Tessler, *A History of the Israeli Palestinian Conflict*, 338.

CHAPTER 8: THE BIG BANG: THE 1967 WAR AND THE REALITY IT CREATED

87 Syria mocked Nasser for his opposition to Fatah's operations: Smith, *Palestine and the Arab-Israeli Conflict*, 190–92.

88 liberate Palestine in a "revolutionary manner.": Smith, *Palestine and the Arab-Israeli Conflict*, 191.

89 It's still unclear why the Soviets did this: Tessler, *A History of the Israeli-Palestinian Conflict*, 385–86.

90 but he still seems to have believed he could make bold moves: Smith, *Palestine and the Arab-Israeli Conflict*, 197.

90 Nasser then announced that Egypt wouldn't fire the first shot: Tessler, *A History of the Israeli-Palestinian Conflict*, 393; Smith, *Palestine and the Arab-Israeli Conflict*, 198.

91 the head of the PLO declared that Israel was about to be destroyed: Tessler, *A History of the Israeli-Palestinian Conflict*, 393.

91 They wanted the opportunity to destroy, once and for all: Gershom Gorenberg, *The Accidental Empire: Israel and the Birth of the Settlements, 1967–1977* (New York: Times Books, 2006), 32.

92 he stammered and mumbled: Gorenberg, *The Accidental Empire*, 29.

95 he knew that joining the war was a mistake: Associated Press, "Jordan's King Calls '67 War a Big Blunder," *New York Times*, June 6, 1997, https://www.nytimes.com/1997/06/06/world/jordan-s-king-calls-67-war-a-big-blunder.html.

95 "Do you want to set the Middle East on fire?": Yossi Klein Halevi, "The Astonishing Israeli Concession of 1967," *Atlantic*, June 7, 2017, https://www.theatlantic.com/international/archive/2017/06/israel-paratroopers-temple-mount-1967/529365/.

97 Israeli leaders declared that Israel would trade at least some of (but not all) the land: Sachar, *A History of Israel*, 673–74.

101 an almost legendary figure emerged from self-imposed retirement to warn his fellow countrymen: Arthur Hertzberg, "The Tragedy of Victory," *New York Review of Books*, May 28, 1987, https://www.nybooks.com/articles/1987/05/28/israel-the-tragedy-of-victory/.

CHAPTER 9: ROLLER COASTER: FROM THE YOM KIPPUR WAR TO THE FIRST INTIFADA (1968–87)

112 "millionaires lolling around their swimming pools": Diana Bahur-Nir, "Swimming in Cash: These Socialist Millionaires Make Robots to Clean the Pools of the World's Wealthy," *Calcalist*, Aug. 22, 2020, https://www.calcalistech.com/ctech/articles/0,7340,L-3846072,00.html.

116 "Have you weaned yourself of your off-putting proclivity for not telling the truth?": Ethan Bronner, "The Bulldozer," review of *ARIK: The Life of Ariel Sharon*, by David Landau, *New York Times*, Feb. 12, 2014, https://www.nytimes.com/2014/02/16/books/review/arik-the-life-of-ariel-sharon-by-david-landau.html.

120 replace the Israeli military administration in the West Bank with a civil administration: Smith, *Palestine and the Arab-Israeli Conflict*, 262–63.

120 Sharon sought to transform Lebanon: Sachar, *A History of Israel*, 901–2; Smith, *Palestine and the Arab-Israeli Conflict*, 267–69.

123 On September 26, four hundred thousand outraged Israelis: William E. Farrell, "Israelis, at Huge Rally in Tel Aviv, Demand Begin and Sharon Resign," *New York Times*, Sept. 26, 1982, https://www .nytimes.com/1982/09/26/world/israelis-at-huge-rally-in-tel-aviv -demand-begin-and-sharon-resign.html.

124 had initiated a war of choice as opposed to necessity: Nathan Thrall, *The Only Language They Understand: Forcing Compromise in Israel and Palestine* (New York: Metropolitan Books, 2017), 29.

124 Begin, broken and depressed, resigned as prime minister: Thrall, *The Only Language They Understand*, 29.

CHAPTER 10: SHAKING IT OFF: THE FIRST INTIFADA

131 land near Palestinian villages was expropriated: Gorenberg, *The Accidental Empire*, 80–86.

131 Israeli control of the aquifers beneath the West Bank: "The Occupation of Water," Amnesty International, Nov. 29, 2017, https:// www.amnesty.org/en/latest/campaigns/2017/11/the-occupation-of -water/; Tessler, *A History of the Israeli-Palestinian Conflict*, 521.

132 a university of sorts, where they learned doctrines of Palestinian nationalism: Khaled al-Azraq, "The Prison as University: The Palestinian Prisoners' Movement and National Education," *Al Majdal* 42 (Autumn 2009), http://www.badil.org/en/publication /periodicals/al-majdal/item/1267-the-prison-as-university-the -palestinian-prisoners'-movement-and-national-education.html.

132 Israel brought back the old British Mandate-era practice of punitive home demolitions: Michael Sfard, *The Gate and the Wall: Israel,*

Palestine, and the Legal Battle for Human Rights (New York: Metropolitan Books, 2018), 49–51.

133 avoided the Arab parts of the city entirely: Tessler, *A History of the Israeli-Palestinian Conflict*, 687.

135 I looked at a series of surveys taken during the 1990s: Elihu Katz, Shlomit Levy, and Jerome M. Segal, "The Status of Jerusalem in the Eyes of Israeli Jews," Center for International and Security Studies, University of Maryland, Baltimore, 1997.

138 The goals of the intifada, the coordinators said: Tessler, *A History of the Israeli-Palestinian Conflict*, 690.

139 Rabin is said to have ordered IDF troops to "break the bones": "Israel Declines to Study Rabin Tie to Beatings," *New York Times*, July 12, 1990, https://www.nytimes.com/1990/07/12/world/israel-declines -to-study-rabin-tie-to-beatings.html.

145 Arafat announced that the PLO had "accepted the existence of Israel as a state in the region": Steve Lohr, "Arafat Says P.L.O. Accepted Israel," *New York Times*, Dec. 8, 1988, https://www.nytimes .com/1988/12/08/world/arafat-says-plo-accepted-israel.html.

CHAPTER 11: ISRAEL IS WAITING FOR RABIN

151 "an important step which is needed in our days": "Yisrael Baytneu Leader Liberman [*sic*] Lauds Public Transport on Shabbat," *Jerusalem Post*, Nov. 23, 2019, https://www.jpost.com/breaking -news/yisrael-beiteinu-leader-liberman-lauds-public-transport-on -shabbat-608730.

152 "In the current reality there are only two options": Itamar Rabinovich, *Yitzhak Rabin: Soldier, Leader, Statesman* (New Haven, CT: Yale University Press, 2017), 174.

152 Rabin believed that Israel could not continue to rule indefinitely: Dan Ephron, *Killing a King: The Assassination of Yitzhak Rabin and the Remaking of Israel* (New York: W. W. Norton, 2015), 30.

153 Rabin ordered a freeze on settlement building: Gershom Gorenberg, *The Unmaking of Israel* (New York: Harper Perennial, 2012), 124–25.

154 "What can we do? Peace you don't make with your friends": Dennis Ross, *The Missing Peace: The Inside Story of the Fight for Middle East Peace* (New York: Farrar, Straus and Giroux, 2004), 92.

156 The goal of the peace process that began at Oslo was a two-state solution: Ephron, *Killing a King*, 31 ("As [Rabin's chief of staff, Eitan] Haber[,] would point out some two decades later, no one internalized this better than Rabin. 'I can tell you that no doubt he understood immediately that signing such an accord … in the end it will [lead to] a Palestinian state'"); Ross, *The Missing Peace*, 104 ("The two struck up an implicit bargain: 'statehood for security'").

158 "I am shamed over the disgrace imposed upon us by a degenerate murderer": Clyde Haberman, "West Bank Massacre," *New York Times*, Mar. 1, 1994, https://www.nytimes.com/1994/03/01/world/west-bank-massacre-overview-rabin-urges-palestinians-put-aside-anger-talk.html.

159 "We must fight terrorism as if there's no peace process": Martin Indyk, "The Strategic Legacy of Yitzhak Rabin," *Wall Street Journal*, Nov. 4, 2020, https://www.wsj.com/articles/the-strategic-legacy-of-yitzhak-rabin-11604512743.

164 Extremist rabbis even issued fatwah-like religious rulings declaring that Rabin was a *rodef* (a "pursuer"): Ephron, *Killing a King*, 106–7.

165 Rabin knew that there would be fierce, even violent, backlash: Uri Savir, *The Process: 1,000 Days that Changed the Middle East* (New

York: Vintage, 1998), 154. Savir, Israel's chief negotiator with the PLO from 1993 to 1996, recounts a meeting between Rabin and Arafat in 1994 in which Rabin said, "Public opinion is rebellious in Israel. There are calls among the Jews to kill me."

165 Some Likud leaders seemed to contribute: Savir, *The Process*, 255; Ephron, *Killing a King*, 143.

165 a mock coffin bearing the inscription RABIN WILL BURY ZIONISM: "Netanyahu Can't Wash His Hands that Led to Rabin's Murder," *Haaretz*, Nov. 13, 2016, https://www.haaretz.com/opinion/editorial -netanyahu-can-t-wash-his-hands-of-incitement-1.5461189.

165 Netanyahu presided from a balcony as supporters burned pictures of Rabin: Ephron, *Killing a King*, 163.

166 They urged him to wear a bulletproof vest: Ephron, *Killing a King*, 145.

168 In his jacket pocket was a pack of Parliaments and a sheet with the lyrics: Serge Schmemann, "Assassination in Israel: The Overview," *New York Times*, Nov. 5, 1995, https://www.nytimes.com/1995/11/05 /world/assassination-israel-overview-rabin-slain-after-peace-rally-tel -aviv-israeli.html; Ephron, *Killing a King*, 185.

168 He recounted how Rabin, the quintessential Israeli, had not known how to wear a tie: "Assassination in Israel; Words of Grief and Resolve from Friends and World Leaders," *New York Times*, Nov. 7, 1995, https://www.nytimes.com/1995/11/07/world/assasination-in-israel -words-of-grief-and-resolve-from-friends-and-world-leaders.html.

170 a quiet condolence call on Rabin's widow: Savir, *The Process*, 261–62.

170 reported that when he heard the news of the assassination, he wept: Dexter Filkins, "Shot in the Heart," *New Yorker*, Oct. 19, 2015, https:// www.newyorker.com/magazine/2015/10/26/shot-in-the-heart.

CHAPTER 12: AS THE CLEVER HOPES EXPIRE:
THE END OF OSLO

173 and felt he knew America well: Anshel Pfeffer, *Bibi: The Turbulent Life and Times of Benjamin Netanyahu* (Toronto: McClelland and Stewart, 2018), 92.

174 Barak was brilliant and cerebral: Ross, *The Missing Peace*, 495.

176 This frustrated the Palestinians: Ross, *The Missing Peace*, 591–92.

177 They didn't feel ready, nor that the time for such a summit was ripe: Ross, *The Missing Peace*, 632–33.

177 Clinton promised him that he would not be blamed: Aaron David Miller (who served as U.S. Deputy Special Middle East Coordinator in the Clinton Administration and as the Senior Advisor on Arab-Israeli Negotiations to Secretary of State Colin Powell), conversation with the author, Mar. 1, 2021.

177 Israel offered the Palestinians the most ambitious proposal yet: Jeremy Pressman, "Visions in Collision: What Happened at Camp David and Taba," *International Security* 28, no. 2 (Fall 2003): 8.

178 The Israeli and American narrative is that Barak offered the Palestinians: Pressman, "Visions in Collision," 9–15.

178 Arafat, this line of reasoning goes, was simply unwilling to close the deal: Ross, *The Missing Peace*, 757–58.

178 The counternarrative put forward both by Palestinian negotiators: Pressman, "Visions in Collision," 33–37.

178 As some Palestinians observed: Pressman, "Visions in Collision," 22.

179 Moreover, the Americans only consulted with and involved key Arab states on the issue: Miller, conversation with the author, Mar. 1, 2021.

179 As is the case with most aspects of this conflict, there is truth to all sides of the story: Pressman, "Visions in Collision," 15–33, 37–40.

180 He owned a house, bedecked by huge Israeli flags: Thomas L. Friedman, "In Jerusalem, Sharon Apartment Creates a Stir," *New York Times*, Dec. 31, 1987, https://www.nytimes.com/1987/12/31/world /in-jerusalem-sharon-apartment-creates-a-stir.html.

180 as an even *bigger* provocation, given who Sharon was: Ari Shavit, "The General," *New Yorker*, Jan. 16, 2006, https://www.newyorker.com /magazine/2006/01/23/the-general-5.

181 an assertion, argued a major Palestinian leader in Jerusalem: Joel Greenberg, "Sharon Touches a Nerve, and Jerusalem Explodes," *New York Times*, Sept. 29, 2000, https://www.nytimes.com/2000/09/29 /world/sharon-touches-a-nerve-and-jerusalem-explodes.html.

182 One of the most harrowing images from the beginning of the unrest: William A. Orme Jr., "A Young Symbol of Mideast Violence," *New York Times*, Oct. 2, 2000, https://www.nytimes.com/2000/10/02 /world/a-young-symbol-of-mideast-violence.html.

183 The image of one of the murderers holding up his bloody hands in triumph: "Palestinians Kill Two Israeli Soldiers in Police Custody," *New York Times*, Oct. 12, 2000, https://www.nytimes .com/2000/10/12/world/palestinians-kill-2-israeli-soldiers-in-police -custody-200010129216405052.html.

183 At the meeting, the outgoing president read aloud out his plan to a rapt room full of American, Palestinian, and Israeli negotiators. He made it clear the proposal would no longer be valid when he left office: Miller, conversation with the author, Mar. 1, 2021. Miller told me that as President Clinton read the proposal out loud (the White House did not provide meeting attendees with copies of the plan), "I'd never seen so many Israelis and Palestinians write so quickly."

184 The "broad principle," as Clinton put it, for Jerusalem was Palestinian sovereignty over Arab parts: Ross, *The Missing Peace*, 743, 752–53.

185 clearly "outside the parameters Clinton offered": Miller, conversation with the author, Mar. 1, 2021.

185 At the end of the Taba Summit, the negotiators issued a joint statement: Pressman, "Visions in Collision," 9.

CHAPTER 13: THE BULLDOZER'S LAST SURPRISE

188 As for Arafat, he and the Palestinian Authority did little to prevent these attacks: Ross, *The Missing Peace*, 730–33.

188 Rather, they attempted to use the unrest to improve their bargaining position: Miller, conversation with the author, Mar. 1, 2021.

191 Sharon rejected the deal out of hand: Marwan Muasher, "The Death of the Arab Peace Initiative?" *Atlantic*, Nov. 23, 2011, https://www.theatlantic.com/international/archive/2011/11/the-death-of-the-arab-peace-initiative/248910/.

191 "The idea that we can continue holding under occupation—and it is occupation; you might not like this word, but it's really an occupation": Kelly Wallace, "Sharon: 'Occupation' Terrible for Israel, Palestinians," CNN.com/world, May 23, 2003, https://www.cnn.com/2003/WORLD/meast/05/26/mideast/.

192 "I have made up my mind to make a real effort to arrive at a real agreement": Shavit, "The General."

192 Israel could not remain a democracy and a Jewish state while holding on to all the territory: Bronner, "The Bulldozer."

194 He, no doubt, intended to withdraw from at least some parts: Shavit, "The General."

195   The Second Lebanon War was something of a debacle for Israel: Amos Harel, "Israel's Second Lebanon War Remains a Resounding Failure," *Haaretz*, Dec. 7, 2016, https://www.haaretz.com/israel-news/.premium.MAGAZINE-israels-second-lebanon-war-remains-a-resounding-failure-1.5407519.

195   The radical Lebanese militant group had increased its power and prestige in Lebanon and beyond: William Booth, "Ten Years After Last Lebanon War, Israel Warns Next One Will Be Far Worse," *Washington Post*, July 23, 2016, https://www.washingtonpost.com/world/middle_east/ten-years-after-last-lebanon-war-israel-warns-next-one-will-be-far-worse/2016/07/23/58d7a6ca-4388-11e6-a76d-3550dba926ac_story.html.

196   at one point, his approval rating stood at 3 percent: Matt Gutman, "Olmert: Should He Stay or Should He Go?" ABC News, Apr. 30, 2007, https://abcnews.go.com/International/story?id=3101808&page=1.

CHAPTER 14: THE DEMOCRACY RECESSION

200   "Democracy Index" has consistently ranked Israel as a "flawed democracy," not a full one: Economist Intelligence Unit, "Democracy Index: 2010," Economist Intelligence Unit, https://graphics.eiu.com/PDF/Democracy_Index_2010_web.pdf.

201   Israel had certainly had rightist coalitions before, but this: Gorenberg, *The Unmaking of Israel*, 213–14; Yossi Alpher, "Who Rules Israel?" *International Herald Tribune*, Apr. 22, 2010, https://www.nytimes.com/2010/04/23/opinion/23iht-edalpher.html.

203   began a campaign of public, political, and legal intimidation: Gorenberg, *The Unmaking of Israel*, 215.

203 Right-wing GONGOs first attacked the New Israel Fund: Gorenberg, *The Unmaking of Israel*, 215–17.

203 right-wing members of the Knesset threatened a parliamentary inquiry: Gorenberg, *The Unmaking of Israel*, 216.

203 GONGOs launched an online video campaign featuring pictures of prominent human rights activists: Peter Beaumont, "Rightwing Israeli Group Accused of McCarthyism over Anti-artist Campaign," *Guardian*, Jan. 28, 2016, https://www.theguardian.com/world/2016/jan/28/israel-im-tirtzu-accused-mccarthyism-anti-artist-campaign.

204 Made it a civil offense for Israelis to call for a boycott of Israel or its settlements: Jonathan Lis, "Israel Passes Law Banning Calls for Boycott," *Haaretz*, Nov. 7, 2011, https://www.haaretz.com/1.5026309; Jonathan Lis, "Israel's Travel Ban: Knesset Bars Entry to Foreigners Who Call for Boycott of Israel or Settlements," https://www.haaretz.com/israel-news/.premium-israel-bars-entry-to-foreigners-who-call-for-boycott-of-settlements-1.5445566.

204 Punished Arab municipalities and institutions for commemorating: Jack Khoury and Jonathan Lis, "Human Rights Groups Petition High Court to Overthrow 'Nakba Law,'" *Haaretz*, Apr. 5, 2011, https://www.haaretz.com/1.5007904.

205 Allowed certain communities to ban "undesirables": Gorenberg, *The Unmaking of Israel*, 218.

205 Restricted the activities of human and civil rights organizations: Holly Young, "Israel: Some NGOs Are Seen as "The Enemy from the Inside," *Guardian*, May 11, 2016, https://www.theguardian.com/global-development-professionals-network/2016/may/11/israel-some-ngos-are-seen-as-the-enemy-from-the-inside.

204 Permanently prioritized Israel's Jewish character over its democratic character: David M. Halbfinger and Isabel Kirschner, "Israeli Law

Declares the Country 'Nation-State of the Jewish People,'" *New York Times*, July 19, 2018, https://www.nytimes.com/2018/07/19/world /middleeast/israel-law-jews-arabic.html.

206 "began with buses, continued with supermarkets and reached the streets": Ruth Pollard, "When Women and Girls Are the Enemy," *Sydney Morning Herald*, Nov. 21, 2011, https://www.smh.com.au /world/when-women-and-girls-are-the-enemy-20111118-1nn4d.html.

206 as Israel became more populist, more ethnonationalist, more illiberal, Netanyahu continued his strong support for the settlement enterprise: Dahlia Scheindlin, "The Logic Behind Israel's Democratic Erosion," The Century Foundation, May 29, 2019, https://tcf.org /content/report/logic-behind-israels-democratic-erosion/.

207 "the establishment of Israeli civilian settlements in the West Bank is not, per se, inconsistent with international law": Josh Lederman and Abigail Williams, "Israeli Settlements Don't Violate International Law, in Major Policy Reversal," NBC News, Nov. 18, 2019, https://www.nbcnews.com/politics/politics-news/u-s-says -israeli-settlements-don-t-violate-international-law-n1085146.

207 in January 2020, the Trump administration released its "Peace to Prosperity" plan: Daniel Estrin, "Netanyahu Plans to Annex Parts of the West Bank. Many Israeli Settlers Want It All," NPR, June 18, 2020, https://www.npr.org/2020/06/18/878305307/netanyahu-plans-to -annex-parts-of-the-west-bank-many-israeli-settlers-want-it-al.

208 By December, the unity government was in a state of collapse: Isabel Kershner, "Israeli Government Collapses, Forcing Fourth Election in Two Years," *New York Times*, December 22, 2020, https:// www.nytimes.com/2020/12/22/world/middleeast/israel-election -netanyahu.html.

208 But as he prepared to present his "Change Coalition" to Israel's president: Mazal Mualem, "Israeli's Security Crisis Has New Political Team Sweating," *Al-Monitor*, May 11, 2021, https://www.al-monitor .com/originals/2021/05/israels-security-crisis-has-new-political -team-sweating.

209 the case was slated to be heard: Nir Hasson, "Sheikh Jarrah Eviction Case Nears Decision: Israel's Top Court Gives Attorney General Two-week Deadline," *Haaretz*, May 26, 2021, https://www.haaretz. com/israel-news/.premium-israel-s-top-court-gives-ag-2-weeks-to -submit-opinion-on-sheikh-jarrah-evictions-1.9843694.

209 Israeli police prevented Palestinians from gathering in the plaza in front of the Damascus Gate: Patrick Kingsley, "After Years of Quiet, Israeli-Palestinian Conflict Exploded. Why Now?" *New York Times*, May 15, 2021, https://www.nytimes.com/2021/05/15/world /middleeast/israel-palestinian-gaza-war.html.

209 Realizing the situation had gotten out of hand: Kingsley, "After Years of Quiet, Israeli-Palestinian Conflict Exploded. Why Now?"

209 Autocratic, increasingly unpopular amongst the Gazans they ruled: Somdeep Sen, "Hamas Wasn't Behind the Jerusalem Protests, So Why Is It Fighting?" *Washington Post*, May 18, 2021, https://www. washingtonpost.com/politics/2021/05/18/hamas-wasnt-behind -jerusalem-protests-so-why-is-it-fighting/

210 the fighting triggered the first serious intercommunal mob violence: Declan Walsh and Eric Nagourney, "Warnings of 'Civil War' as Arabs and Jews Face Off Violently in Israel's Streets," *New York Times*, May 13, 2021, https://www.nytimes.com/live/2021/05/13/world/israel -gaza-news.

210 But that message was tempered this time by other voices: Nicholas Fandos and Catie Edmendson, "Democrats, Growing More Skeptical

of Israel, Pressure Biden," *New York Times*, May 17, 2021, https://www
.nytimes.com/2021/05/17/us/politics/israel-gaza-democrats-biden.
html.

CHAPTER 15: THE MAP IS NOT THE TERRITORY

213 a dedicated effort at political and demographic wishful thinking: The
battle over language, place names, and signs continues to this day,
although it's moved from graffiti and vandalism to the highest levels
of the Israeli government. Barak Ravid, "In Arabic and in Hebrew,
a Name Is More than Just a Name," *Haaretz*, Dec. 15, 2011, https://
www.haaretz.com/1.5219712.

214 "there isn't even a single stone of the Old City of Jerusalem that is
Jewish": Jeffrey Goldberg, "Arafat's Gift," *New Yorker*, Jan. 22, 2001,
https://www.newyorker.com/magazine/2001/01/29/arafats-gift.

214 Yasser Arafat alleged, completely falsely, that there was no evidence
that a Jewish Temple: Ross, *The Missing Peace*, 718.

214 insisting that there is no such thing as a Palestinian people: Tessler, *A
History of the Israeli-Palestinian Conflict*, 444.

214 Palestinian Arabs all came to the region in the last couple of
centuries: Many examples of this ahistorical claim can be found
in right-wing media outlets. Here's an example: Daniel Grynglas,
"Debunking the Claim that 'Palestinians' Are the Indigenous People
of Israel," *Jerusalem Post*, May 12, 2015, https://www.jpost.com/blogs
/why-world-opinion-matters/are-arabs-the-indigenous-people-of
-palestine-402785.

214 Official Israeli and Palestinian Authority maps of the territory often
neglect to show the Green Line: "For long periods of time since
1967, the Green Line has been removed from many official and
educational maps. This policy was adopted by David Levy when, as

housing minister back in the 1980s, he wished to make a political statement about the government's intentions to gradually expand the construction of settlements in the West Bank[,] which would effectively constitute a de facto annexation of parts of the area even if the government did not undertake any de jure (legal) moves in this respect." David Newman, "Borderline Views: Putting the Green Line on the Map," *Jerusalem Post*, Feb. 24, 2014, https://www.jpost.com /opinion/columnists/borderline-views-putting-the-green-line-on -the-map-342434.

215 Generations of Palestinian and Israeli kids grow up with maps: Gorenberg, *The Unmaking of Israel*, 67. ("The future of the occupied territories was already the most important political issue in Israel, but maps no longer showed where the occupied territories began. Bored school-children staring at the map on the classroom wall would not learn the shape of their own country. Tel Aviv and Hebron would appear to be part of the same entity.") There is also a debate within the American Jewish community about the use of maps of Israel and the West Bank that do not show the Green Line. Yardain Amron, "Why Do Jewish Camps Erase the Green Line on Israel Maps?" June 30, 2015, https://forward.com/news/310838/how-do-jewish-camps-draw -the-green-line/; Mira Sucharov, "Why Is the Green Line Not on Our School's Maps?" *Canadian Jewish News*, May 6, 2005, https://www .cjnews.com/perspectives/opinions/green-line-not-schools-maps.

215 established by the Ir David Foundation, a right-wing religious- nationalist organization: Bari Weiss, "Can an Archaeological Dig Change the Future of Jerusalem?" *New York Times*, Mar. 30, 2019, https://www.nytimes.com/interactive/2019/03/30/opinion/sunday /jerusalem-city-of-david-israel-dig.html.

216 "a clear political intent, which is to cement permanent Israeli control. And that isn't good for anyone who still has hope for a resolution": Weiss, "Can an Archaeological Dig Change the Future of Jerusalem?"

no actual archaeological evidence: Sarah Wildman, "The Fight for Jerusalem's Past, and Future," *New Yorker*, Aug. 2, 2013, https://www.newyorker.com/news/news-desk/the-fight-for-jerusalems-past-and-future.

216 Israeli archaeologists, concerned about attempts to manipulate the rich archaeological record: Wildman, "The Fight for Jerusalem's Past, and Future." Emek Shaveh (which is supported by the New Israel Fund) describes itself this way: "Emek Shaveh is an Israeli NGO working to defend cultural heritage rights and to protect ancient sites as public assets that belong to members of all communities, faiths and peoples. We object to the fact that the ruins of the past have become a political tool in the Israeli-Palestinian conflict and work to challenge those who use archaeological sites to dispossess disenfranchised communities. We view heritage site as resources for building bridges and strengthening bonds between peoples and cultures and believe that archaeological sites cannot constitute proof of precedence or ownership by any one nation, ethnic group or religion over a given place." https://emekshaveh.org/en/about-us/.

218 Everybody still referred to it by its old Arabic name, "Musrara": David Kroyanker, "Entrepreneur's Dream, Historian's Nightmare," *Haaretz*, Jan. 5, 2006, https://www.haaretz.com/1.4903994.

218 that would have forced the Jerusalem municipality to use the Hebraized neighborhood names: Ofer Aderet, "A Stir Over Sign Language," *Haaretz*, July 29, 2011, https://www.haaretz.com/1.5037062.

CHAPTER 16: ISRAEL'S ARAB CITIZENS: SHARED SOCIETY OR SEGREGATION?

221 Israel's founding document, the Declaration of the Establishment of the State of Israel: "Full Text of Israel's Proclamation of Independence Issued in Tel Aviv," *Jewish Telegraphic Agency*, May 16, 1948.

221 it also extended martial law to those areas: Hussein Ibish, "The Specter of an Arab Israel," *Politico*, Mar. 19, 2015, https://www.politico.com /magazine/story/2015/03/israeli-election-arab-israel-116243_Page2 .html; Sachar, *A History of Israel*, 382–86.

223 But while they are officially equal, in many ways they are not: Tessler, *A History of the Israeli-Palestinian Conflict*, 470.

223 Arab citizens are subject to many kinds of discrimination, informal and official: Ibish, "The Specter of an Arab Israel." Two of the most prominent Israeli NGOs working to catalogue and combat discrimination against Arab citizens of Israel are the Association for Civil Rights in Israel (the Israeli version of the ACLU) and Adalah (Israel's premier Arab civil rights organization). Both have extensive databases about their work on behalf of Israel's Arab citizens. You can access them here: https://law.acri.org.il/en/category/arab-citizens -of-israel/arab-minority-rights/ and https://www.adalah.org/en/tag /index/517?page=4.

224 Arab citizens of Israel are routinely subjected to casual discrimination, humiliating treatment, and interrogation and detention: Noa Landau, "Israeli Diplomat Said Humiliated by Racial Profiling at Ben-Gurion Airport: 'Makes Me Sick,'" *Haaretz*, Apr. 8, 2019, https://www .haaretz.com/israel-news/.premium-israeli-diplomat-humiliated-by -profiling-airport-authority-says-nothingwrong-1.7617552.

225 "the right-wing government is in danger. Arabs are coming out to the polls in droves." Ishaan Tharoor, "On Israeli Election Day, Netanyahu Warns of 'Arabs Voting in Droves,'" *Washington Post*, Mar. 17, 2015, https://www.washingtonpost.com/news/worldviews/wp/2015/03/17 /on-israeli-election-day-netanyahu-warns-of-arabs-voting-in-droves/.

225 "disloyal" Arabs: "Lieberman: Disloyal Israeli Arabs Should Be Beheaded," *Haaretz*, Jan. 10, 2018, https://www.haaretz.com. lieberman-disloyal-israeli-arabs-should-be-beheaded-1.5334458.

225 is now trying to extend the Admissions Committees Law to apply to larger communities: Jonathan Lis, "Bill Expanding Residential Screening Law in Israel Passes Preliminary Vote," *Haaretz*, Dec. 12, 2018, https://www.haaretz.com/israel-news/.premium-bill-to-boost -israeli-community-insularity-passes-preliminary-vote-1.6743230.

226 The true intention of the law: Amir Fuchs, "Israel's Nation-State Law Isn't 'Declarative,' It Does Real Damage," *Haaretz*, Apr. 12, 2020, https://www.haaretz.com/opinion/.premium-israel-s-nation-state -law-isn-t-declarative-it-does-real-damage-1.9345944.

226 that threatens to upend the decades-long, carefully calibrated balance between the Jewish and democratic aspects of Israel's identity: "Nation-State Law Explainer," Israel Democracy Institute, July 18, 2018, https://en.idi.org.il/articles/24241.

227 to register his disapproval: Noga Tarnopolsky, "Israeli President Rebukes Bibi, Signs Controversial 'Nation-State Law' in Arabic," *Daily Beast*, Apr. 9, 2019, https://www.thedailybeast.com/netanyahu -denigrates-arabs-to-try-to-win-re-election-but-israeli-president -rivlin-signs-the-controversial-nation-state-law-in-arabic.

228 Arab Israelis voted at lower rates from 1967 onward: David Halbfinger and Allison McCann, "As Israel Votes Again (and Again), Arabs See an Opportunity, *New York Times*, Feb. 28, 2020, https://www .nytimes.com/2020/02/28/world/middleeast/israel-arabs-election -vote.html.

230 Odeh stands for something new in Israel: David Remnick, "Seeds of Peace: Ayman Odeh's Unlikely Crusade," *New Yorker*, Jan. 25, 2016, https://www.newyorker.com/magazine/2016/01/25/seeds-of-peace.

230 "The day in which hundreds of thousands fill the streets": Ayman Odeh, "Guardian of Democracy," keynote speech, Sept. 13, 2020, New Israel Fund.

CHAPTER 17: A LOVE STORY?
ISRAEL AND THE AMERICAN JEWISH COMMUNITY

234 "The Citizens of the United States of America have a right to applaud": George Washington, "A Reply to the Hebrew Congregation of Newport (c. August 17, 1790)," in Paul R. Mendes-Flohr and Jehuda Reinharz, eds., *The Jew in the Modern World: A Documentary History* (New York: Oxford University Press, 1980), 363.

235 the fiercest critics: J. J. Goldberg, *Jewish Power: Inside the American Jewish Establishment* (New York: Basic Books, 1997), 151.

235 "We consider ourselves no longer a nation, but a religious community": Conference of Reform Rabbis, "The Pittsburgh Platform (1885)," in Mendes-Flohr and Reinharz, eds., *The Jew in the Modern World*, 371–72.

235 "In the rehabilitation of Palestine, the land hallowed by memories and hopes": "The Columbus Platform (1937)," in Mendes-Flohr and Reinharz, eds., *The Jew in the Modern World*, 410–12.

237 couldn't say no to his old friend: Sachar, *A History of Israel*, 302–3.

237 support for and defense of the new country became perhaps *the* central organizing principle: Mendes-Flohr and Reinharz, eds., *The Jew in the Modern World*, 356.

238 American Jewish identity might be a victim of the success of American Jews themselves: Goldberg, *Jewish Power*, 65–67.

239 Today, AIPAC is viewed by many: Goldberg, *Jewish Power*, 224.

240 By 1975, American Jews were giving $1.5 billion: Hannah Shaul Bar Nissim, "Why Jewish Giving to Israel Is Losing Ground," The Conversation, Aug. 15, 2018, https://theconversation.com/why -jewish-giving-to-israel-is-losing-ground-100946.

242 despite tensions: Goldberg, *Jewish Power*, 337–46.

245 highly educated, and overwhelmingly liberal: Frank Newport, "American Jews, Politics, and Israel," Gallup, Aug. 27, 2019, https://news.gallup.com/opinion/polling-matters/265898/american-jews-politics-israel.aspx.

247 Beinart, an observant Jew and the former wunderkind editor: Peter Beinart, "The Failure of the American Jewish Establishment," *New York Review of Books*, June 10, 2010, https://www.nybooks.com/articles/2010/06/10/failure-american-jewish-establishment/.

247 Poll after poll, study after study, showed: Dov Waxman, "As Israel Turns 70, Many Young Jews Turn Away," The Conversation, May 3, 2018, https://theconversation.com/as-israel-turns-70-many-young-american-jews-turn-away-95271; "A Portrait of Jewish Americans," Pew Research Center, Oct. 1, 2013, https://www.pewforum.org/2013/10/01/jewish-american-beliefs-attitudes-culture-survey/.

247 A plurality of American Jews, however: Scott Clement, "Jewish Americans Support the Iran Deal," *Washington Post*, July 27, 2015, https://www.washingtonpost.com/news/the-fix/wp/2015/07/27/jewish-americans-support-the-iran-nuclear-deal/. A 2015 poll found that 48 percent of American Jews supported the deal, while 28 percent opposed it and 25 percent hadn't heard enough to form an opinion.

248 Donald Trump and his subsequent "bromance" with Netanyahu: TOI Staff, "'You Are Great!': Trump's Handwritten Praise for Ally Netanyahu on 70th Birthday," *Times of Israel*, Oct. 22, 2019, https://www.timesofisrael.com/you-are-great-trump-congratulates-ally-netanyahu-on-70th-birthday/.

248 Sheldon Adelson (who donated over $180 million to Trump and the GOP for the 2020 election): Michela Tindera and Will Yakowicz, "No Dividends, No Problem: Sheldon Adelson Has Given at Least 180 Million This Year Despite Troubles at His Company," *Forbes*, Oct. 27, 2020, https://www.forbes.com/sites

/michelatindera/2020/10/27/no-dividends-no-problem-trump
-megadonor-sheldon-adelson-has-given-at-least-180-million-this
-year-despite-troubles-at-his-company/?sh=51c0d8b92ec4.

249 American Jews couldn't stand him: A 2017 survey by the centrist American Jewish Committee found that 77 percent of American Jews held an unfavorable opinion of Trump: "AJC Survey of American Jewish Opinion 2017," AJC, Sept. 13, 2017, https://www.ajc.org/survey2017. A 2019 survey by the liberal organization Bend the Arc found essentially the same thing: "Bend the Arc's National Survey of American Jewish Voters," Bend the Arc, n.d., https://www.bendthearc.us/votersurvey.

249 They did not feel safe in Donald Trump's America: The Bend the Arc survey found that 73 percent of American Jews said they felt "less safe today in America than they did four years ago. Nine in ten Jewish voters believe antisemitism has increased in the last four years." "Bend the Arc's National Survey of American Jewish Voters."

249 refused to utter a word of criticism at Trump's winks and nods to antisemites: Josef Federman, "As Trump Questions Loyalty of US Jews, Israeli PM Is Silent," Associated Press, Aug. 21, 2019, https://apnews.com/article/ef631bdba5674540be35b59c4db361da.

250 But did Netanyahu support his ambassador's move?: Barak Ravid, "On Netanyahu's Orders: Israel's Foreign Ministry Retracts Criticism of anti-Semitism in Hungary and Slams George Soros," Haaretz, Oct. 7, 2017, https://www.haaretz.com/israel-news/israel-retracts-criticism-of-hungary-s-anti-soros-campaign-1.5492668.

250 institutions of the American Jewish community seemed paralyzed: Uriel Heilman, "What Jewish Groups Have (and Haven't) Said About Trump," Times of Israel, Dec. 16, 2015, https://www.timesofisrael.com/what-jewish-groups-have-and-havent-said-about-trump/.

251 Meanwhile, newer organizations less concerned with defending Israel: Some of these newer organizations (e.g., J Street, IfNotNow, and Open Hillel) sought to offer new ways for liberal American Jews to engage, often from a place of constructive criticism, with Israel. Others (e.g., Bend the Arc) avoided the issue of Israel altogether.

CHAPTER 18: THE SETTLEMENTS

252 More than 440,000 Jewish Israeli civilians live in the settlements: "Settlement Watch," Peace Now, https://peacenow.org.il/en /settlements-watch/settlements-data/population.

253 They were built, and intended, to be permanent communities: Tessler, *A History of the Israeli-Palestinian Conflict*, 505–6.

254 Almost every country aside from Israel considers the Israeli settlements illegal: A good primer on the status of the settlements under international law can be found in Isabel Kershner, "Are West Bank Settlements Illegal? Who Decides?" *New York Times*, Nov. 18, 2019, https://www.nytimes.com/2019/11/18/world/middleeast /israel-west-bank-settlements.html.

254 Israel disputes this: Gorenberg, *The Unmaking of Israel*, 73–77.

255 the United States had determined that the settlements did not violate international law: Lara Jakes and David M. Halbfinger, "In Shift, U.S. Says Israeli Settlements in West Bank Do Not Violate International Law," *New York Times*, Nov. 18, 2019, https://www.nytimes .com/2019/11/18/world/middleeast/trump-israel-west-bank-settlements .html?action=click&module=RelatedLinks&pgtype=Article.

255 American support for Israel's annexation of parts of the West Bank: David M. Halbfinger and Isabel Kershner, "Trump Plan's First Result: Israel Will Claim Sovereignty Over Part of West Bank," *New York*

Times, Jan. 28, 2020, https://www.nytimes.com/2020/01/28/world/middleeast/israel-west-bank-annex-sovereignty.html.

255 including the European Union, Israel's biggest trading partner: Reuters staff, "EU Rejects Trump Middle East Peace Plan, Annexation," Reuters, Feb. 4, 2020, https://www.reuters.com/article/us-israel-palestinians-eu/eu-rejects-trump-middle-east-peace-plan-annexation-idUSKBN1ZY1I9.

255 enjoy the same rights: Gorenberg, *The Unmaking of Israel*, 73–80.

255 Yet they are subject to Israeli military law: Limor Yehuda et al, *One Rule, Two Legal Systems: Israel's Regime of Laws in the West Bank*, Tel Aviv: Association for Civil Rights in Israel, Oct. 2014, p. 7, https://law.acri.org.il/en/wp-content/uploads/2015/02/Two-Systems-of-Law-English-FINAL.pdf.

256 who were no longer permitted even to walk on some of the city center's sidewalks or drive on certain streets reserved for settlers: Elior Levy, "Hebron: Separate Roads for Jews and Palestinians," *Ynet*, Mar. 6, 2013, https://www.ynetnews.com/articles/0,7340,L-4353235,00.html; Jonathan Freedland, "An Exclusive Corner of Hebron, *New York Review of Books*, Feb. 23, 2012, https://www.nybooks.com/articles/2012/02/23/exclusive-corner-hebron/.

258 enmity of many of its neighbors: Tessler, *A History of the Israeli-Palestinian Conflict*, 403.

258 turning what it calls Judea and Samaria into new districts of the State of Israel: Tessler, *A History of the Israeli-Palestinian Conflict*, 521–23.

259 Israel set up army bases and built civilian settlements: Tessler, *A History of the Israeli-Palestinian Conflict*, 466–67.

259 was intoxicating for many Israelis finally to be able to trace their footsteps: Gorenberg, *The Accidental Empire*, 83–84. Gorenberg

writes, "*Euphoria* is the word most often used by Israelis describing the summer of 1967. The biblical verse cited most, in a season when the Bible was quoted constantly, was from Psalms: 'When the Lord brought back those who returned to Zion, we were like dreamers.'"

259 originally called Gush Emunim: Gorenberg, *The Unmaking of Israel*, 71–72.

260 the Nahal, made up largely of soldiers from kibbutzim and other collective communities: Gorenberg, *The Unmaking of Israel*, 74.

260 Some Labor Party officials: Gorenberg, *The Accidental Empire*, 4.

261 the settler population comprised about 4,200: "Population," Settlement Watch, Peace Now, https://peacenow.org.il/en settlements -watch/settlements-data/population.

261 leaders had long been proponents of Israeli annexation: Gorenberg, *The Accidental Empire*, 267.

262 erasing the Green Line from the mental maps of many Israelis: Tessler, *A History of the Israeli-Palestinian Conflict*, 523. "Likud's [the largest right-wing party and chief champion of the settlement enterprise] explicit goal was to erase the Green Line, and its activities aimed at creating facts were vigorously pursued with this objective in mind."

264 a radical and violent movement of militant Jewish settler "hilltop youth": Naomi Zevelof, "The Radical New Face of the Jewish Settler Movement," *Forward*, Jan. 11, 2016, https://forward.com /news/328981/the-radical-new-face-of-the-jewish-settler-movement/.

266 in late 2018, it stood at about 43 percent: Adam Rasgon, "Support for Two-State Solution at Lowest in Nearly 20 Years—Poll," *Times of Israel*, Aug. 13, 2018, https://www.timesofisrael.com/support-for-two -state-solution-at-lowest-in-nearly-20-years-poll/.

266 who say they support annexation of either Area C or the whole West Bank: Dahlia Scheindlin, "Here's What the Israeli Public Thinks About Netanyahu's Campaign Promise to Annex Parts of the West Bank," *Washington Post*, Sept. 12, 2019, https://www.washingtonpost .com/politics/2019/09/12/heres-what-israeli-public-thinks-about -netanyahus-campaign-promise-annex-parts-west-bank/.

266 For example, Naftali Bennett, Israel's former minister of education: Naftali Bennett, "For Israel, Two-State Is No Solution," *New York Times*, Nov. 5, 2014, https://www.nytimes.com/2014/11/06/opinion /naftali-bennett-for-israel-two-state-is-no-solution.html.

267 Recent polls put the level of Palestinian support for a two-state solution: Rasgon, "Support for Two-State Solution at Lowest in Nearly 20 Years—Poll."

268 their demand is simple: Haidar Eid, "The Two-State Solution: The Opium of the Palestinian People," Al Jazeera, Dec. 29, 2020, https:// www.aljazeera.comopinions/2020/12/29/the-two-state-solution-the -opium-of-the-palestinian-people.

269 Bassem Tamimi told me he no longer supports a two-state solution: Bassam Tamimi, conversation with the author, Feb. 19, 2019.

269 "I want to take my children to the beach": Tamimi, conversation with the author, Feb. 19, 2019.

CHAPTER 19: WHAT WE TALK ABOUT
WHEN WE TALK ABOUT BDS

271 in the BDS movement's own words: "Palestinian Civil Society Calls for BDS," BDS, https://www.bdsmovement.net/call.

271 keep in mind that the BDS movement is nonviolent: "What is BDS?" BDS, https://bdsmovement.net/what-is-bds. The BDS website reads, "Inspired by the South African anti-apartheid movement,

the Palestinian BDS call urges nonviolent pressure on Israel until it
complies with international law by meeting three demands . . ."

271 So, why is a movement that rejects violence and terror labeled as
unacceptable, anti-Israel, and even antisemitic: David M. Halbfinger
et al., "Is B.D.S. Anti-Semitic? A Closer Look at the Boycott Israel
Campaign," *New York Times*, July 27, 2019, https://www.nytimes
.com/2019/07/27/world/middleeast/bds-israel-boycott-antisemitic
.html.

272 "strategic threat": Peter Beaumont, "Israel Brands Palestinian-led
Boycott Movement a 'Strategic Threat,'" *Guardian*, June 3, 2015,
https://www.theguardian.com/world/2015/jun/03/israel-brands
-palestinian-boycott-strategic-threat-netanyahu.

274 more U.S. military aid than all other countries combined: "US
Military Aid: Israel Gets More than Everybody Else Combined,"
Statista, https://www.statista.com/chart/3487/us-military-aid/.

275 In 2010, a group of Israeli artists, writers, and performers: Chaim
Levinson and Or Kashti, "150 Academics, Artists Back Actors'
Boycott of Settlement Arts Center," *Haaretz*, Aug. 30, 2010, https://
www.haaretz.com/1.5107218.

276 label products from settlements as MADE IN ISRAELI SETTLEMENTS,
not MADE IN ISRAEL: Associated Press, "Products from Israeli
Settlements Must Be Labelled, EU Court Rules," *Guardian*, Nov. 12,
2019, https://www.theguardian.com/world/2019/nov/12/products
-israeli-settlements-labelled-eu-court.

276 Differentiation [between Israel and its settlements] disincentivizes
Israel's illegal acquisition: Hugh Lovett, "EU Differentiation
and the Push for Peace in Israel-Palestine," European Council on
Foreign Relations, Oct. 31, 2016, https://ecfr.eu/publication/eu
_differentiation_and_the_push_for_peace_in_israel_palestine7163/.

277 who said, "The EU decision to label Israeli products is antisemitic": Gil Stern Stern Hoffman, "MK Oren Labels EU Products at Supermarket in Protest over Anticipated Guidelines," *Jerusalem Post*, Nov. 4, 2015, https://www.jpost.com/israel-news/politics-and-diplomacy/oren-labels-eu-products-at-supermarket-432060.

279 several major philanthropists were embarrassed: Josefin Dolsten, "LA Jewish Group Pulls Funding for Canary Mission–linked NGO," *Times of Israel*, Oct. 15, 2018, https://www.timesofisrael.com/la-jewish-group-pulls-funding-for-canary-mission-linked-ngo/.

281 more than thirty states have passed or considered laws: "Antisemitism: State Anti-BDS Legislation," Jewish Virtual Library, https://www.jewishvirtuallibrary.org/anti-bds-legislation.

281 Critics argue that they are misguided attempts: One of those critics is me. Daniel Sokatch, "Congress's Un-American, Bad-for-Israel Agenda," *New York Times*, Oct. 12, 2017, https://www.nytimes.com/2017/10/12/opinion/israel-congress-bds.html.

CHAPTER 21: THE *OTHER A*-WORD

287 activist Rabbi Jill Jacobs has come up with: Jill Jacobs, "How to Tell When Criticism of Israel Is Actually Anti-Semitism," *Washington Post*, May 18, 2018, https://www.washingtonpost.com/outlook/how-to-tell-when-criticism-of-israel-is-actually-anti-semitism/2018/05/17/cb58bf10-59eb-11e8-b656-a5f8c2a9295d_story.html.

290 nobody at the IHRA *ever* intended: Kenneth Stern, "I Drafted the Definition of Antisemitism. Rightwing Jews are Weaponizing It," *Guardian*, Dec. 13, 2019, https://www.theguardian.com/commentisfree/2019/dec/13/antisemitism-executive-order-trump-chilling-effect. Here, the author of the IHRA definition of antisemitism sharply criticizes its adoption into legislation and its "weaponization" by Trump and right-wing Jewish organizations.

290 when it announced that it planned to label leading international human rights organizations: Lara Friedman, "Weaponizing Anti-Semitism, State Department Delegitimizes Human Rights Groups," *American Prospect*, Nov. 12, 2020, https://prospect.org/politics/weaponizing-anti-semitism-state-department-delegitimizes-human-rights-groups/.

290 a group of 122 Palestinian and Arab academics wrote: David N. Myers, "Yes, Palestinians Have the Right to Speak About Antisemitism," *Forward*, Dec. 4, 2020, https://forward.com/opinion/459654/yes-palestinians-have-the-right-to-speak-about-antisemitism/.

CHAPTER 22: RED COWS IN THE HEARTLAND: ISRAEL AND ARMAGEDDON

292 In 2014, a red heifer was born: Raphael Poch, "Holy Cow! Red Heifer Born in the US," *Israel365 News*, June 29, 2014, https://www.israel365news.com/17303/holy-cow-red-heifer-born-us/.

292 going so far as to re-create Temple garments and rehearse sacrificial rites: "Update on the Building of the Third Temple," *Jewish Voice*, https://www.jewishvoice.org/read/article/update-building-third-temple.

293 a quarter of Americans identify: David Masci and Gregory A. Smith, "5 Facts About US Evangelical Protestants," FactTank, Pew Research Center, Mar. 1, 2018, https://www.pewresearch.org/fact-tank/2018/03/01/5-facts-about-u-s-evangelical-protestants/.

293 80 percent of those who do say they believe that the Jewish return to Israel: Joel C. Rosenberg, "Evangelical Attitudes Toward Israel, Research Study," Chosen People Ministries, 2017, https://lifewayresearch.com/wp-content/uploads/2017/12/Evangelical-Attitudes-Toward-Israel-Research-Study-Report.pdf.

293 within today's Republican Party: Jeffrey Rosario, "Mainstreaming Christian Zionism Could Warp Foreign Policy," *Washington Post*, June 30, 2020, https://www.washingtonpost.com/outlook/2020/06/30/mainstreaming-christian-zionism-could-warp-foreign-policy/.

294 As conservative evangelical icon Rev. Jerry Falwell: Kahlid Amayreh, "Against Israel, Against God," Al Jazeera, Sept. 2, 2003, https://www.aljazeera.com/news/2003/9/2/against-israel-against-god.

294 "my passion for Israel springs from my Christian faith": The White House, Remarks by the Vice President at Christians United for Israel Washington Summit, Washington, D.C., July 17, 2017, https://www.whitehouse.gov/briefings-statements/remarks-vice-president-christians-united-israel-washington-summit/.

294 And when Trump's secretary of state Mike Pompeo: Edward Wong, "The Rapture and the Real World: Mike Pompeo Blends Beliefs and Policy," *New York Times*, Mar. 30, 2019, https://www.nytimes.com/2019/03/30/us/politics/pompeo-christian-policy.html.

294 the 2014 Ebola outbreak was God's punishment for Obama's Israel policy: Ariel Cohen, "Pastor Warns Ebola Is God's Punishment for Obama Dividing Jerusalem," *Jerusalem Post*, Oct. 19, 2014, https://www.jpost.com/christian-news/christian-pastor-warns-ebola-is-gods-punishment-for-obama-dividing-jerusalem-379207.

294 CUFI, which claims to have more than nine million followers: "Mission," Christians United for Israel, https://cufi.org/about/mission/.

294 "I consider CUFI a vital part of Israel's national security": "On Anniversary of Jerusalem Embassy Dedication, CUFI Reaches Six Million Members," Christians United for Israel, https://cufi.org

/press-releases/on-anniversary-of-jerusalem-embassy-dedication-cufi
-reaches-six-million-members/.

296 It seemed that biblical prophecy was being fulfilled: Jessica Steinberg,
"Christian Docudrama Sees Six Day War as Prophecy Fulfilled,"
Times of Israel, June 7, 2017, https://www.timesofisrael.com/christian
-docudrama-sees-six-day-war-as-prophecy-fulfilled/.

296 so supportive of Israel, no matter what: Mimi Kirk, "Countering
Christian Zionism in the Age of Trump," Middle East Research
and Information Project, Aug. 8, 2019, https://merip.org/2019/08
/countering-christian-zionism-in-the-age-of-trump/.

296 Trump was a modern-day Cyrus: Daniel Block, "Is Trump Our
Cyrus? The Old Testament Case for Yes and No," *Christianity Today*,
Oct. 29, 2018, https://www.christianitytoday.com/ct/2018/october
-web-only/donald-trump-cyrus-prophecy-old-testament.html.

297 Indeed, the very character flaws: Tara Isabella Burton, "The Biblical
Story the Christian Right Uses to Defend Trump," *Vox*, Mar. 5, 2018,
https://www.vox.com/identities/2018/3/5/16796892/trump-cyrus
-christian-right-bible-cbn-evangelical-propaganda.

297 remember Trump as the Jewish people remember Cyrus: Burton,
"The Biblical Story the Christian Right Uses to Defend Trump."

297 Mike Pompeo told a crowd at a church in Kansas: Wong, "The
Rapture and the Real World."

INDEX

A NOTE on the AUTHOR and ILLUSTRATOR

DANIEL SOKATCH is the chief executive officer of the New Israel Fund (NIF), the leading organization committed to equality and democracy for all Israelis (not just Jews). Before joining NIF, he served as the executive director of the Jewish Community Federation of San Francisco, the Peninsula, Marin and Sonoma Counties and as the founding executive director of the Los Angeles–based Progressive Jewish Alliance. He was named to the *Forward*'s "Forward 50," an annual list of the fifty leading Jewish decision makers and opinion shapers, in 2002, 2005, 2008, and 2010. His writing has appeared in the *New York Times*, the *Washington Post*, the *Los Angeles Times*, and other publications. Sokatch has an MA from the Fletcher School at Tufts University, a JD from Boston College Law School, and a BA from Brandeis University. He is married with two daughters and lives in San Francisco.

CHRISTOPHER NOXON is a journalist and illustrator whose work has appeared in the *New Yorker*, the *Atlantic*, the *New York Times Magazine*, *Salon*, and his book *Good Trouble: Lessons from the Civil Rights Playbook*. He writes and draws in Ojai, California.